Science Fiction:
A Literary History

Science Fiction:
A Literary History

Edited by Roger Luckhurst

BRITISH LIBRARY

First published 2017 by
The British Library
96 Euston Road
London NW1 2DB

Text copyright © the authors 2017
Illustrations copyright © the British Library Board and other named
copyright-holders 2017

Cataloguing in Publication Data
A catalogue record for this book is available from the British Library

ISBN 978 0 7123 5692 3

Cover design by Rawshock Design
Typeset by IDSUK (DataConnection) Ltd
Printed in Malta by Gutenberg Press

Contents

Preface　　　　　　　　　　　　　　　　　　　　6
Adam Roberts

Introduction　　　　　　　　　　　　　　　　　8
Roger Luckhurst

Chapter 1. The Beginnings: Early Forms of Science Fiction　　11
Arthur B. Evans

Chapter 2. From Scientific Romance to Science Fiction: 1870–1914　　44
Roger Luckhurst

Chapter 3. Utopian Prospects, 1900–49　　　　　72
Caroline Edwards

Chapter 4. Pulp SF and its Others, 1918–39　　102
Mark Bould

Chapter 5. After the War, 1945–65　　　　　　130
Malisa Kurtz

Chapter 6. The New Wave 'Revolution,' 1960–76　　157
Rob Latham

Chapter 7. From the New Wave into the Twenty-First Century　　181
Sherryl Vint

Chapter 8. New Paradigms, After 2001　　　　208
Gerry Canavan

Notes on Contributors　　　　　　　　　　　235
Picture Credits　　　　　　　　　　　　　　237
Index　　　　　　　　　　　　　　　　　　238

Preface

Adam Roberts

Science fiction is now a global culture. Tens of thousands of novels and short stories, countless films and TV shows, graphic novels, games and music are loved and discussed and celebrated and reviled and kept alive by myriad fans and fan communities. And it's getting bigger every year. But it wasn't always like this. Once upon a time SF was a subculture haunted by small populations of nerds and geeks. *Star Wars* (1977) changed that, setting in motion a worldwide popularisation of the genre that grew through the 80s and 90s. Nowadays, from *Avatar* to the Marvel Comics Universe, from *Doctor Who* to *The Hunger Games*, from high culture to low, almost *everybody* loves SF.

Of course, that means that the scholar who wants to study this field has her work cut out: how to summarize so vast, and still expanding, a field? How even to define SF when any gathering of three experts will produce four mutually exclusive definitions? There's no shortage of critics willing to give it a go, of course; many critical histories have been written and a lively world of academic scholarship continues to pore over the genre; but I don't know any introduction to science fiction that does as much, so usefully and illuminatingly, in such a small space, as the British Library History you hold in your hands.

This book's real achievement is to give a sense of the sheer *diversity* of the mode – never just a monoculture of white men, always more than a simplistic binary of two polarized political positions (the progressive, alien-hugging left and the militaristic bug-blasting right). To read these essays is to start to understand just how many branching paths – editor Roger Luckhurst's well-chosen Borgesian trope, from his introduction – add up to the composite way, the *tao*, of science fiction.

The essays themselves, though compact, take care not to stint on the detail, and use their space to focus more directly on their various topics. Arthur Evans provides a survey of what he calls 'early SF', showing just how richly the genre was supplied with subterranean exploration, interplanetary adventure, and time travel well before the twentieth century. These deep roots for the genre help explain both the variety and the vigour of the myriad scientific romances published between 1870 and 1914, a period expertly interrogated in Roger Luckhurst's chapter. That fecundity continues to define the genre throughout the century. Caroline Edwards surveys the many varieties of utopia published internationally across the first half of the twentieth century, and Mark Bould's marshalling of the explosive energies and sprawling cultural production of early-century pulp SF – something he shows to be much more politically engaged than previous scholarship has acknowledged. Malisa Kurtz takes us deftly through the so-called 'Golden Age', and Rob Latham continues the story into the 'New Wave' of the 1960s and 1970s, when many-sidedness, howsoever contested at the time, came to define the genre itself. If the turf-wars fought over the genre that Latham summarises look a little distant now, that is in part because – as Sherryl Vint comprehensively shows in her chapter on SF in the later decades of the century – the genre's river was about to expand into a global delta, mixing high culture and low, postmodernism and traditionalism, science and art, technology and culture, and increasingly 'cyberizing' and, indeed, defining our age itself. Finally Gerry Canavan boldly goes into the new century, and traces the way science fiction and actual reality are increasingly shaped by their mutual ongoing collision.

If one thing is clear from this history it is that the genre is still characterised by a restless and creative energy. SF has a long history (it has *seen* things you wouldn't believe – attack ships on fire off the shoulder of Orion), but so far from being exhausted it is gearing up for its next blast-off. No better guide is available as to where it has come from, and no better short book gives a better sense of where it is going.

Introduction

Roger Luckhurst

In Jorge Luis Borges's short story, 'The Garden of Forking Paths' (1941), the Chinese governor Ts'ui Pen abandons public life and announces that he is retiring to write a book and make a labyrinth. He dies, however, some time later, leaving only an enigmatic muddle of notes towards a novel, and no sign of his maze. It is only later that the puzzle is solved: the book *is* the labyrinth, for the plot proceeds by trying to include every possible future that branches from every decisive action. Ts'ui Pen, it is explained, 'did not believe in uniform, absolute time. He believed in an infinite series of times, in a growing, dizzying net of divergent, convergent and parallel times. This network of times which approached one another, forked, broke off, or were unaware of one another for centuries, embraces *all* possibilities of time' (Borges 1987: 53).

This was the first short story by Borges to be translated into English by Anthony Boucher, who published it in what might seem an unlikely location: *Ellery Queen's Mystery Magazine.* Boucher had written witty and paradoxical stories for science fiction magazines in the 1940s, and went on to be the founding editor of one of the most important magazines in the 1950s, *Fantasy and Science Fiction,* home to important writers like Philip K. Dick, Frederik Pohl and Walter M. Miller. Borges, although considered the height of post-war experimental fiction (even, sometimes, one of those dreaded 'postmodernists'), also wrote science fiction stories – and even a homage to the king of pulp horror, H. P. Lovecraft.

'The Garden of Forking Paths' is sometimes considered an anticipation of the theory of 'many worlds' in quantum physics. This idea, first proposed by Hugh Everett in 1957, was that there are infinite universes, each branching off at every juncture of possibility. The popularisation of such ideas has lent some scientific gravitas to the large subgenre of alternative or parallel worlds in science fiction. Science and fiction have always been gloriously interwoven in the wackiest speculative reaches of theoretical physics.

I think of this Borges story every time I read a history of science fiction (a term that, to save space, we'll contract to SF in this volume). It came back to me again and again as I edited this collection of essays. The eight authors have brought their specialist knowledge to bear on this task, but SF is such a vast and diverse field by now that any single volume can only be haunted by all the choices *not* made, the books *not* mentioned. In an alternative world, every sentence of the history you hold contains a different example, and forks on another path with every new sentence added.

There are rigid designators to every history, you might think: Verne to Wells, Heinlein to Ballard, Delany to Atwood. But our knowledge of the archive shifts and changes over time. Historians have long tried to displace the 'great man' history that has Verne or Wells as the fountainhead of SF, and have found multiple points of origin within the chaotic nineteenth-century print cultures that birthed them, and unearthed parallel developments across the world, in China, Japan, Latin America, Russia, not just in America and Europe. Long-forgotten utopias by African Americans such as Pauline Hopkins or George Schuyler have only relatively recently been recovered and reassessed. Our standard lines of historical narrative have exploded into a garden of forking paths.

Boundaries, too, have relaxed a little. The true pioneers of SF history writing only really started in the 1960s – Kingsley Amis, Brian Aldiss, Darko Suvin. They kept quite a tight rein on definitions, and sought justification for paying attention to lowly popular fiction by fiercely separating out worthies from the awful anonymous mass. The SF tradition was great in Britain, but trash in America – so Aldiss said. SF was properly 'cognitive' and political fiction, but fantasy and the Gothic was opium for the masses – so Suvin said.

Nowadays, we have relaxed the border patrols, and are kind to all sorts of migrants and mongrels. Readers *embrace* genre mash-ups, revel in them:

we are in the era of what Gary Wolfe has termed the 'evaporation of genres'. Nowadays, rather than drawing up strict protocols, critics begin, to quote a recent essay title by John Rieder, 'on defining SF or not', tending very definitely to the looseness and improvisations of the latter. This is another liberation from artificial boundaries, but only contributes ever more routes through the garden of forking paths.

All of which is an elaborate way of holding up my hands in apology as the editor before we start if this history does not include every stone-cold classic, every criminally overlooked minor masterpiece. We are surely guilty of these misdemeanours. But rather than aim for an insistence that we have solved the puzzle and found the one true path, we have aspired to map some of the important routes through the labyrinthine history of this extraordinary, protean and constantly shifting genre. The chapters follow in a broadly chronological order and seek to map out the major highways, but these are not the only way to get to your destination. Each chapter hints at alternative scenic routes, intriguing roads less travelled, even as they necessarily speed along. All we can hope for is that readers new to the genre find some orientation here, and old hands come across some new finds. If this history inspires you to start a new author or revisit an old favourite with fresh eyes, each page a reader turns contributes once again to the cunning labyrinths of Borges's vision of endless textual proliferation.

References

Aldiss, Brian (1973), *Billion Year Spree*. London: Weidenfeld & Nicolson.

Amis, Kingsley (1961), *New Maps of Hell: A Survey of Science Fiction*. London: Gollancz.

Borges, Jorge Luis (1987), *Labyrinths*. Harmondsworth: Penguin.

Rieder, John (2010), 'On Defining SF, or Not: Genre Theory, SF, and History', *Science Fiction Studies* 37: 2, pp. 191–209.

Suvin, Darko (2016), *Metamorphoses of Science Fiction: On the Poetics and History of a Literary Genre,* originally 1979, new edition edited Gerry Canavan. London: Peter Lang.

Wolfe, Gary K. (2011), *Evaporating Genres: Essays on Fantastic Literature*. Middletown, CT: Wesleyan University Press.

Chapter 1

The Beginnings: Early Forms of Science Fiction

Arthur B. Evans

This chapter will focus on science fiction *avant la lettre* – forms of SF that predate the American pulp-magazine era of the 1930s when the label 'science fiction' finally became the accepted appellation (and social identity) for the genre. SF scholars sometimes use the term 'proto SF' to designate these stories, as if to imply that no *real* SF could have existed before the twentieth century. I prefer instead to use the term 'early SF', arguing that it is possible for something to exist before it has an official name; that early SF texts must be considered on their own merits and in their own historical contexts rather than as immature 'pre-versions' of a later narrative form; and, finally, that SF did not slowly emerge (like a butterfly from its chrysalis) from other genres but, rather, already existed as a recognisable literary tradition, clearly evident in a host of rationally speculative tales dating from at least the seventeenth century and perhaps before.

Probably more than any other literary genre, science fiction has been known by many different names. For example, it has been called the 'marvellous romance' by Sir Walter Scott, the 'scientific miraculous' by the Goncourt Brothers, the 'extraordinary voyage' and the 'scientific novel' by Jules Verne, the 'scientific romance' by Charles Howard

Hinton and H. G. Wells, the 'realistic romance' by Edgar Fawcett, the 'scientific-marvellous' and the 'hypothesis novel' by Maurice Renard, 'scientifiction' by Hugo Gernsback, 'speculative fiction' by Robert A. Heinlein and Judith Merril, 'sci-fi' by Forrest Ackerman, 'structural fabulation' by Robert Scholes, and, of course, 'SF' or 'sf' as a form of shorthand by most readers and critics since the 1960s.

Definitions

How can science fiction be defined? SF has always been a 'fuzzily-edged, multi-dimensional, and constantly shifting discursive object' (Bould and Vint 2011: 5) with no single, agreed-upon definition. Over the years, many SF writers, critics, and readers have attempted to stake out its boundaries using various criteria. Some, such as Hugo Gernsback or J. O. Bailey, have restricted the label of SF only to those works that contain extrapolated scientific content, or that recount the adventures and events resulting from a specific, imagined scientific breakthrough. Others, such as Judith Merril, have seen it as a kind of thought experiment that examines some version of reality using the traditional 'scientific method' (observation, hypothesis, experimentation). Still others have used narratological and linguistic theory to demonstrate the genre's unique ways of signifying, focusing on the 'distinct level of subjunctivity [that] informs all the words in an SF story' (Delany 2009: 10) or on how SF's 'necessary and sufficient conditions are the presence and interaction of estrangement and cognition, and whose main formal device is an imaginative framework alternative to the author's empirical environment' (Suvin 1979: 7–8). Some have opted for the purely subjective approach: 'Science fiction is what we point to when we say it,' suggested Damon Knight in 1967.

In today's world, traditionally understood SF may meld and overlap with fantasy, horror, surrealism and other literary genres, and for some critics, the very notion of a single 'genre' has become increasingly suspect. But one fact is certain: SF does exist, and it has a long tradition. Further, the rationally conjectural fictions belonging to this tradition do not stand alone. They are part of a complex network of literary intertextuality, social contexts, and cultural production that stretches back at least to the birth of modern science in the seventeenth century. The SF genre cannot be defined as a single, fixed conceptual object; it is a continually shifting matrix of megatexts 'rooted in past practices and shared protocols, tropes, and traditions ... generated across a multiplicity of media, including centuries of diverse literary fictions and, more recently, video and computer games, graphic novels, big-budget films, and even advertising' (Evans et al. 2010: xiii).

Histories

In much the same way that there exists no single, agreed-upon definition of SF, there can be no single, agreed-upon history of SF. This is mostly due to a lack of consensus about the genre's origins. As one critic summed it up: '[W]here we place that starting point inevitably affects what we see as the history (and the prehistory) of the genre, which in turn changes our perception of what science fiction is. It is a Möbius loop: the definition affects the perception of the historical starting point, which in turn affects the definition' (Kincaid 2003: 45). Some have argued that SF's roots lie in sources as ancient as the fantastic voyages of Ancient Greek myth or the ancient Mesopotamian epic of Gilgamesh. Other influential writers and critics have contended that the 'first' SF story was, variously, Sir Thomas More's *Utopia* (1516); Johannes Kepler's *Somnium* (1634); or the British cleric Francis Godwin's lunar voyage *The Man in the Moone* (1638). Brian W. Aldiss, in his popular SF history *Billion Year Spree* (1973), makes a case for Mary Shelley's *Frankenstein* (1818) as the first SF novel. As one might suppose, the two nineteenth-century authors often identified as the 'founding fathers' of the genre, Jules Verne and H. G. Wells, figure prominently in many SF histories, such as Kingsley Amis's *New Maps of Hell* (1960), Sam Moskowitz's *Explorers of the Infinite* (1963), David Ketterer's *New Worlds for Old* (1974), John J. Pierce's *Foundations of Science Fiction* (1987), and Edward James's *Science Fiction in the 20th Century* (1994). Roger Luckhurst, in his 2005 'cultural history' of SF, asserted that 'science fiction' cannot be said to exist before 1880. Finally, the notion that SF was born in the American pulp magazines of the 1920s to 1930s, midwifed by editor Hugo Gernsback, has long been promoted by SF critic Gary

Westfahl, especially in his *The Mechanics of Wonder* (1998). This view has found some traction in recent SF histories, such as Mark Bould and Sherryl Vint's *The Routledge Concise History of Science Fiction* (2011).

As mentioned, for much of its history, science fiction was a literary genre without a fixed label, known by different names at different times and in different cultural milieus. But, as early as the eighteenth century, a number of European science-fictional texts were already being recognised as constituting a distinct narrative tradition, occupying a separate branch on the literary tree. In 1787, the French publisher Charles-Georges-Thomas Garnier gathered into one enormous thirty-six-volume series many of these speculative fictions. He included stories such as Lucian of Samosata's *True History* (*c.* 120–80), Cyrano de Bergerac's *Other Worlds: The Comical History of the States and Empires of the Moon and Sun* (1657, 1662), Daniel Defoe's *Robinson Crusoe* (1719), Jonathan Swift's *Gulliver's Travels* (1726), Chevalier de Mouhy's *Lamekis* (1735), Ludvig Holberg's *The Journey of Niels Klim to the World Underground* (1741), Robert Paltock's *The Life and Adventures of Peter Wilkins* (1750), Voltaire's *Micromégas* (1752), Marie-Anne de Roumier-Robert's *The Voyages of Lord Seaton to the Seven Planets* (1765), and dozens of others. Garnier titled his collection *Imaginary Voyages, Dreams, Visions, and Cabalistic Novels* and divided its contents into these same four categories, with *Imaginary Voyages* taking up thirty volumes, *Dreams and Visions* two volumes, and *Cabalistic* (mystic, occult) *Novels* four volumes. In his preface to the collection, Garnier explains what he means by the term 'imaginary voyage':

> History portrays for us men as they have been or as they are. Novels portray them as they ought to be. The traveller tells us of the lands he has explored, gives an account of his discoveries, and recounts what happened to him among previously unknown peoples whose customs and practices he describes. But the *philosophe* has a different way of travelling. With no other guide than his imagination, he transports himself to new worlds, where he collects observations that are no less interesting and useful … Such will be the kind of stories that we shall present to our readers in these imaginary voyages … We intend to speak first to the mind in order to amuse and instruct it, and then to the heart in order to touch it. (Garnier, 1787: 1–4, quoted in Gove 1941: 29–31, my translation)

The 'interesting and useful' (from Horace's *utile dulci*) message in Garnier's preface highlights two fundamental attributes that can be found in most SF texts: diversion (imagination) and didacticism (cognition). Consider, for example, how Garnier's words prefigure a similar preface written by Jules Verne's editor/publisher Pierre-Jules Hetzel, as he promoted Verne's newly conceived book series called the *Voyages extraordinaires*:

> The two-fold merit of the works of M. Jules Verne is that the reading of these charming books has all the flavor of a spicy dish while providing the substance of a nourishing meal ... Verne has succeeded in creating a new genre. What is promised so often and what is delivered so rarely, instruction that entertains and entertainment that instructs, Verne gives both unsparingly in each one of his exciting narratives. (Hetzel 1866: 7, translated by and quoted in Evans 1988: 30)

It is also important to note that Garnier, as editor, enriched the texts included in his collection by adding this own critical observations about them, amounting to over 180 pages. It might be argued that Garnier, through his extensive commentaries on the works appearing in his *Imaginary Voyages*, was establishing his own 'genealogy' of early SF history and criticism, much as Hugo Gernsback would later do in the editorial pages of his magazine *Amazing Stories*.

The imaginary voyages of the seventeenth and eighteenth centuries can perhaps be best understood as a fictional expression of the dominant ideologies of their historical eras. Emulating the travelogues of early European explorers, these narratives also reflect the rise of modern science – the profound religious and cultural revolutions sparked by the discoveries of Copernicus, Galileo, Newton, and others – as well as the significant social impact (both positive and negative) of the emerging Industrial Revolution.

The new heliocentric explanation of the solar system and the debates it encouraged about 'cosmic pluralism' soon generated a multitude of interplanetary travel narratives. Most were strongly didactic, seeking to teach either scientific or socio-political lessons. Examples of the former include Johannes Kepler's *Somnium* (1634), which gives a detailed and astronomically accurate – yet still very estranging – description of the

Earth as viewed from the Moon through the eyes of its lunar inhabitants; or John Wilkins's *The Discovery of a World in the Moon* (1638) and David Russen's *Iter Lunare, or A Voyage to the Moon* (1703), who both offer 'serious' arguments about the technological feasibility of human travel to the Earth's nearest celestial neighbour; or finally the delightful book that became an international bestseller by Bernard le Bovier de Fontenelle called *Conversations on the Plurality of Worlds* (1686), which depicts a series of evening conversations between a young marquise and the author (a 'natural philosopher') about the marvels of astronomy and the possible existence of alien life on other worlds. Examples of the socio-political type include Sir Thomas More's watershed *Utopia* (1516), whose story about the discovery of an unknown island containing a perfect society launched the SF subgenre of the same name; Tommaso Campanella's *The City of the Sun* (1623), which describes an ideal city encircled by seven walls and ruled by an enlightened philosopher-king, where class divisions and private property do not exist, and where the arts and sciences are accessible to all; and Francis Bacon's *New Atlantis* (1627), an unfinished novel visualising a utopian city of the future and its university-like research institution called 'Salomon's House', specialising in applied science and technology.

Early SF Speculations

Other early SF tales were more fanciful, depicting adventurous heroes who explore faraway places inhabited by exotic life forms. These narratives often combine both the scientific and socio-political didacticism mentioned above but replace the island setting with an extra-terrestrial one. And from this estranged perspective, they offer (sometimes biting) satirical commentary on their own contemporary societies. One of the earliest fictions of this sort was Francis Godwin's *The Man in the Moone* (1638), an imaginary voyage to the Moon that, according to Marjorie Hope Nicolson 'proved immensely popular ... for here were all the elements of the kind of romance in which our ancestors delighted ... it foreshadowed *Robinson Crusoe* and *Gulliver's Travels*, both of which drew from it' (Nicolson 1948 71). In Godwin's tale, the castaway narrator escapes from his deserted island by harnessing a flock of wild geese, which carry him to the Moon. There he discovers an advanced utopian civilisation – a race of Christian beings who live in perfect harmony, without hunger or disease, and whose individual heights and longevity correspond to their levels of intelligence and goodness.

The French author Savinien de Cyrano de Bergerac's two-book series *Other Worlds: The Comical History of the States and Empires of the Moon and Sun* (1657, 1662) **[1.1]** is often cited as one of the foundational starting-points for the science fiction genre. Apart from his SF, published posthumously after his premature death at age thirty-six, the author was also a well-known dramatist and swordsman, mostly remembered as the chivalrous, large-nosed protagonist of Edmond Rostand's *fin-de-siècle* play *Cyrano de Bergerac* (1897). The real Cyrano's *Other Worlds* are at times strongly reminiscent of Godwin's novel – he even made Godwin's narrator, Domingo Gonsales, one of his fictional characters. But Cyrano's imaginary visits to the Moon and Sun are more deliberative in their promotion of Copernican astronomy and more provocative in their use of wit and bawdy humour (at one point comparing the serpent in the Garden of Eden with the human penis). They tend to be more extrapolative in their portrayal of technology, utilising rockets to propel the traveller toward the Moon and a solar-powered flying machine equipped with a sail, special mirrors, and an 'icosahedron crystal' to carry him to the Sun. Their plots are also more openly anti-clerical in spirit and tone, attacking religious dogmatism with mocking parody and Cartesian logic. A gifted freethinker, Cyrano opened the imaginary voyage to new conceptual frontiers and 'deserves to be recognised as one of the first to no longer view Man as a marvel of Creation, and to put him in his place' (Versins 1972: 219, my translation).

For many years after Cyrano, other imaginary voyages to the beyond – some intended as social satires, some not – continued to appear in print with surprising regularity. For example, in 1687, English playwright Aphra Behn wrote a Molièresque farce called *Emperor of the Moon*, in which her anti-hero Doctor Baliardo becomes obsessed with the idea of travelling to the Moon and establishing an empire there. His friends and family attribute his lunar 'disease' to the many 'foolish Books' that Baliardo has been reading – a clear indication of just how

Figure 1.1 Frontispiece from Cyrano de Bergerac, *Comical History of the States and Empires of the Worlds of the Moon and Sun*.

popular these Moon stories had become during this time. Another faraway destination depicted in these fictions was the unexplored continent of Australia, discovered by the Dutch in 1606. The mysterious 'land down under' became home to a variety of exotic peoples, whose societies and governments were often depicted as home-grown utopias. For example, Dénis Vairasse d'Alais's *The History of the Sevarambians* (1675) describes a race of tall, blond, Sun-worshipping natives who believe in education for all – including women – and in the practice of eugenics for improving the species; Gabriel de Foigny's *The Southern Land, Known* (1676) portrays an enlightened society of hermaphrodites; and Nicolas Restif de la Bretonne's *The Discovery of the Austral Continent by a Flying Man* (1781) tells of a young hero named Victorin who invents a mechanical flying suit with artificial wings that eventually carries him to 'Megapatagonia' (Australia) where he visits the antipodal utopian city named 'Sirap' (Paris).

But it is Voltaire's famous *conte philosophique* entitled *Micromégas* (1752) that best illustrates not only the extent to which imaginary voyages had become 'mainstream' literature by the middle of the eighteenth century, but also how a master satirist was able to rejuvenate this traditional SF trope of the encounter with the Other. In Voltaire's version, the roles of the protagonists are reversed: it is now the alien who, travelling through the cosmos, discovers a strange and perplexing world called Earth. Originally from a colossal planet circling the star Sirius (the brightest in the sky), Micromégas is a Gargantuan giant over 20 miles (32 kilometres) tall and extremely learned. On Earth, he comes into contact with a group of microscopically tiny but highly intelligent beings who seem very proficient in geometry, astronomy, and other 'outside' sciences but who are incapable of understanding the 'inside' sciences pertaining to the human spirit. The fictional character of Micromégas himself – whose very name is an oxymoron, reinforcing the many 'all-is-relative' motifs contained in the story – was no doubt intended to be a nod to the British scientist Isaac Newton, whom Voltaire idolised and who is also reputed to have popularised the phrase 'If I have seen further, it is by standing on the shoulders of Giants'.

Subterranean Worlds

Another popular 'beyond' for such imaginary voyages was the interior of the Earth. Margaret Cavendish's *The Blazing World* (1666) started the trend, but it was especially the renowned astronomer Edmund Halley's hollow-Earth theories of 1692 that gave impetus, and 'scientific' plausibility, to these new fictional journeys underground. Examples include Charles de Fieux Chevalier de Mouhy's *Lamekis* (1735), whose eponymous hero, the son of a high priest of ancient Egypt, explores an underground world inhabited by intelligent worm-men; Ludvig Holberg's *The Journey of Niels Klim to the World Underground* (1741), which recounts the underground adventures of the young Norwegian

Niels Klim who falls through the hollow Earth's crust and lands in the kingdom of Potu (utop[ia]) on a planet named Nazar which circles a small sun at the Earth's core; Robert Paltock's *The Life and Adventures of Peter Wilkins* (1750), whose lengthy subtitle offers a convenient summary of the novel's plot: 'A Cornish Man, Relating Particularly His Shipwreck Near the South Pole, His Wonderful Passage Through a Subterraneous Cavern into a Kind of New World, His There Meeting with a Gawrey, or Flying Woman, Whose Life He Preserved, and Afterwards Married Her: His Extraordinary Conveyance to the Country of Glumms and Gawreys, or Men and Women That Fly'; and finally Giacomo Casanova de Seingalt's *The Icosameron* (1788), also lengthily subtitled as 'The Story of Edward and Elizabeth who Spent Eighty-One Years in the Land of the Megamicres, Original Inhabitants of Protocosmos in the Interior of the Globe'.

The proliferation of hollow-Earth narratives continued unabated into the nineteenth and early twentieth centuries. One of America's earliest utopias is *Symzonia* (1820) by Captain Adam Seaborn (most likely a pseudonym for John Cleves Symmes, creator of the 'Symmes Theory of Concentric Spheres') who sails to the interior of the Earth through an opening at the South Pole and discovers there a thriving civilisation of intelligent humanoids who are vegetarians, pacifistic, very inventive (they have flying machines), and governed by an enlightened ruler who is elected by a council of the 'Wise, Good, and Useful'. A similarly advanced underground alien population, the Vril-ya, is described in Edward Bulwer-Lytton's *The Coming Race* (1871), where the narrator, going deep within a mine shaft, comes upon a subterranean city containing a highly evolved species far superior to humans who make use of a special electromagnetic energy called *vril* to heal, to kill, and to power their machines. Jules Verne renovated this hollow-Earth SF subgenre – making its focus more geologically scientific and less politically satiric – in his hugely popular *Journey to the Center of the Earth* (1864) [1.2], in which the young narrator Axel, his uncle Professor Lidenbrock, and their guide Hans go on a danger-filled trek toward the Earth's core by descending into the extinct Icelandic volcano Mount Snaeffels. Other notable underground SF

Figure 1.2 Illustration of mushroom forest in *Journey to the Centre of the Earth* by Jules Verne (Griffith & Farran, 1872).

tales include Mary E. Bradley Lane's *Mizora: A Prophecy* (1890), an early women-only utopia where children are produced by parthenogenesis, where life spans are very long because all disease has been eliminated, where all religions have been banned, and where advanced technology provides for all their physical needs. William R. Bradshaw's *The Goddess of Atvatabar* (1892) is a jingoistic SF fantasy about an intrepid American explorer who leads an expedition to the North Pole, sails into a Symmes's hole, discovers inside the Earth a highly advanced nation called Atvatabar, falls in love with and then abducts their queen/goddess, precipitating a bloody civil war, from which – thanks mostly to the in-the-nick-of-time arrival of two American and

British warships – he triumphs in the end and is crowned king of the realm. Famously, of course, the series of six novels starting with *At the Earth's Core* (1914) by Edgar Rice Burroughs are set deep inside the hollow Earth in Pellucidar, a land of prehistoric dinosaurs, primitive humans, and a dominant race of cunning winged reptilian beings called the Mahars. In these Pellucidar stories, Burroughs was also drawing on themes of exploration and discovery popularised in a variety of nineteenth-century 'lost-world' novels, including many works of prehistoric fiction – such as Elie Berthet's *The Pre-Historic World* (1879), J.-H. Rosny *aîné*'s *The Xipehuz* (1887), *Vamireh* (1892), and *Quest for Fire* (1911), Jack London's *Before Adam* (1906), and Arthur Conan Doyle's *The Lost World* (1912) – as well as H. Rider Haggard's many internationally best-selling 'exotic' adventure novels (see Chapter 2).

Interplanetary Voyages

As early as the mid-eighteenth century, authors of imaginary voyages no longer felt restricted to limiting their narratives to the undiscovered regions of the Moon, the Sun, and/or the Earth and began to set their sights on all the known planets of our solar system and the universe beyond. Such is the case, for example, in Charles-François Tiphaigne de la Roche's novel about panspermia (the seeding of life throughout the universe by asteroids, comets and spacecraft) called *Amilec* (1753). In Marie-Anne de Roumier-Robert's *The Voyages of Lord Seaton to the Seven Planets* (1765), her hero visits the Moon as well as the Sun, Venus, Mars, Jupiter, and Saturn. Charlemagne-Ischir Defontenay's *Star: Psi Cassiopeia* (1854) recounts the history of a race of humans in a distant galaxy; and the French astronomer and writer Camille Flammarion's *Real and Imaginary Worlds* (1864) speculates about what types of extra-terrestrial life might inhabit the different planets of our solar system or nearby stars.

Consider too Percy Greg's *Across the Zodiac* (1880), whose protagonist journeys to Mars in a spaceship powered by an anti-gravity force called 'apergy' (a substance that H. G. Wells would later call 'cavorite' in his 1901 novel *The First Men in the Moon*), where he discovers a technologically advanced but decadent Martian civilisation. This theme, following on from Giovanni Schiaparelli's 1877 observations of the supposed Martian 'channels', and with the help of amateur astronomer Percival Lowell's *Mars* (1895), would trigger a public 'Mars mania' that would last for decades on both sides of the Atlantic.

Travels through Time

One final permutation of this 'encounter-with-the-Other' theme takes the form of an imaginary voyage not to a distant *place* but rather to a distant *time*. Traditionally, 'the future was reserved as a topic for [religious] prophets, astrologers, and practitioners of deliberative rhetoric' (Alkon 1987: 3) and was not considered to be a viable topic for writers of fiction. However, as Western society began to experience the sometimes jarring, transformative effects of the Industrial Revolution – e.g., technological growth, the spread of railways and factories, political upheaval – a new and radical idea took hold: that the future could be very different from the past. From this basic realisation emerged the new subgenre of futuristic SF. It first appeared in such extrapolative works as Samuel Madden's *Memoirs of the Twentieth Century* (1733), where diplomatic documents from the reign of George VI in 1997–8 are transported back to the author's era, and Louis-Sébastien Mercier's extremely influential *Memoirs of the Year Two Thousand Five Hundred* (1771), which features a French *philosophe* who falls asleep and awakens several centuries later in an idealised Paris of 2440. Mercier's book became an international bestseller in the late eighteenth century, a popularity that would be duplicated over a hundred years later by another famous utopia of the future, Edward Bellamy's *Looking Backward 2000–1887* (1888) **[1.3]**.

In early-nineteenth-century Romantic fiction, futuristic settings became widespread. In his 1834 novel/manifesto *The Novel of the Future*, Félix Bodin underscored the importance of this new 'epic' literature to showcase the wonders of the scientific age. A few years earlier, Jean-Baptiste Cousin de Grainville had already renovated the end-of-times Christian apocalypse story by visualising it in

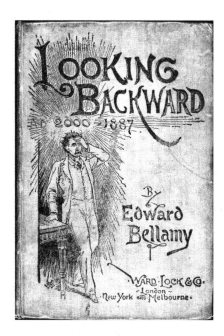

Figure 1.3 Cover of first British edition of Edward Bellamy's *Looking Backward 2000–1887* (1889).

secular terms in his 1805 novel *The Last Man*. This same end–of–the-world scenario was also used by Mary Shelley in her 1826 novel of the same name, in which she imagines the world's population being wiped out by a lethal plague. It was taken up by Edgar Allan Poe in his 'The Conversation of Eiros and Charmion' (1839), by Camille Flammarion in *Omega: The Last Days of the World* (1893), and in J.-H. Rosny *aîné*'s *The Death of the Earth* (1910), where *Homo sapiens* are superseded by a mineral-based life form called the 'ferromagnetics'. On a much lighter note, Jane Webb Loudon's *The Mummy! A Tale of the Twenty-Second Century* (1827) tells of an archaeologist-scientist who resuscitates (via galvanism) the mummy of the Egyptian pharaoh Cheops who then serves as the improbable hero of a series of comically picaresque adventures in the highly technologised world of 2126. Emile Souvestre's satiric *The World as It Shall Be* (1846), one of the first dystopias of the future in Western literature, tells the story of two young French newlyweds, Marthe and Maurice, who awaken from a mesmerised sleep to find themselves in the year 3000 in a hyper-industrialised Earth composed of one single nation-state called the 'Republic of United Interests'. The remainder of the novel gives an account of Marthe's and Maurice's many adventures in this hilarious and horrifying world of consumerism and technology gone mad. Another cautionary dystopia that proved to be enormously influential was George Tomkyns Chesney's *The Battle of Dorking* (1871), a future-war novel that details how an ill-prepared England was invaded and soundly defeated by high-tech armies from Germany. This seminal novel gave rise to many other stories of future war, including such works as Hugh Arnold-Foster's *In a Conning Tower* (1888), George Griffith's *The Raid of the Le Vengeur* (1901), H. G. Wells's 'The Land Ironclads' (1903), among many others, before the actual outbreak of World War I.

Albert Robida

One of the more fanciful examples of this new future-war SF subgenre is *War in the Twentieth Century* (1887) by the French author, caricaturist, and illustrator Albert Robida. The story includes an assortment of heavily armed flying machines, attack submarines, tank-like 'rolling blockhouses', biochemical weapons, and even mind-benders, mesmerists, and mediums, all integrated into a fast-moving and lavishly illustrated narrative about a young French draftee and his military (and amorous) escapades. Despite its ostensibly grim subject-matter, the narrative voice of the story and its many comedic episodes give it a light-hearted tone. The same is true of Robida's other illustrated SF novels, beginning with the tongue-in-cheek parody of Jules Verne's famous *Voyages extraordinaires* in *The Very Extraordinary Adventures of Saturnin Farandoul in the World's Five or Six Continents and in All the Countries Known and even Unknown to Monsieur Jules Verne* (1879) in which, in his travels around the world, the hero Farandoul meets a variety of Vernian protagonists such as Captain Nemo, Phileas Fogg, Hector Servadac, Michel Strogoff, and Captain Hatteras.

Robida's most well-known novel is his wonderfully illustrated *The Twentieth Century* (1882), which is set in 1952 and portrays the day-to-day humorous tribulations of a young Parisian woman, Hélène Colobry, who has just graduated from school and is experimenting with different career prospects – in law, politics, academe, journalism, and business – providing the author with ample fodder to satirise each of these professions. Hélène's world is highly technologised: homes contain ultra-modern amenities such as electric light and heat, 'telephonoscopes' (large-screen interactive televisions), elevators in lieu of stairs, anti-burglar alarms, and piped-in gourmet food and fine wines; the skies are filled with aerocars and dirigible aerobuses, power lines, and aerial advertising; the cities are clean, architecturally innovative, and linked by efficient high-speed tube trains. But all is not perfect: there are still acts of terrorism, fatal accidents, and many incidents of petty crime. Robida's omnipresent high-tech gadgetry and other 'futurisms' are always treated as a given: they are rarely explained, they often malfunction, and the fictional characters accept them as an ordinary part of their everyday lives. It is this oxymoronic (and at times very funny) juxtaposition of advanced technology and nineteenth-century bourgeois lifestyles and social institutions that makes Robida's narrative style so appealing and unique. A cross between *The Jetsons* and the novels of Charles Dickens (as the publicist at Wesleyan University Press once described the novel), *The Twentieth Century* is not a straightforward satire of 1882 'but a genuinely extrapolative study, injecting a good deal of thought into its humor' (Stableford 2016: 289). Society in Robida's *The Twentieth Century* is neither utopian nor dystopian; it is simply different. Despite the futuristic landscape and the ubiquitous technology, ordinary people – with all their joys, heartaches, and foibles – remain very much the same.

In 1892 Robida published a sequel to *The Twentieth Century* entitled *The Electric Life* **[1.4]**, which is set in 1955 and returns the reader to the same hyper-technologised future that was explored in his earlier novel. The storyline focuses on a wealthy Parisian scientist-engineer Philoxène Lorris and his wayward son Georges, who refuses to follow his father's 'practical' vocational choices or accept his proposed 'rational marriage' to a woman of impeccable genetic pedigree. Like its predecessor, the tone of *The Electric Life* is generally light and humorous, and

Figure 1.4 Illustration from *The Electric Life* by
Albert Robida.

the text is punctuated with dozens of marvellous drawings, reinforcing
Robida's reputation as the founder of the genre of SF illustration, the
first to create a consistent, believable future iconography. Unlike its
predecessor, *The Electric Life* contains embedded in its plot a discern-
ible critique of the hectic pace ('freneticism') of daily life controlled by
ever-more-rapid-and-efficient mechanical systems. This hint of scepti-
cism in Robida's attitudes concerning the overall benefits of technological progress would soon metamorphose into overt antipathy in one
of his last – and aggressively dystopian – futuristic novels, *The Engineer
Von Satanas*, published in 1919, immediately following the horrors of
World War I.

Mary Shelley and Romanticism

One way to understand the evolution of science fiction during the nine-teenth century is to view it as an expression of two ideological reactions to the social upheavals of the Industrial Revolution: Positivism and Roman-ticism. The partisans of Positivism, emulating the doctrines of Francis Bacon and Henri de Saint-Simon, contended that the physical world was an intellectually analysable object governed by mathematical laws, that nature was non-anthropomorphic and infinitely exploitable, and that human 'progress' (material and moral) was achievable through science, technology, and capitalism. In contrast, the proponents of Romanticism, following the path of Jean-Jacques Rousseau and William Blake, believed that the physical world was an organic whole not reducible to a codified body of empirical knowledge, that nature was an *état d'âme* and compre-hensible only through emotional communion, and that human 'Progress' was an illusion privileging the material over the spiritual, leading only to psychological alienation and commodity fetishism. The exemplary SF hero for the Positivist was a scientist or engineer in the mould of Jules Verne's Professor Lidenbrock or Cyrus Smith. The exemplary SF anti-hero for the Romantic was a mad (or amoral) scientist in the mould of Goethe's Faust or Mary Shelley's Victor Frankenstein.

Mary Shelley's *Frankenstein, or the Modern Prometheus* (1818), a novel at the crossroads of Gothic horror, mythological fantasy, and science fiction, almost single-handedly upended the stereotype, in vogue since the dawn of the age of Enlightenment, of the noble scientist pursuing truth for the common good. A significant and in many ways watershed work, it raised profound questions about the wisdom of unfettered scientific experimentation, the use of new and powerful technolo-gies, and the social responsibility of scientists. The plot of *Frankenstein* – famously conceived by Shelley in 1816 in response to a challenge to write a 'ghost' story – is well known: a young, ambitious Swiss scientist named Victor Frankenstein creates a living, sentient human being from dead body parts and then, repelled by what he has done, abandons the creature to its fate. But the creature soon returns and takes vengeance on Frankenstein by slaying members of his family, his best friend, and eventually his fiancée. The 'monster' then flees into the ice fields of the Arctic where its creator tries to track it down to destroy it. But he ultimately perishes in the attempt, after telling his story to another young scientist, Robert Walton, whose letters to his sister transcribing Frankenstein's autobiographical narrative constitute the majority of the text.

Shelley's novel portrays, for the first time in Western literature, the use of modern science and technology – rather than magic and/or the supernatural – for creating human life. Although the scientific methodology used in *Frankenstein* remains murky, the much-discussed experiments on electricity and galvanism by Erasmus Darwin during this time (outlined by Shelley in her 1831 preface) give enough scientific verisimilitude to the story to permit the reader to suspend disbelief and accept *Frankenstein*'s plot as marginally plausible. It is this hint of scientific credibility that moves Shelley's speculative tale out of world of pure fantasy and into the realm of SF.

The drama and many conflicting moral issues in *Frankenstein* are effectively presented by the author's use of multiple first-person narrators: Walton, Victor Frankenstein, and especially the 'demon' (as Victor calls it). Looking at the world and humanity through the eyes of the monster triggers in the reader what Darko Suvin has called a kind of 'cognitive estrangement' (Suvin 1979: 6–7) as the reader experiences first-hand the creature's hopes, fears, and rage. As one scholar has described this identification process, 'Shelley collapses the distinction between alien and human, although not by Defoe's method of assimilating the alien to ourselves as in Crusoe's conversion of Friday, but by the opposite method of assimilating ourselves to the alien' (Alkon 1994: 34–5).

The media rapidly popularised Mary Shelley's Frankenstein story, first in the theatre (Richard Brinsley Peake's *Presumption; or The Fate of Frankenstein* in 1823 and Henry M. Milner's *Frankenstein; or The Man and The Monster* in 1826 **[1.5a, 1.5b]**, among others) and later in film: the Edison Studio's *Frankenstein* in 1910, James Whale's highly influential *Frankenstein* in 1931 (with Boris Karloff as the memorable monster), Terence Fisher's *The Curse of Frankenstein* in 1957, and dozens of others throughout the twentieth century. One common trait shared by

MR Q. SMITH AS THE MONSTER.

in

FRANKENSTEIN.

London Pub.ᵈ by J. Duncombe, 19 Little Queen Street, Holborn.

Figure 1.5a The unnamed being created by Baron Frankenstein as portrayed in the melodrama, *The Man and The Monster; or, the Fate of Frankenstein* (1852) by Henry M. Milner, adapted from Shelley's novel.

virtually all these theatrical and cinematic adaptations of Shelley's novel, however, is that the word 'Frankenstein' came to designate in the public mind not the scientist and his out-of-control experiment but rather the nameless creature itself. In consequence – and perhaps appropriately given its 'ghostly' origins – Shelley's *Frankenstein* has become immortalised most often as a work of horror fiction, rather than SF.

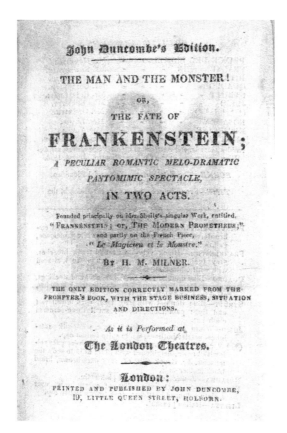

Figure 1.5b Title page of *The Man and The Monster; or, the Fate of Frankenstein* (1852).

Mad Scientists

Shelley's Romantic-infused portrayal of a mad scientist is only one of many that have appeared in literature both before and after her novel. And the range of their characterisations is surprisingly broad. At one end of the spectrum are mad scientists who seem little more than amusing clowns, who are easily fixated and oblivious to their surroundings: for example, the 'flappered' scientists on the floating island of Laputa in Jonathan Swift's *Gulliver's Travels* (1726) or Jules Verne's absent-minded professor Paganel in *The Children of Captain Grant* (1867). At the other end of the spectrum are mad scientists depicted as evil and dangerous, such as Coppelius in E. T. A. Hoffmann's 'The Sandman' (1816), or the diabolical scientist in Honoré de Balzac's *The Centenarian* (1822), who speculates that if he could only discover a way to achieve immortality, he would be able to 'hoard the treasures of science, lose nothing of individual discoveries, constantly pursuing, unceasingly and forever, his investigations of nature; making all powers his [... and ultimately becoming] almost God!' (Balzac 2005: 225–6). In the middle of the spectrum are mad scientists so obsessed with their research that they willingly sacrifice their families or friends: e.g., Balzac's *The Quest of the Absolute* (1834), Nathaniel Hawthorne's 'Rappaccini's Daughter' (1844) or Fitz-James O'Brien's 'The Diamond Lens' (1858), in which the young microbiologist rationalises the murder of his best friend, saying 'After all, what was the life of a little peddling Jew, in comparison with the interests of science?' (O'Brien 1966: 297). It is also interesting to note that, in the majority of post-Darwin nineteenth-century SF, not all sciences are equal: physics and astronomy have been replaced by chemistry and biology as their preferred fields – for example, in Robert Louis Stevenson's *Strange Case of Dr. Jekyll and Mr. Hyde* (1886) or H. G. Wells's *The Island of Dr. Moreau* (1896) – no doubt because these sciences are more fertile for evoking the horrors of lab experimentation gone awry.

Poe and Verne

Another nineteenth-century author whose literary reputation in the US and the UK has identified him primarily – and some believe, erroneously – as a writer of horror literature is Edgar Allan Poe. In point of fact, Poe's historical importance in world literature is rooted in three different genres: Gothic fiction, detective fiction, and SF. Although he will always be remembered for such frightening stories as 'The Black Cat' (1845), 'The Masque of the Red Death' (1850), and 'The Pit and the Pendulum' (1850), Poe's most original works are less about creating fear in the reader and more about speculation and problem solving. He virtually invented detective fiction, which he labelled 'tales of ratiocination', featuring a brilliantly deductive sleuth named C. Auguste Dupin (originating the template for Conan Doyle's Sherlock Holmes) in 'The

Murders in the Rue Morgue' (1841), 'The Mystery of Marie Roget' (1842), and 'The Purloined Letter' (1844). And, although only about a quarter of Poe's literary output can be considered science-fictional, it was deemed so important to the emerging social identity of the SF genre in the 1920s that Hugo Gernsback cited him as one of its founders in his inaugural issue of *Amazing Stories*: 'By "scientifiction" I mean the Jules Verne, H. G. Wells, and Edgar Allan Poe type of story' (Gernsback 1926: 3).

In his SF, Poe pioneered a narrative technique that was central to what would later come to be known as 'hard SF': using real science to enhance the credibility of a fantastic storyline. For example, in a lengthy note added to his 'The Unparalleled Adventure of One Hans Pfaal' (1835), Poe criticises earlier authors of lunar voyages, observing that: 'In none is there any effort at *plausibility* in the details of the voyage itself. The writers seem, in each instance, to be utterly uninformed in respect to astronomy. In "Hans Pfaal" the design is original inasmuch as regards an attempt at *verisimilitude* in the application of scientific principles' (Poe 1938: 41, emphasis in original). This attention to detail can be seen in how Poe portrays the mechanics of hot-air balloon flight in 'The Balloon Hoax' (1844); the effects of mesmerism in 'A Tale of the Ragged Mountains' (1844) and 'The Facts in the Case of M. Valdemar' (1845); sea voyages to lost worlds in 'MS Found in a Bottle' (1833) and *The Narrative of Arthur Gordon Pym of Nantucket* (1838); an airship journey across the Atlantic in the year 2848 in 'Mellonta Tauta' (1849); and the future destruction of Earth by a comet in 'The Conversation of Eiros and Charmion' (1839), among others. SF writers and historians sometimes disagree about Edgar Allan Poe's impact on the genre. Noted author and critic Thomas Disch, for example, states flatly that 'Poe is the source' (Disch 1998: 34), whereas SF scholar Everett F. Bleiler offers much fainter praise: 'One can admire the . . . remarkable blend of wild imagination and sober rationality . . . but one must still admit that the evolution of science fiction would have been much the same had Poe never written these stories' (Bleiler 1999: 603). The truth of the matter no doubt lies between these two extremes. But it is undeniable that Poe's influence was powerfully felt by one young SF writer: Jules Verne.

After reading the French poet Charles Baudelaire's superb 1856 translation of Poe's stories (titled, significantly, *Histoires extraordinaires* – perhaps a source for Verne's own series title *Voyages extraordinaires*), Verne wrote his only piece of literary criticism: an essay called 'Edgard [*sic*] Poe and his Works', published in the French periodical *Musée des Familles* in 1864. In it, Verne praises Poe and his fiction and describes it as occupying 'a high position in the history of the imagination' because Poe had created 'a distinct species' of literature, which might be described as 'the Cult of the Unusual' (Verne 1864: 194). But it was not Poe's taste for the macabre, nor his love of twisted hoax-humour, nor his belief in a kind of mystic supernatural that attracted Verne. It was, rather, Poe's ability to make the uncanny believable and the unreal real. In other words, it was Poe's use of scientific verisimilitude that impressed Verne. It is true that, in terms of his most favoured themes, Verne borrowed repeatedly from Poe – balloons, cryptograms, maelstroms, mesmerism, even the entire narrative of *Arthur Gordon Pym* – but it was nevertheless Poe's *style* that had the greatest impact on him.

Jules Verne has often been dubbed the 'Father of Science Fiction' because, more than any other SF writer, he was both enormously prolific and the first to popularise the SF genre around the world. Even today, imprints of the more than sixty novels in his *Voyages extraordinaires* continue to rank Verne as one of the most translated authors of all time according to UNESCO's *Index Translationum* – more than Mark Twain, Charles Dickens, or even Shakespeare. The SF variant that Verne made famous was the *roman scientifique* (scientific novel), a hybrid fictional genre whose narrative recipe features a fast-paced adventure tale heavily flavoured with scientific didacticism and technology, mixing equal parts of drama, humour, and 'sense of wonder' and seasoned with large pinches of Romantic exoticism and Positivistic *Weltanschauung*. Verne's editor, publisher, mentor, and 'spiritual father' Pierre-Jules Hetzel played a large role in guiding his young protégé toward this successful formula. He also effectively marketed Verne's *Voyages extraordinaires* **[1.6a and 1.6b]**, most often having them appear first in serial format in Hetzel's family periodical the *Magasin d'Éducation et de Récréation* and reprinted later in luxury red and gold, illustrated octavo editions. Hetzel never ceased to promote Verne's books in hyperbolic terms, such as when

Figure 1.6a Cover of one of Jules Hetzel's luxurious editions of Jules Verne's *Voyages extraordinaires.*

Figure 1.6b Nemo viewing the giant octopus in Jules Verne's *Twenty Thousand Leagues Under the Sea.*

he announced the creation of Verne's series: 'The goal of this series is, in fact, to outline all the geographical, geological, physical, and astronomical knowledge amassed by modern science and to recount, in an entertaining and picturesque format that is his own, the history of the universe' (Hetzel 1866: 8, translated by and quoted in Evans 1988: 30).

Marketing exaggerations aside, Hetzel never lost an opportunity to underscore the value of Verne's stories as both entertainment and education. Seeking to compensate for a lack of science instruction in France's Catholic-controlled schools, he viewed Verne's novels as an ideal way to achieve this goal by taking readers on imaginary 'Journeys to Known and Unknown Worlds' (the subtitle of the series). It was partly this pedagogical social function that allowed Verne's SF to attain what one literary scholar has called a successful 'sociological implantation', establishing for the genre as a whole a credible 'institutional landing point and ideological model' (Angenot 1978: 64). From the geographical discoveries of an aerial trek across Africa in *Five Weeks in a Balloon* (1863) to the geology and palaeontology of *Journey to the Center of the Earth* (1864), from the astronomy and physics of space flight in *From the Earth to the Moon* (1865) to the oceanography and marine biology of *Twenty Thousand Leagues under the Seas* (1870), and from the chemistry of *The Mysterious Island* (1875) to the aeronautics of *Robur the Conqueror* (1886), Verne's most popular narratives always sought to interweave *real* science into their fictional storylines. In a 1903 interview toward the end of his life, when Verne was asked to compare his own work with that of his younger rival H. G. Wells, he identified this role of science as the greatest single difference between their two approaches:

> 'No, there is no *rapport* between his work and mine. I make use of physics. He invents. I go to the moon in a cannonball discharged from a cannon. Here there is no invention. He goes to the Mars [*sic*] in an airship which he constructs of a metal which does away with the law of gravitation. *Ça c'est très joli*,' cried Monsieur Verne in an animated way. 'But show me this metal. Let him produce it.' (Sherard 1903: 589, emphasis in original)

Three other attributes of Verne's *romans scientifiques* that enhanced their appeal were their ability to evoke unlimited mobility, their 'quest' narrative structure, and their frequent use of powerful but anthropo-morphised technology – what I have referred to elsewhere as his 'dream machines' (Evans 2013: 129–46). By portraying exciting journeys to destinations 'where no man has gone before', Verne's novels transport readers to the farthest reaches of the Earth and beyond: to such richly mythic locales as the North and South Poles in *The Adventures of Captain Hatteras* (1866) and *The Ice Sphinx* (1897), the Amazon jungles in *The Jangada* (1881), the hidden depths of the oceans in *Twenty Thousand Leagues under the Seas* (1870), the dark side of the Moon in *Around the Moon* (1870), and even the distant planets of our solar system in *Hector Servadac* (1877). Many of the journeys depicted are structured around a specific quest motif. This may be to find a missing loved one, as in *The Children of Captain Grant* (1867), *Mistress Branican* (1891), or *The Mighty Orinoco* (1898); to map an unexplored region, as in *Meridiana: The Adventures of Three Englishmen and Three Russians in South Africa* (1872); to transform part of the Sahara into an inland sea, as in *The Invasion of the Sea* (1905); or to survive as castaways on a deserted Pacific island, as in *The Mysterious Island* (1875) or *A Two-Year Vacation* (1888). And most include an intriguing piece of vehicular technology: Captain Nemo's futuristic submarine *Nautilus*; Barbicane and Nicholl's aluminium space-bullet (so similar to the Apollo 11 capsule); the electricity-powered helicopter airship *Albatross* in *Robur the Conqueror* (1886); the steam-driven overland locomotive (designed to resemble an Indian elephant) in *The Steam House* (1880); the many different modes of transport (both hi-tech and low) used by Phileas Fogg and Passepartout in their circumnavigation of the globe in *Around the World in 80 Days* (1873); and finally the polymorphic car/boat/airplane named *The Terror*, invented by a now-insane Robur in *Master of the World* (1904). Such imaginary vehicles incarnated the Industrial-age utopian ideal of facility of movement within a rapidly moving world – or *Mobilis in mobili*, as Captain Nemo aptly put it. If the scientific didacticism of Verne's *romans scientifiques* helped to form their social identity, it was their visionary content that made them truly memorable. As one critic has observed, Verne's 'best work transcends pedagogy and subverts its own conservatism. . . . Instruction and adventure are put in the foreground but then yield to symbolism in the service of a new "mythology of the Machine" that stays to haunt our imagination when his science lessons are forgotten' (Alkon 1994: 66–7).

It is important to acknowledge that many of Verne's later works, published after Hetzel's death in 1886, show a dramatic change of tone when compared to his earlier and more celebrated *Voyages extraordinaires*. In general, they tend to be more pessimistic about the ultimate benefits of science and sceptical about the moral integrity of scientists, who are increasingly depicted as irresponsible, untrustworthy, or crazed. These novels often reflect 'unVernian' attitudes such as Romantic angst, Juvenalian satire, or anger over social injustice, recalling some of Verne's pre-Hetzel short stories such as 'Master Zacharius' (1854) or his 'lost' novel, the dystopian *Paris in the Twentieth Century* (1994), rejected by Hetzel in 1863. Consider, for example, the story *The Purchase of the North Pole* (1889), in which the members of Verne's Baltimore Gun Club, famous for their trip around the Moon, now seek to alter the angle of the Earth's axis with a gigantic cannon blast. Indifferent to the environmental and human devastation that would result from such a project, their scheme is to melt the Earth's polar ice cap in order to uncover vast mineral wealth for themselves. Thanks to a serendipitous *deus ex machina*, they fail miserably in their attempt and end up being universally ridiculed and socially ostracised. The final sentence makes clear the intended moral of the story: 'It is not given to mankind to change the order established by the Creator in the system of the Universe' (Verne 1889: 143). The same message resonates in the destruction of Verne's giant floating island in his novel *The Self-Propelled Island* (1895), which concludes with a similar rhetorical question, asking whether humanity has 'not been forbidden to usurp so recklessly the power of the Creator?' (Verne 1895: 323). And finally, note Verne's cautionary tale *Master of the World* (1904) – a dark sequel to his literary homage to heavier-than-air flight in *Robur the Conqueror* (1886) – in which the once-heroic engineer Robur has now become an insane megalomaniac intent on world domination, until he and his flying machine are blasted out of the skies by a Providential lightning bolt. Verne's other post-1886 works also highlight a broad range of social and environmental issues: the cruel oppression of the Québécois in Canada in *Family without a Name* (1889); the harm caused by superstitious belief in *The Castle of the Carpathians* (1892); the inhumane treatment of Irish orphans in *Foundling Mick* (1893); the environmental pollution caused by the American oil industry in *The Last Will of an Eccentric* (1899); and the slaughter of elephants for their ivory in *The Village in the Treetops* (1901), among others.

After Verne

Verne and his *Voyages extraordinaires* made a deep impact on the ever-evolving genre of SF during the the mid- to late nineteenth century. Their influence was international in scope as many speculative writers from around the world, seeking to emulate Verne's commercial success, adopted his 'hard science' narrative style. Examples include, in France, Louis Boussenard's *Monsieur Synthesis* (1888), Henry de Graffigny and Georges Le Faure's multi-volume *Extraordinary Adventures of a Russian Scientist Across the Solar System* (1889–96), and Paul d'Ivoi's action-packed series of novels called the *Voyages excentriques* (1894–1914). Russia, always one of the most lucrative foreign markets for Verne's books, saw the publication of Konstantin Tsiolkovsky's *On the Moon* (1887) and *The Call of the Cosmos* (1895) and Vladimir Obruchev's *Plutonia* (1915). James de Mille's *A Strange Manuscript Found in a Copper Cylinder* (1888), Robert Cromie's *A Plunge into Space* (1890), and George Griffith's *The Angel of the Revolution* (1893) appeared in pre-Wells England. In Germany, the 'German Jules Verne' Robert Kraft's young-adult SF series *From the Realms of the Imagination* appeared in 1901 and Friedrich Wilhelm Mader's *Distant Worlds* in 1911. Spain and Latin America saw Eduardo Holmberg's *The Marvellous Voyage of Mr. Nic-Nac* (1876), Enrique Gaspar's pre-Wells time-machine story *The Time Ship* (1887) **[1.7]**, and Nilo María Fabra's 'On the Planet Mars' (1890). Finally, in the pre-Gernsback United States, we find Edward S. Ellis's frontier SF western *The Steam Man of the Prairies* (1868), E. E. Hale's satellite story *The Brick Moon* (1869), Frank R. Stockton's *The Great War Syndicate* (1889), and the many Frank Reade dime novels by Luis P. Senarens and others that flourished from the 1870s through to the *fin-de-siècle*.

Figure 1.7 Cover of Enrique Gaspar's *Novelas* (1887) for 'El Anacronópete'
depicting the earliest known portrayal of a time machine.

But the SF genre would soon take a dramatic new turn with the
publication of H. G. Wells's first 'scientific romances' from 1895 to
1914, visionary works that bridge two centuries both literally and
narratologically and whose popularity would inspire new generations
of SF readers and writers. Wells's genius was to change the role played
by science in the discursive structure of his SF texts. Rather than
seeking to teach science or to adhere closely to known scientific law
in his stories (as per the Vernian model), he chose instead to speculate
on more fantastical 'what-if' scenarios and to use what he called 'scientific patter' to enhance their verisimilitude. In other words, Wells
shifted the primary focus of his SF thought experiments away from
their scientific plausibility and more toward their social, political, and
psychological outcomes. And, in so doing, he pushed the SF genre
into new cognitive and aesthetic territory, opening new frontiers of
the beyond to explore.

References

Alkon, Paul K. (1987), *Origins of Futuristic Fiction*. Athens, GA: University of Georgia Press.

———— (1994), *Science Fiction Before 1900*. New York: Twayne.

Angenot, Marc (1978), 'Science Fiction Before Verne', *Science Fiction Studies* 5: 1, pp. 58–66.

Bailey, J. O. (1947), *Pilgrims Through Space and Time: Trends and Patterns in Scientific and Utopian Fiction*. New York: Argus.

Balzac, Honoré de (2005), *The Centenarian* [1822]. Middletown, CT: Wesleyan University Press.

Bleiler, Everett F. (1990), *Science-Fiction: The Early Years*. Kent, OH: Kent State University Press.

———— (1999), 'Edgar Allan Poe', in *Science Fiction Writers*, ed. Richard Bleiler. New York: Charles Scribner's Sons, pp. 595–604.

Bould, Mark, and Sherryl Vint (2011), *The Routledge Concise History of Science Fiction* London: Routledge.

Clarke, I. F. (1995), *The Tale of the Next Great War, 1871–1914*. Liverpool: Liverpool University Press.

Clute, John, and Peter Nicholls, eds (1993), *The Encyclopedia of Science Fiction*. New York: St. Martin's Press.

Delany, Samuel R. (2009), *The Jewel-Hinged Jaw* [1978]. Middletown, CT: Wesleyan University Press.

Disch, Thomas M. (1998), *The Dreams Our Stuff Is Made of: How Science Fiction Conquered the World*. New York: Simon & Schuster.

Evans, Arthur B. (1988), *Jules Verne Rediscovered: Didacticism and the Scientific Novel*. Westport, CT: Greenwood Press.

———— (2013), 'Jules Verne's Dream Machines: Technology and Transcendence', *Extrapolation* 54: 2 (summer), pp. 129–46.

————, Istvan Csicsery-Ronay, Joan Gordon, Veronica Hollinger, Rob Latham, and Carol McGuirk, eds (2010), *The Wesleyan Anthology of Science Fiction*. Middletown, CT: Wesleyan University Press.

Garnier, Charles-Georges-Thomas, ed. (1787–9), *Voyages imaginaires, songes, visions et romans cabalistiques*. 36 vols. Paris: Hôtel Serpente.

Gernsback, Hugo (1926), 'A New Sort of Magazine', *Amazing Stories* 1: 1 (April), p. 3.

Gove, Philip Babcock (1941), *The Imaginary Voyage in Prose Fiction*. New York: Columbia University Press.

Hetzel, Pierre-Jules (1866), 'Avertissement de l'Editeur' in *Voyages et aventures du capitaine Hatteras* by Jules Verne. Hetzel: Paris, pp. 7–8.

Kincaid, Paul (2003), 'On the Origins of Genre', *Extrapolation* 44, pp. 409–19.

Knight, Damon (1967), *In Search of Wonder: Essays on Modern Science Fiction*. Chicago: Advent.

Luckhurst, Roger (2005), *Science Fiction*. Cambridge: Polity.

Merril, Judith (1971), 'What Do You Mean: Science? Fiction?' [1966], in *SF: The Other Side of Realism: Essays on Modern Science Fiction and Fantasy*, ed. Thomas D. Clareson. Bowling Green, OH: Bowling Green University Press, pp. 53–95.

Nicolson, Marjorie Hope (1960), *Voyages to the Moon* [1948]. New York: Macmillan.

O'Brien, Fitz-James (1966), 'The Diamond Lens' [1858], in *Future Perfect: American Science Fiction in the Nineteenth Century*, ed. H. Bruce Franklin. New York: Oxford University Press, pp. 328–51.

Poe, Edgar Allan (1938), *The Complete Tales and Poems of Edgar Allan Poe*, ed. Hervey Allen. New York: Random House.

Roberts, Adam (2006), *The History of Science Fiction*. New York: Palgrave Macmillan.

Sherard, Robert H. (1903), 'Jules Verne Re-visited', *T.P.'s Weekly* (9 October), p. 589.

Stableford, Brian (2016), *The Plurality of Imaginary Worlds: The Evolution of French Roman Scientifique*. Encino, CA: Black Coat Press.

Suvin, Darko (1979), *Metamorphoses of Science Fiction: On the Poetics and History of a Literary Genre*. New Haven, CT: Yale University Press.

Verne, Jules (1864), 'Edgard Poë et ses oeuvres', *Musée des Familles* 31: 7 (April), pp. 193–208. Translated by I. O. Evans as 'The Bizarre Genius of Edgar Poe', in *The Jules Verne Companion*, ed. Peter Haining. London: Souvenir Press, 1978, pp. 26–30.

—— (1864), *Five Weeks in a Balloon*. Trans. F. P. Walter, ed. A. B. Evans. Middletown: Wesleyan University Press, 2015.

—— (1889), *Sans dessus dessous*. Paris: Hetzel. Trans. (anonymously) as *The Purchase of the North Pole*. London: Sampson Low, 1890.

———— (1895), *L'Île à hélice*. Paris: Hetzel. Trans. Marie-Thérèse Noiset as *The Self- Propelled Island*. Lincoln, NE: The University of Nebraska Press, 2015.

Versins, Pierre (1972), *Encyclopédie de l'utopie, des voyages extraordinaires, et de la science fiction*. Lausanne: L'Âge d'homme.

Wells, H. G. (1934), 'Preface', in *Seven Famous Novels by H. G. Wells*. New York: Alfred A. Knopf, pp. vii–x.

What to Read Next

Cyrano de Bergerac, *Other Worlds: The Comical History of the States and Empires of the Moon and Sun*. Translated and with an Introduction by Geoffrey Strachan (London: New English Library, 1976).

Peter Fitting (ed.), *Subterranean Worlds: A Critical Anthology* (Middletown, CT: Wesleyan University Press, 2004).

Edgar Allan Poe, *Poetry and Tales*. Edited by Patrick Quinn (New York: Library of America, 1984).

Albert Robida, *The Twentieth Century*. Translated by Philippe Willems and edited by Arthur B. Evans (Middletown, CT: Wesleyan University Press, 2004).

Mary Shelley, *Frankenstein, or the Modern Prometheus*. Edited with an Introduction and Notes by Maurice Hindle (London: Penguin, 2003).

Jules Verne, *The Mysterious Island*. Translated by Sidney Kravitz with an Introduction and Notes by William Butcher (Middletown, CT: Wesleyan University Press, 2001).

H. G. Wells, *The Time Machine and The Island of Dr. Moreau*. Edited with an Introduction by Patrick Parrinder (London: Oxford University Press, 1996).

Chapter 2

From Scientific Romance to Science Fiction: 1870–1914

Roger Luckhurst

Contexts

An extraordinary set of conditions in British and American print culture came together in the latter half of the nineteenth century to produce a great flowering of popular literary forms. There was an explosion of newspapers and cheap weekly and monthly magazines and journals. This expansion was partly driven by a new mass audience from compulsory education, but also innovations in printing technologies that pushed costs down. The launch of national papers such as the *Daily Mirror* and the *Daily Mail* created powerful publishing empires for influential magnates such as Alfred Harmsworth and George Newnes in Britain, or William Randolph Hearst in the US.

Newnes was a pioneer, creating the weekly *Tit-Bits* in 1881 expressly as 'light' reading for the mass working population, involving a mix of short columns, news stories, jokes, gossip, and fiction. It started with a circulation of 12,000, but ended the century with nearly 700,000. Newnes then went after the lower middle-class 'monthly' magazine market too, launching the *Strand Magazine* in 1890. The success of this mix of heavily illustrated essays and short serial stories was secured when Newnes published the first Sherlock Holmes serial story, 'A Scandal in Bohemia', in 1891. Newnes paid Arthur Conan Doyle vast sums through the years to secure the return of the detective, while other writers and journals tried to imitate the formula. In the US, the newspaper magnate Frank Munsey published various forms of the *Argosy* magazine from 1882, hitting on an all-story format in the 1890s that is often considered one of the first pulp magazines. By the 1930s, pulp magazines were produced in their hundreds from the print works of New York and were read in their tens of millions.

The demand for short and serial fiction in this new environment rapidly established a whole new literary world. Middle-class Victorians read three-volume novels borrowed from circulating libraries that held a monopoly over publishers. There were a handful of respectable monthly journals that were considered arbiters of taste. In the 1880s, shorter books in one volume began to be sold cheaply and directly to the mass public. By 1897, the three-volume novel had entirely vanished. Instead, terms like 'bestseller' and 'short story' were coined. Writers made deals through a brand-new profession of agents, struggled to secure international copyright, and became public celebrities who featured in the newspaper gossip columns. There were 'booms' about exciting new authors – Robert Louis Stevenson, Henry Rider Haggard, Rudyard Kipling, Marie Corelli, Arthur Conan Doyle. In the 1890s, H. G. Wells was a representative figure of this new generation; a young man from the shopkeeping classes who had escaped a miserable apprenticeship to a draper but failed at schoolmastering, and who returned to London with less than £5 in his pocket in 1888. His breakthrough into professional writing came in 1893, when he started earning a steady, if precarious, income writing pieces of journalism for the new press. In the year that he published his first fiction, *The Time Machine: An Invention,* he earned several hundred pounds and was by 1900 wealthy enough to build his own house.

This was the world of *New Grub Street,* described in George Gissing's 1891 novel about the penurious life of hack writers and journalists, many of whom subsisted at or below the poverty line as they slaved over copy. Gissing regarded the popular press as addressing the 'quarter-educated', 'the great new generation being turned out by the Board Schools, the young men and women who can just read, but are incapable of sustained attention' (Gissing 1993: 460). *New Grub Street* was a bitter portrait of artistic failure and cynical success in the merciless commercial marketplace of professional writing.

Writers such as Haggard or Wells were creations of this new marketplace, often not writing in the stolid tradition of domestic realism but presenting wild, exotic revivals of the older romance form, often in thrilling, headlong prose that abandoned classical rhetorical structures for a more demotic style. Traditional defenders of literary culture largely despised this new generation as the barbarians at the gate. The fore-runner of the *Times Literary Supplement* was established in 1897 to distinguish the 'better authors' from 'the rubbish heap of incompetence' that was flooding the market and debasing the moral virtues of literature (Keating 2011: 76). Crucially, then, this was also the era when the modern distribution of the relative value of high and low culture, and the pejorative notion of 'middlebrow' literature, emerged.

What Wells and others started to call the 'scientific romance' is one of the popular genre forms that arose in this very particular context, along with spy fiction, detective fiction, the colonial romance, and the mutation of old school eighteenth-century Gothic romance into weird tales, occult fiction, and modern horror. All of these forms had forebears, of course, but I am emphasising the publishing conditions that allowed for the structures of genre to emerge in their distinct mass modern forms in this era. 'Science fiction' would stabilise around that name and in its own magazines only at the end of the 1920s. 'Early SF' existed in lots of different forms, as Arthur Evans explored in Chapter 1, but modern, commercial SF was clearly taking shape in this late-nineteenth-century ecology of new mass literature.

Why is the scientific romance one of these emergent genres? The other crucial contexts to consider are the significant shift of the cultural authority of science and the transformation of everyday life by electrical technologies after 1870. In Britain, a series of government commissions in the 1870s resulted in research funding, scientific institutions, and the teaching of science for the first time in any systematic way. It made the idea of a career in science, the professional 'scientist', rather than the gentleman amateur, possible ('scientist' was a term coined by William Whewell in 1833, but remained largely unused for the rest of the nineteenth century). The confidence of this generation of scientific men that there had been a decisive shift from theology to science was signalled by the physicist John Tyndall, when he declared as newly elected president of the British Association for the Advancement of Science in 1874:

'The impregnable position of science may be described in a few words. All religious theories, schemes, and systems, which embrace notions of cosmogony, or which otherwise reach into its domain must, in so far as they do this, submit to the control of science' (Tyndall 1874: 318). This assertion caused splenetic outrage, and the struggle to include scientific ideas in schools, especially in church-funded schools (but also in state education), in fact continued long afterwards.

Perhaps even more significant was the visible transformation of everyday experience by technology. Steamships, newspapers, express trains, telegrams, and telephones compressed time and space, turning the globe into an interlinked network. Populations, cities, empires, tele-technologies, machines, and arms multiplied and accelerated at speeds that seemed at once exhilarating and potentially disastrous. Contemporary commentators on the late nineteenth century self-consciously regarded their era as one of restless innovation, a modernity that risked spiralling out of control. The future – its promises and cataclysms – seemed to be increasingly folded into the present.

In the 1890s, the transatlantic *McClure's Magazine* began its monthly issue with a round-up called 'The Edge of the Future'. 'The edge of the electric future is bright with immediate promise', ran the New Year message for 1894, with headlines that included: 'LIFE PROLONGED BY THE MASTERY OF ELECTRICITY', 'SEEING A THOUSAND MILES', 'AN APPARATUS FOR THE AUTOMATIC REGISTRATION OF UNWRITTEN, UNSPOKEN THOUGHT', 'WARS AND HUNGER TO CEASE'. The magazine made culture heroes of inventors such as Thomas Edison and Alexander Graham Bell, who seemed to speak with absolute conviction from somewhere in the near future, where the promise of 'THOUGHT TRANSFERENCE BY ELECTRICITY' blurred with the actual discovery, in 1896, of Wilhelm Röntgen's 'X-Rays', 'a new kind of light' that revealed the astounding possibilities of the invisible world that lay beyond the narrow spectrum of the human senses.

At the same time that this utopian, promissory discourse flooded the press, there were also voices predicting the imminent collapse of the Western world, often precisely as a result of this accelerated modernity. If the arms race between the European powers didn't end it, or fears of a future world war, the intricate inner secrets of human biology might. The German journalist Max Nordau made a splash with *Degeneration*

(1892, translated into English 1895), which began with a vision of 'The Dusk of Nations' in the Western world and went on to detail symptoms of over-stimulation, moral and nervous collapse, and growing hysteria, all of which would result in rapid racial degeneracy. Decadence was the name of the leading aesthetic movement of the era, a group that fantasised repeatedly about corruption and collapse, decline and fall. '*Fin de siècle*', mutters one of Oscar Wilde's jaded dandies in *The Picture of Dorian Gray* (1890). '*Fin du globe*', comes the reply, in an exchange that neatly captures the equal mix of neurosis, boredom, and dread that circulated in the 1890s. No wonder Wilde was presented as a prime example of Nordau's 'degeneration'. When the clash of Europe's imperial powers arrived in the cataclysm of the Great War in 1914, it came in a technological form that this strange, prophetic era had long predicted, almost willing its own destruction into being.

Many fictions that we now identify as SF were part of the heady brew of stories bubbling in the cauldron of this era. It was one of the key forms of commercial mass literature that turned the bewildering contradictions of this period into narrative form, particularly responding to scientific and technological breakthroughs, but often as much a symptom of processing these rapid changes as an attempt to diagnose them. Histories of the genre (including my own) tend to try to isolate the passage from the 'scientific romance' of the 1880s, via H. G. Wells's famous first fictions in the 1890s, to the 'science fiction' of the 1920s. This is obviously an important strand, but in this chapter I want to emphasise that this was an era that produced – and across the world – a whole host of different, overlapping forms of fantastical fictions, all of which fed into what was always a quintessentially hybrid literature with blurred boundaries.

'Scientific Romance'

Edwin Abbott published the eccentric mathematical/fictional folly about the two-dimensional world, *Flatland,* in 1884. In response a peculiar maths teacher at Uppingham School, Charles Howard Hinton, seized the opportunity to publish a pamphlet about his theory of the *fourth* dimension. This became one of a series of pamphlets published over the following year and collected together under the title *Scientific Romances* in 1886. 'What is the Fourth Dimension?' was an exercise in speculation involving non-Euclidean geometries and the higher mathematics, which were used to challenge the limits of senses 'continually narrowed by the ever-increasing complications of our civilisation', Hinton said (1886: 4). He explained how a four-dimensional being might 'suddenly appear as a complete and finite body, and as suddenly disappear, leaving no trace of himself, in space' (Hinton 1886: 25). The fourth dimension was explored as a theoretical possibility but also as a question of perception and psychology – and indeed Hinton was then spending much of his time trying to train his students to *see* into the fourth dimension. This first scientific romance was followed by a far more unclassifiable piece of speculation called 'The Persian King' that mixed mathematical exposition in awkward fictionalised dialogues and interludes.

Hinton's scientific romances were well received by scientific and literary reviewers alike. He would go on to publish a grand philosophical synthesis of his ideas, *A New Era of Thought* (1888), an occult novel, *Stella, and an Unfinished Communication (Studies in the Unseen)* where a scientist working 'on the borderland between chemistry and physics' (Hinton 1895: 17) conjures a presence invisible in three dimensions because of the 'coefficient of refraction in the body' (Hinton 1895: 29), but present in four, and debates the possibility of this alternate plane of reality with chemists, mathematicians, occultists, and spiritualists. Hinton published a second eclectic volume of *Scientific Romances* in 1898.

Hinton fell from grace early when he was found guilty of bigamy in 1886, and after a very public trial and conviction in London he spent the rest of his life in various posts in Japan and America. Marginalised by this scandal, his speculative ideas about the fourth dimension nevertheless had a wide cultural influence, becoming not just a convention in science-fictional stories, but also influencing mainstream literature, as in Joseph Conrad and Ford Madox Hueffer's romance, *The Inheritors,* which used the premise of visitors from the fourth dimension to critique the degeneracy of three-dimensional society in 1901. Its main impact, though, was on the late Victorian occult revival. The fourth dimension became a mathematical proof of spirit worlds in the works of spiritualists such as W. T. Stead or the German physicist Johann Zöllner, who mixed up mathematical calculations and practical experiments with the spiritualist medium Henry Slade to come up with a proof of the fourth dimension. This higher-dimensional space was the locus for alternate, higher realities, which could be rendered visible through gnostic training in the influential writing and practice of mystics such as P. D. Ouspensky and Rudolf Steiner. The rigours of the higher mathematics were coterminous with higher spiritual planes to Hinton and many of his readers. This mixing up of science, occultism, fiction, and imaginative speculation was the ambiguous legacy buried in the term Hinton chose, the 'scientific romance'.

H. G. Wells opens *The Time Machine* with a differently framed discussion of the fourth dimension, which he suggests is temporal not spatial (the fourth dimension was an idea he had encountered as a student at the Normal School of Science in the 1880s). He also explored these ideas in his early short stories, such as 'The Plattner Story' (1896), in which a German scientist is blasted into the fourth dimension in a laboratory accident, and 'The Remarkable Case of Davidson's Eyes' (1896). When *The Time Machine* was published in May 1895, Wells sent a copy to the fellow science journalist and popular author Grant Allen, writing: 'I flatter myself that I have a certain affinity with you. I believe that this field of scientific romance with a philosophical element which I am trying to cultivate, belongs properly to you' (Smith 1998: I, 245–6). Wells was already following a nascent genre.

Allen is another exemplary product of the late Victorian publishing explosion. His first book was a dry biological tome called *Physiological Aesthetics* (1877), written in strict accord with the developmental theories of evolutionary thinker Herbert Spencer. Like Wells, Allen became too ill to teach and was forced into journalism from 1880, where he became a prolific writer of popular science articles for the burgeoning middle- and lower-class journal market. Almost by accident, he discovered that writing ghost stories paid considerably more, and despite a disgust with the lesser mode of fiction almost as great as his materialist disdain for superstitious beliefs in ghosts and spirits (which he saw as an evolutionary regression to 'savage' thought), he produced enough of these lurid shockers to publish *Strange Stories* in 1884. He soon learnt that the three-volume Realist novel was not his forte (*Philistia* was an utter failure), so instead returned to a sequence of romances, all conceived within a strict social Darwinian frame. For one of these, *What's Bred in the Bone* (1890), he even won a prize of £1,000 and serial publication from Newnes's *Tit-Bits* magazine. In the 1890s, Allen became a studied controversialist, addressing sexual freedom and women's rights in the much-debated *The Woman Who Did* (1894). The follow-up, *The British Barbarians* (1895) was a satirical inversion of utopia, detailing the fieldwork of an anthropologist from the twenty-fifth century who has travelled back in time to undertake a study of the peculiarly primitive social and sexual taboos of England in the 1890s. It was exactly the kind of inversion Wells would use in *The War of the Worlds,* dethroning the arrogance of an imperial metropole that considered its population to be the most advanced beings on the planet. Allen called these romances 'hill-top novels', rising above the cesspool of the Thames Valley, to observe and critique modern mores of London society. In one memorable short story, 'The Thames Valley Catastrophe' (published in the *Strand* in 1901), Allen delightedly destroyed London and its western suburbs with a violent volcanic eruption.

Wells's 'scientific romances' began with *The Time Machine* **[2.1]**, which borrowed quite a lot of this 'hill-top' sermonising, sending the Time Traveller forward to the year 802,701 to find not evolutionary progress but exactly the sort of degeneracy of the race then being discussed by Max Nordau and others. After the profound disappointment of meeting his simple-minded savage descendants, the Eloi, the traveller sits on a hill to reflect on the suicide of the race, a decadence arising from too much ease and comfort, a loss of the energy provided by the Darwinian struggle to survive. His pompous theorising is wrong, of course, because he has yet to encounter his other descendants, the Morlocks, who live below the bucolic hills in workshops and tunnels underground. The Morlocks are the ambiguous remainder of the industrial working classes who have taken revenge for their oppression by their effete capitalist overlords by turning them into supper. This is the barely articulable final horrific secret of this future London, for cannibalism was the mark of the most primitive in nineteenth-century hierarchies of race. The traveller barely escapes this awful fate himself, scrambling on to his time machine and plunging a further thirty million years into the future to witness the apocalyptic heat death of the planet, a desolate

Figure 2.1 Frontispiece illustrated by W.B. Russell from the first edition
of *The Time Machine*.

rock falling towards an exhausted Sun. It was this sublime extension of
a rigorous evolutionary extrapolation into the far future that signalled
a new kind of cosmological time-scale for the apocalyptic imagination.
The French astronomer (and occultist) Camille Flammarion had just
imagined a similar entropic end of the world in *Omega* (1894).

Wells's early years were marked by an impish pleasure in using
advances in the sciences and innovations in machinery to undermine
the security of his readers. Early journalistic pieces were full of jarring
extrapolations from biology, warning, for instance, that humanity may be
the dominant animal on the planet, but: 'Its reign may be brief or long,
but, brief or long, at the end of it, awaiting it, is the absolute certainty

Figure 2.2 The Martians from H. G. Wells's *The War of the Worlds*, as depicted by Alvim-Correa in the Belgian edition, *La Guerre des mondes* (1906).

of death' (Wells 1894: 656). *The War of the Worlds* (1898) **[2.2]** combined this biological dethronement with an exploitation of the renewed fascination with the planet Mars after an Italian astronomer, Giovanni Schiaparelli, in the 1870s spotted *canali* or striations on the Martian surface that many interpreted as artificial structures and, therefore, signs of life. Wells imagined an older race, more advanced than humans, reversing the anthropological gaze with menacing effect: 'intellects vast and cool and unsympathetic, regarded this earth with envious eyes, and slowly and surely drew their plans against us' (Wells 1993: 5). The depiction of the destruction of London that follows and the instant collapse of civilisation so outraged the astronomer and popular science writer Garrett Serviss in America that he composed an immediate sequel for the *Boston Post*, in which the world teams up around the inventor Thomas Edison to build rockets and weapons strong enough to ensure a decisive counter strike against Mars. Wells's scientific romance is redolent with British irony and fear of degeneration; Serviss's *Edison's Conquest of Mars,* in contrast, is exemplary of the can-do engineering paradigm that became central to American pulp SF.

None of Wells's early scientists or engineers are especially sympathetic: Dr Griffin of *The Invisible Man* (1897) is secretive, angry, and too morally feeble to cope with his chemical discovery of invisibility, instead indulging in an inept crime spree. One of the pioneers of flying machines in the short story 'Filmer' ends up committing suicide. Wells's brilliant but unhinged vivisectionist Dr Moreau is perhaps the most amoral scientist since Shelley's Frankenstein. Chased out of Europe for offending civilised sensibilities, he conducts grotesque experiments in splicing animals together in a doomed attempt to uplift creatures into men. He creates hybrid monsters that defy category and who overthrow their cruel master only to inevitably regress back towards the animal again. *The Island of Dr Moreau* was received as a queasy Gothic horror rather than a progressive scientific romance. It is a nightmare of eugenics (controlled breeding) that is teased out as a perverse twist hidden in the logic of Darwinian theory.

Brian Stableford argues persuasively that there is a distinctive British tradition of the scientific romance, imbued with the biological imagination, that was consolidated by Wells and which was continued in Wellsian vein by J. D. Beresford, who wrote *The Hampdenshire Wonder* in 1911, a satire about an evolutionary 'sport' hounded by his dullard human contemporaries. The Darwinian underpinning of the British scientific romance feeds into the extraordinary visionary fiction of Olaf Stapledon, whose *Last and First Men* (1930) covers no less than eighteen generations of human evolution into the far distant future. Stapledon corresponded with Wells; Stapledon was also a guest speaker to a gathering organised by a very young Arthur C. Clarke in the 1930s, a writer who was to become far more adept at fusing the British scientific romance with American conventions in the post-1945 consolidation of SF. Clarke's story

'The Sentinel' (1951), which became the basis for Stanley Kubrick's film *2001: A Space Odyssey* (1968), remains discernably Wellsian, however, as does the evolutionary uplift envisaged in Clarke's key novel, *Childhood's End* (1951).

But there are strong hints even in this brief summary to suggest that Wells was not constrained by the very nascent genre of the scientific romance, and indeed was writing simultaneously in wildly diverse forms, including comedy (*The Wheels of Chance,* 1896), fantasy (an angelic arrival in *The Wonderful Visit,* 1895), social realism (*Love and Mr Lewisham,* 1900), scientific reportage, futurological prediction (*Anticipations,* 1901), the ghost story, weird fiction, and Gothic horror. *The Time Machine* was recognisably embedded in an argument with contemporary utopian fiction. The traveller arrives in a London suspiciously like that of William Morris's *News from Nowhere* from 1890, only with a far nastier underside; it also mocks the glib social solutions to class conflict influentially proposed by Edward Bellamy's American utopia in *Looking Backward 2000–1887* (1888). For all the apparently mordant rejections of utopian hope in these early romances, Wells turned towards utopia in *A Story of the Days to Come* (1899) and *A Modern Utopia* (1905). After the turn of the century, Wells became very invested in the idea of a cadre of engineers taking over ailing nationalist democracies and providing carefully administered, rational solutions to global problems of wasteful rivalry and deadly conflict (an idea similarly pursued in Rudyard Kipling's stories about the Aerial Board of Control, a benign dictatorship of technicians starting with 'As Easy as A. B. C.' in 1905). Such technocratic fictions themselves became targets for writers appalled by the anti-human, totalitarian implications of Wells's writing. E. M. Forster's 'The Machine Stops' (1906) was an explicit riposte to Wells, as was Aldous Huxley's famous dystopia, *Brave New World* (1932). These engagements identified Wells with certain modes of literary genre, but also determinedly marginalised him from the formation of the English Literature canon. When the influential literature academic F. R. Leavis created the 'great tradition', it was formed against the crudities of 'mass culture' and explicitly named Wells as a danger to the refinement of literary taste.

We should read figures like Hinton, Allen, and Wells, then, as restless experimentalists in different residual and emergent forms, and see the scientific romance as only one strand that led towards the consolidation of SF. And in the late nineteenth century, these scientific and technological visions were always thoroughly intertwined with the Gothic and occult revivals.

Late Victorian Gothic Revival

In his second preface to *The Castle of Otranto* (1764), the author Horace Walpole confessed that his delirious medieval tale was not, after all, a recently discovered mouldering manuscript, but a fantasy from his own pen. He complained that the norm for the new kind of literature, called the novel, was fast becoming 'a strict adherence to common life' but that this dammed up and denigrated 'the great resources of fancy' (Walpole 2008: 9). The Gothic revival was, as SF was to be, the protest of fantasy against social realism that aligned moral virtue in literature with mimesis.

There have long been attempts to make a rigid conceptual opposition between SF and the Gothic: the former rational, scientific, and premised on natural law; the latter irrational, magical, and obsessed with the supernatural. This rarely works well: they are both products of the same industrial and scientific modernity of the eighteenth century. They share the context of modernity's ceaseless creative destruction, sometimes inflecting it in different ways, but often in fantastical forms that are very difficult to distinguish. This is why Mary Shelley's *Frankenstein* is at once a Gothic horror and early SF. And the accelerations of the second Industrial Revolution of the 1870s also provided a rich context for another burst of Gothic unease and outright horror.

The late Victorian romance revival was kick-started by Robert Louis Stevenson's *Treasure Island* (1883) and Henry Rider Haggard's *King Solomon's Mines* (1885), both huge successes in cheap editions sold directly to the public and praised by their defenders for restoring health and vitality to a novelistic tradition turned inward and neurotic by godless Naturalists (Emile Zola) or suspicious aesthetes with an unhealthy knowledge of women (Henry James). Stevenson was a bohemian avant-gardist, yet totally willing to exploit commercial possibilities in the new fiction ecology. In 1884, he published the ghost story 'Markheim' and the lurid horror 'The Body Snatchers', based on the notorious Burke and Hare crimes of the 1820s. The latter tale, for a Christmas special, was advertised in London by hiring six men dressed in white surplices to carry coffin-shaped boards – a vulgar marketing tactic soon curtailed by the police. The following Christmas, Stevenson was meant to deliver another seasonal Gothic tale, but being ill and uncertain about what he had written, just missed the deadline. *Strange Case of Dr Jekyll and Mr Hyde* **[2.3]** was instead published in January 1886, but this did not affect its instant global success.

The nature of Dr Henry Jekyll's (al)chemical experiments in his secret laboratory is not especially a focal point of the novella – in this,

Figure 2.3 Illustration by S.G. Hulme-Beaman to the 1930 edition of Robert Louis Stevenson's *Strange Case of Dr Jekyll and Mr Hyde*.

it follows Shelley's *Frankenstein*'s lack of interest in the mechanics of the science, but more in the ethical consequences that follow. Yet at the same time, Stevenson was picking up on extraordinary findings in experimental psychology that suggested that the model of mind bound together by unifying Will was incorrect, and that certain forms of fever, mental illness, natural trance states, and artificially induced somnambulism could weirdly split mental activity into multiple streams, even with their own partial identities and separate memory chains. Obscure French doctors toying with dubious 'Mesmeric' treatments had termed this '*dédoublement*' or 'double personality', a highly unorthodox and marginal area of research. However, in 1882, the leading European neurologist, Jean–Martin Charcot, accepted the experimental proof that hypnotic states were an objective phenomenon that reproduced the dissociations associated with certain kinds of mental illness. Stevenson's short, nasty fiction about a respectable doctor able to isolate and express his savage inner beast in Mr Hyde, was both a moral tale (although an ambiguous one, either about the dangers of too much or too little repression) and on the cutting edge of mental science. A pioneering psychologist of the 'subliminal' mind, Frederic Myers, wrote ecstatically to Stevenson that he had just formulated a case history crucial to the advance of experimental psychology. Indeed, the novella was soon incorporated into psychological studies around the world. Myers was perhaps Stevenson's perfect reader, since he was also a founder of the Society for Psychical Research, which had been set up to theorise 'supernatural' phenomena such as ghosts, second sight, psychic projections, doubles, and telepathy as explicable in the frameworks of emergent sciences of dynamic psychology and energy physics. *Jekyll and Hyde* was the significant success of the late Victorian Gothic revival; unnerving horrors would now emerge from the context of scientific advance.

A whole subgenre of 'psychic detectives', from Sheridan Le Fanu's Dr Hesselius from 'In A Glass Darkly' (1872), via Bram Stoker's Professor Van Helsing in *Dracula* (1897), to Algernon Blackwood's *John Silence, Physician Extraordinary* stories (1908) and William Hope Hodgson's *Carnacki, The Ghost-Finder* (1913), mixed the patina of psychical science with outright occultism. In contrast, Charlotte Perkins Gilman generated effective horror in her Gothic tale 'The Yellow Wall-Paper' (1892) by simply adhering to the latest medical advice for the psychological cure recommended for women suffering post-natal depression. Arthur Machen's controversial horror stories in *The Great God Pan* (1894) and *The Three Impostors* (1895) mimicked Stevenson's intricate plotting, and although saturated in fears of degeneration and a dread of pagan forces pushing through from the remote past, the stories also shadowed contemporary science – if only to mock the fragility of the empirical method. His recurrent character, Mr. Phillipps, is described as a 'student of physical science, and something of an ethnologist, [who] insisted that all literature ought to have a scientific basis' (Machen 1995: 8), and yet it is Phillipps who proves to be the most credulous and easily persuaded by the supernatural. The writer and critic Andrew Lang, ardent supporter of the romance revival, saw a simple dialectic at work in these fictions: 'As the visible world is measured, mapped, tested, and weighed, we seem to hope more and more that a world of invisible romance may not be far from us, or, at least, we care more and more to follow fancy into these airy regions' (Lang 1905: 279). And even the magical discoveries of 'dark matter' and invisible energies such as radiation, 'X-rays' and Hertzian waves seemed to exist in the vanishing point between the natural and the supernatural. A scientific romancer such as H. G. Wells also willingly exploited these marginal sciences to generate his fictions.

The Occult Scientific Romance

Another key figure in this twilight zone of scientific romance was the author Marie Corelli, whose first book, *A Romance of Two Worlds* (1886), started a career of astounding success, far outselling any of her popular rivals in Britain by many factors. *A Romance* is the story of the treatment of a neurotic young artist by a mysterious Chaldean healer in Paris. Heliobas propounds an esoteric 'Electric Creed', and is an adept at manipulating the physical electricity of the body, so repairing its 'delicate networks of fine threads – electric wires on which run messages of thought, impulse, affection and emotion' (Corelli 1931: 51). This spiritual treatment (very different from vulgar Mesmerism) produces a new health and creativity, but also leads towards a transcendent spiritual revelation of the astral world, taking the narrator on a journey through the solar system that drops in on the refined spiritual beings that inhabit Saturn and Jupiter. Earth, having turned away from God, is in contrast a 'doomed star' (Corelli 1931: 180). The book's foreword and afterword, added to later editions, affirmed this Electric Creed as the perfect fusion of modern science and religion. The 1896 edition used a *McClure's Magazine* interview with Röntgen about his newly discovered X-rays as an objective proof in science of this mystical Christian belief.

Corelli was continuously mocked and lambasted by critics, often in the same class terms as Wells (Edmund Gosse, the critic, called her 'that little milliner'). But her melodramatic romances, uplifting spiritual message, and moral denunciations of decadent culture and corrupt institutions were a phenomenon of the new mass market. 'Corelli' – herself an elaborate fictitious construct of an author by the lowly writer Minnie Mackay – was selling 100,000 copies of new books a year by 1900. It has been noted that these works 'cross genres, mixing the conventions of romance, gothic, historical and society novels', but also 'anticipate feminist science fiction' (Federico 2000: 2). *A Romance* and its sequel, *Ardath: The Story of a Dead Self* (1889) were occult scientific romances that echoed the mystical writings of Emma Hardinge Britten, whose *Ghost Land, or Researches into the Mysteries of Occultism* (1876) also contained interstellar journeys and amazing mystical revelations. (Britten was a medium who claimed to have had these 'truths' communicated to her in trance.) Corelli shared the same ambitions as the influential Theosophical Society, whose founder Helena Blavatsky lived in London in the late 1880s. Blavatsky's ambition was to synthesise all religions, East and West, with the modern sciences, spinning an extraordinary evolutionary fantasy of biological, racial, and spiritual development that stretched from the pre-human, prehistoric past to the far future.

Theosophists, like spiritualists and psychical researchers, eagerly followed scientific and technological developments, because they wanted 'to legitimate occult knowledge in the dominant public sphere in quasi-scientific terms of validation' (Morrisson 2008: 4). The promise of esoteric wisdom, wrapped up in the patina of invisible energies and magical electricity, was communicated through the vehicles of popular romances and the newspaper melodrama of notorious figures such as Blavatsky and Corelli. Corelli's tales too were part of the emergence of SF, although they are often written out of histories that are more comfortable with stricter lines of demarcation between SF, the Gothic, and the occult. Nevertheless, the visionary, mystical interplanetary mythologies constructed by, say, David Lindsay in *A Voyage to Arcturus* (1920) or in C. S. Lewis's Cosmic Trilogy, *Out of the Silent Planet* (1938), *Perelandra* (1943), and *That Hideous Strength* (1945), owe a debt to this tradition of travelling through the astral spheres, long embedded in the Christian conception of the universe.

The promise of Hermetic occult wisdom often exoticised the East as a space of mystery and forgotten scientific knowledge (Hermes was constructed by many in the West as a single, ancient Egyptian magus and the author of actually very diverse ancient magical texts). Hence Corelli's healer Heliobas was a Chaldean and Blavatsky made her occult guides to her grand occult works initially Egyptian and later 'Mahatmas' hidden away in the fastness of Tibet.

Of course, SF has a long prehistory embedded in the fantastical tall tales of travellers such as Marco Polo and John Mandeville. Again in the late nineteenth century, colonial expansion reignited this kind of exotic writing and fed into the emergence of SF.

The Colonial Romance and Global Modernity

This era saw the compression of global space through communication technologies: the Atlantic telegraph cable was laid in 1866 to much fanfare, but the Pacific cable that linked Australia and New Zealand only arrived in 1903. In Britain, the 'all-red' imperial telegraph route was often referred to as 'the nerves of empire'. New diesel engines in ships and horseless carriages also slashed travel times. The international agreement to organise the world into standard time zones measured from Greenwich in London was first proposed at the International Meridian Conference of 1884. This helped trade and travel and geopolitical arrangements at a time when rival European and American empires were busily carving up the world into colonial territories (Africa was divided between the European powers at the Berlin Conference of 1885).

In this era of newly aggressive imperialism, to travel in space, from West to East, was perceived as travelling back in time. As Marlow travels up the Congo River in Joseph Conrad's *Heart of Darkness* (1899), he describes a regression into the 'savage' origins of the world. That is why it is such a horror to find Kurtz, a white European, in the Congo's dark heart.

The colonial romance, with its exotic encounters of unknown races and territories weirdly disjunct from modern time (mostly behind, but sometimes ahead of Western modernity), is intrinsically science-fictional, as John Rieder has argued. Hence the exotic romances of Henry Rider Haggard, often set in the unknown interior of Africa, parallel the spiritual journeys of Corelli's occult romances. Haggard was the other massive-selling romancer of the era, producing at least one romance a year for forty years after his first success, *King Solomon's Mines* (1885) **[2.4]**. This tale, based on Haggard's extraordinary experience as a frontier colonial official

Figure 2.4 Frontispiece illustrated by Walter Paget for the 1887 edition of Sir H. Rider Haggard's *King Solomon's Mines*.

in Natal and the Transvaal provinces of southern Africa as a very young man, set up a formula. A group of Englishmen venture into the interior after the trace of a missing brother. Beyond the boundary of the administered world, they find an unknown race of Africans, highly organised and militarily powerful. The splendidly engineered ruins and noble natives are associated with the Biblical story of the city of Ophir, which mined the gold that was transported to King Solomon. The Englishmen incidentally help re-set a system of rule perverted by a corrupt, ageless (possibly supernatural) crone who tyrannises the society through witchcraft. The men fight for the rightful crown from principle in the face of certain death but survive and are rewarded with impossible wealth in diamonds.

The violent, bloody nature of the descriptions and the rush of demotic prose again singled out Haggard for huge commercial success and loud critical disdain. The *Church Quarterly Review* was appalled and declared Haggard the leading offender of 'the cult of the horrible'. After Haggard's own attack in a leading journal on the debased, neurotic literature he hoped to revitalise, he was utterly ignored by literary circles. Until recently, his large body of work was dismissed as straightforward ideological weapons of pro-imperialist popular culture. In fact, *King Solomon's Mines* was mournful compensation for the British destruction of the Zulu uprising against the British in 1879, a momentary success of a disciplined military force that humiliated the British Army and inevitably led to a punitive war and the annihilation of an African culture Haggard had come to admire, admittedly with the sentimentalism of the 'noble savage' mythos. The book promised adventure 'to all the big and little boys who read it' (as the dedication ran), but that doesn't stop it being a complex, ambiguous engagement with contemporary imperial politics. *She* (1886) was an even bigger success, another African fantasy that comes to reflect on the deathliness of whites in their dealings with their colonial others. The late Victorian romances of Rider Haggard can be seen as crucial switching points between genres, because his depictions of travel through the unevenly distributed time of modernity around the globe generate moments of wonder but often also slide towards Gothic feelings of horror and the uncanny.

While Haggard shaded gently from his real experiences of southern Africa into the fantasy world of Kukuanaland, others used the colonial frontier to create spaces of outright weirdness. Another writer with experience of South Africa, Bertram Mitford, merged his frontier fiction more overtly with the Gothic, in tales such as *The Weird of Deadly Hollow* (1891) and *The Sign of the Spider* (1896), the latter culminating in a hallucinatory encounter with a giant man-eating spider that is worshipped as the god of an African tribe that demands sacrificial tribute. In *The Lost World* (1912) **[2.5]**, Conan Doyle used a remote plateau in South America as an isolated ecosystem where dinosaurs have survived. One of the first and most influential of these adventures into exotic space was Edward Bulwer-Lytton's *The Coming Race* (1871), with adventurers who this time find a much more advanced race inside the hollow Earth. There is a direct line of descent from these kinds of colonial romances to the adventures of John Carter on Mars in the Barsoom series started by Edgar Rice Burroughs in *All-Story Magazine* in 1912. The series repeats

Figure 2.5 Illustration by Harry Rountree for Arthur Conan Doyle's *Lost World* from *The Strand*, July 1912.

the romance structure of Haggard's tale almost precisely, and is obsessed with distinguishing the hierarchy of races amongst the tribes of Mars. It is not surprising to find interplanetary spaces modelled on colonial spaces. After all, Cecil Rhodes, the agent of many dubious land-grabs in southern Africa in the 1880s and 1890s, who annexed the territory of Zambesia (renamed Rhodesia in his honour) once famously lamented: 'I would annex the planets if I could; I often think of that. It makes me sad to see them so clear and yet so far' (quoted in Millin 1933: 138). The expansive logic of space opera in the 1930s, and the interminable adventures of empires and rebels of the *Star Wars* movies from 1977 onwards, find their origins here.

I sometimes define SF as the literature of technologically saturated societies, but this comes with the implication that it limits the genre to advanced industrial contexts. In fact, the experience of modernity could be even sharper where uneven development meant less an immersive experience and more a jagged confrontation of different speeds and temporalities that accompany processes of globalisation. As genre historians have begun to show, the late nineteenth century was a crucial period for the development of SF around the world: in Japan (where Verne was translated first in 1878); China (where Huangjiang Diaosuo's *Tales from the Moon Colony* appeared the year after Verne's *From Earth to the Moon* was translated in 1903); in India (where Rokheya Shekhawat Hossain's gender-inverted utopia was published in 1905); and in Latin America, where *literatura fantástica* has been dated by Rachel Haywood Ferreira from Fósforos Cerillas' 'Mexico in the Year 1970' (1844), Dos Santos's *Pages from the History of Brazil Written in the Year 2000* (1868–72), and in Argentina, Eduardo Ladislao Holmberg's *The Marvellous Journey of Mr. Nic-Nac* (1875). In Russia, *Nature and People* magazine announced in 1894:

> Science and technology are defining modern reality by transforming not just everyday life, but the very ways in which we can think and imagine. A new kind of writing, called *nauchnaia fantastika,* scientific fantasy, is playing a not inconsequential role in the process ... Is it not in the imagination where bold theories and amazing fictions are first born? (cited Banerjee 2012: 1)

The refusal of Russian society to advance in accord with the objective developmental laws defined by confident social Darwinists in the nineteenth century made the eruption of the Revolution in 1917 even more startling. No wonder the Soviet revolutionaries were saturated with science-fictional ideas as they accelerated towards what they fervently believed was utopian futurity.

Future Wars

The last element I want to investigate here is directly linked to the age of empire and the growing tensions between rival European powers. In 1871, a year after the shockingly rapid victory of the newly organised and highly mobile Prussian army over disorderly French forces, the British soldier George Chesney imagined the invasion of Britain by the Germans in a short story masquerading as reportage for *Blackwood's Magazine*. 'The Battle of Dorking' **[2.6]** (there was something brilliant about choosing such an unexceptional locale) was a publishing sensation. It was

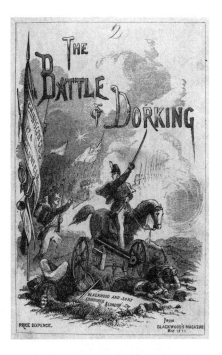

Figure 2.6 Illustration for *The Battle of Dorking* by George Chesney, from *Blackwood's Magazine*, May 1871.

followed by over 3,000 near-future war fictions and anxious invasion fantasies across Europe, all the way to the novel by Saki (H. H. Munro), *When William Came* (1913). The genre seemed nothing less than a slow and deadly conjuring into being of the apocalyptic Great War of 1914–18. Saki was killed by a German sniper in November 1916, shouting at his troops to put their cigarettes out: he had anticipated his own death.

Most of the contributions to this genre were overtly polemical attempts to whip up nationalist sentiment and force governments to spend more on armaments, barely stepping into the near future to project a theoretical invasion. The British Navy, central to imperial self-identity, was felt by conservatives to be under-funded, over-stretched, and falling behind the technological innovations of the newly unified German state. The British Army suffered humiliation in 1879 in southern Africa, failed to rescue the beloved (and reckless) General Gordon from an Islamic uprising in Khartoum in 1885, despite spending millions of pounds on a relief expedition, and was further humiliated by Boer farmers and irregulars using guerrilla tactics at the start of the Second Boer War in 1899. In this context, future-war scenarios were often thinly veiled propagandist demands for an increased budget for the War Office. The author and journalist William Le Queux developed a specialism in these fictions, many of which were serialised in the *Daily Mail*. *The Great War in England in 1897* (1894) was his first commission by the proprietor, but *The Invasion of 1910* (1906) – later published under the title *If England Were Invaded* – sold over a million copies as anxieties about a belligerent Germany increased. 'The object of this book is to illustrate our utter unpreparedness for war from a military standpoint; to show how, under certain conditions which may easily occur, England can be successfully invaded by Germany; and to present a picture of the ruin which must inevitably fall on us on the evening of that not far-distant day' (Le Queux 2014: xi). Like Chesney, Le Queux made this scenario extremely concrete, plotting out the swift night-time invasion along the East Anglian coast, the cutting of telegraph communications, and the starvation tactics of submarines sinking merchant vessels around the British coast. The prose slotted into the journalism surrounding its first publication, using military reports, journalist's accounts, and eye-witness narratives.

Wells's *The War of the Worlds* (1898) in this context looks like a generic exercise. The politics is very different, however, depicting only useless human defences against the heat rays of the Martians, the rapid disintegration of advanced civilisation into mass death and feral groups of survivors, and the insipid consolations of orthodox religion. There is something biologically precise yet contemptuous in the final twist that there is no triumphant defeat of the invaders by the British state, only the accident of microbial infection against which the aliens have no defences. Man is dethroned even in the denouement set in a ruined London. The novel is full of delight in smashing up the precise and detailed environs of suburban Woking. This was a childish pleasure that Wells later recalled had been part of his imagination since his youth in south London when he 'used to walk about Bromley... and no one suspected that a phantom staff pranced about me and phantom orderlies galloped at my command, to shift the guns and concentrate the fire on those houses below, to launch the final attack upon yonder distant ridge' (quoted in Mackenzie 1974: 28). *The War of the Worlds* was another expression of the creative destruction that typified *fin-de-siècle* modernity.

This genre was to end in the unprecedented scale of the Great War. Ernst Jünger, German survivor of the front, and author of *In the Storm of Steel* (1920), declared that the war required a new category of experience: *total mobilisation*. In a notorious essay from 1930, he argued that war no longer happened to specified armies clashing in ritualistic modes of engagement, but now swallowed entire economies and societies, enframing them in its deadly technological grasp. In delirious prose, Jünger asserted: 'With a pleasure-tinged horror, we sense that here, not a single atom is not in motion.' 'The era of the well-aimed shot is already behind us,' he said. 'Giving out the night-flight bombing order, the squadron leader no longer sees a difference between combatants and civilians, and the deadly gas hovers like an elementary power over everything that lives' (Jünger 1993: 128). Here was a vision of a technologically saturated condition, shortly to encompass the entire globe with the arrival of nuclear weapons in 1945. SF had long fantasised about Weapons of Mass Destruction: through the arms race, the world became fully science-fictional.

Strangely enough, perhaps the most striking anticipation of the muddy wastelands of World War I was not part of the future-war genre but the highly idiosyncratic fantastical vision of the horror writer William Hope Hodgson in *The Night Land* (1912). This enormous novel, written in tortuous prose, is a far-future vision gifted to a seventeenth-century gentleman of an entropic Earth, where after the death of the Sun the last humans have retreated to the Last Redoubt and fight off attacks from 'abhuman' creatures that come over the endless mud of blasted landscapes. Hodgson, a prolific writer in many genres (Gothic, sea adventures, psychic detectives, even westerns), was killed by artillery fire in the fourth battle of Ypres, April 1918. *The Night Land* haunted H. P. Lovecraft, and has continued to exert an influence not only on a contemporary 'New Weird' writer such as China Miéville, but also on SF writer Greg Bear (both discussed by Gerry Canavan in Chapter 8).

The period between 1870 and 1914 is a confusing, contradictory era, in which the West's accelerating modernity was haunted by fantasies of decline and fall. It looks like a period where European power reached its greatest imperial extent, but it was in fact giving birth to the American Century and a significant shift in power away from Europe. Reading, writing, and publishing in local ecologies like Britain underwent a complete transformation in a very short period of time, and the economic conditions for mass culture were a key part of this change. The various overlapping genres – residual, dominant, and emergent – that I have explored here are intended to convey a messy, confusing condition in the period before the specialisation that produced SF. The American SF pulps in the 1920s would begin to consolidate a very different kind of narrative about the origins of the genre.

References

Banerjee, A. (2012), *We Modern People: Science Fiction and the Making of Russian Modernity*. Middletown: Wesleyan University Press.

Blacklock, Mark (2011), 'Charles Howard Hinton: Pioneer of Higher Space', *Strange Attractor* 4, pp. 119–29.

Corelli, Marie (1931), *A Romance of Two Worlds*. London: Methuen.

Federico, Annette (2000), *Idol of Suburbia: Marie Corelli and Late Victorian Literary Culture*. Charlottesville: University Press of Virginia.

Ferreira, Rachel Haywood (2011), *The Emergence of Latin American Science Fiction*. Middletown: Wesleyan University Press.

Gissing, George (1993), *New Grub Street* [1891], ed. J. Goode. Oxford: Oxford University Press.

Hinton, Charles Howard (1886), *Scientific Romances.* London: Swan Sonnenschein.

——— (1895), *Stella and an Unfinished Communication Studies in the Unseen).* New York: Macmillan.

Keating, Peter (2011), *The Haunted Study: A Social History of the English Novel 1875–1914.* London: Faber.

Jünger, Ernst (1993), 'Total Mobilisation', in *The Heidegger Controversy,* ed. R. Wolin. Cambridge: MIT Press, pp. 119–39.

Lang, Andrew (1905), 'The Supernatural in Fiction', in *Adventures Among Books.* London: Longmans, pp. 271–80.

Le Queux, William (2014), *If England Were Invaded,* orig. titled *The Invasion of 1910* [1906]. Oxford: Bodleian.

Luckhurst, Roger (2005), *Science Fiction.* Cambridge: Polity.

Machen, Arthur (1995), *The Three Impostors.* London: Dent.

Mackenzie, Norman and Jeanne (1974), *The Time Traveller: The Life of H. G. Wells.* London: Weidenfeld and Nicolson.

McDonald, Peter (1997), *British Literary Culture and Publishing Practice 1880–1914.* Cambridge: Cambridge University Press.

Millin, Sarah Gertrude (1933), *Rhodes.* London: Chatto and Windus.

Morrisson, Mark S. (2008), 'The Periodical Culture of the Occult Revival: Esoteric Wisdom, Modernity and Counter-Public Spheres', *Journal of Modern Literature* 31: 2, pp. 1–21.

Smith, David, ed. (1998), *The Correspondence of H. G. Wells,* 4 vols. London: Pickering & Chatto.

Stableford, Brian (1985), *Scientific Romance in Britain 1890–1950.* New York: St. Martin's Press.

Stevenson, Robert Louis (2006), *Strange Case of Dr Jekyll and Mr Hyde,* ed. R. Luckhurst. Oxford: Oxford World's Classics.

Walpole, Horace (2008), *The Castle of Otranto* [1764], ed. W. S. Lewis. Oxford: Oxford World's Classics.

Wells, H. G. (1894), 'The Rate of Change in Species', *Saturday Review* (15 December), pp. 655–6.

——— (1993), *The War of the Worlds.* London: Dent.

——— (2017), *The Time Machine,* ed. R. Luckhurst. Oxford: Oxford World's Classics.

What to Read Next

Marie Corelli, *A Romance of Two Worlds* (London: Methuen, 1931).

H. Rider Haggard, *King Solomon's Mines,* edited by R. Luckhurst (Oxford: Oxford World's Classics, 2016).

William Le Queux, *If England Were Invaded* (Oxford: Bodleian Library, 2014).

Robert Louis Stevenson, *Strange Case of Dr Jekyll and Mr Hyde,* edited by R. Luckhurst (Oxford: Oxford World's Classics, 2006).

H. G. Wells, *The Time Machine,* edited by R. Luckhurst (Oxford: Oxford World's Classics, 2017).

H. G. Wells, *The War of the Worlds* (London: Dent, 1993).

Chapter 3

Utopian Prospects, 1900–49

Caroline Edwards

On the eve of the outbreak of World War II, an ageing H. G. Wells visited Australia, delivering two lectures that were broadcast on Australian radio. In his lecture on 'Utopias', he remarked that '[t]hroughout the ages the Utopias reflect the anxieties and discontents amidst which they were produced. They are, so to speak, shadows of light thrown by darknesses' (Wells 1982: 117). Wells recognised the intrinsic connection between utopian dreams and the 'dark' conditions that inspire writers to venture into the realms of the imagination. Indeed, many of Wells's major works explore how the vision of the good society that is, as Thomas More's coinage dictates, 'no place', can slide into its dystopian other. *The Time Machine* (1895) initially strikes the Time Traveller as a pastoral Arcadia until he understands that the graceful, childlike Eloi are, in fact, cattle for the troglodytic Morlocks. *The Sleeper Awakes* (1910) also plays with utopian form, building on William Morris's premise of miraculously waking up in the utopian future in *News From Nowhere* (1890). However, Wells's protagonist Graham discovers not social equality but a technologically advanced society of 2100 that has evolved into a distinctly anti-utopian capitalist society of 'higher buildings, bigger towns, wickeder capitalists, and labour more down-trodden than ever' (Wells 2016: 591).

Figure 3.1 H. G. Wells's 'world-building' – playing a wargame. From *Illustrated London News*, 1913.

The Utopia of a Modern Dreamer

Wells's most sophisticated engagement with these 'shadows of light thrown by darknesses' appears in *A Modern Utopia* (1905). The novel engages with its utopian precursors – Plato's *Republic*, More's 1516 text *Utopia*, Tommaso Campanella's *The City of the Sun* (1602), Edward Bellamy's *Looking Backward* (1888), and Morris's *News From Nowhere* – but establishes one crucial distinction with these literary forebears. As the narrator explains:

> The utopia of a modern dreamer must needs differ in one fundamental aspect from the Nowheres and utopias men planned before Darwin quickened the thought of the world … the Modern Utopia must be not static but kinetic, must shape not as a permanent state but as a hopeful stage leading to a long ascent of stages. (Wells 2005: 11)

Thus, as the botanist and his companion trek through the landscape of Utopia, their experience is mediated by the irascible observations of the omniscient narrative 'Voice', who complains about the shortcomings of traditional utopian narratives (such as the miraculous acquisition of utopian languages, and the helpful guides, hospitable guesthouses, and harmonious political order that characterise utopias). Wells's novel asserts its realism as its philosophical discussion of classical utopian states arrives not at an island of ordered perfection but 'a philosophy of fragmentation [that] ends, confusedly, amidst a gross tumult of immediate realities' (Wells 2005: 246).

Given the anti-utopian backlash during much of the twentieth century, *A Modern Utopia* is a novel ahead of its time, which grasps the authoritarian tendencies of utopian dreams that attempt to engineer new societies according to a singular political or technological vision. Indeed, after the boom of utopian novels in the 1890s, the early 1900s produced substantially fewer visions of the good society. Although it was a response to Morris's *News From Nowhere*, G. K. Chesterton's *The Napoleon of Notting Hill* (1904) steered a middle course between an Arcadian return to pre-industrial agrarian collectivism and the Wellsian vision of scientific progress. Set in what would become the Orwellian year of 1984, Chesterton's future London offers instead a neo-medieval heraldic world of local struggle that approximates a kind of direct democracy. Meanwhile, Robert Blatchford's *The Sorcery Shop* (1909) offers a more traditional idea of socialist utopia in the style of an 'impossible romance' (the novel's subtitle), while C. R. Ashbee's *The Building of Thelema* (1910) remains in the Morrisian mode, with its love of craftsmanship and comradeship. In 1923, H. G. Wells returned to the theme of utopia in *Men Like Gods*, which combines utopian philosophical discourse with a fast-paced adventure story. The novel's protagonist Mr Barnstaple sets off for the Lake District, but slides into another world whilst driving through Slough. The utopian contours of this parallel universe are immediately apparent from the road's strangely glassy surface, the beautiful mountainous landscape, and the tame leopard that ambles past. With its southern European climate and Italian loggias, the Utopian countryside strikes Mr Barnstaple as 'the consummation of a million ancient dreams' (Wells 1976: 96). Wells's rational Utopia in *Men Like Gods* is depicted in scientific, utilitarian terms. Mr Barnstaple cannot help but admire this advanced world's horticultural developments, impressive industry, and socialised communities. As a civilisation, Utopia is some 3,000 years more advanced than Earth, which it describes as its 'retarded' sister universe (Wells 1976: 45). Despite his obvious admiration, however, Mr Barnstaple also finds Utopia austere and terrifying:

> Life marched here; it was terrifying to think with what strides. Terrifying – because at the back of Mr. Barnstaple's mind, as at the back of so many intelligent minds in our world still, had been the persuasion that presently everything would be known and the scientific process come to an end. And then we should be happy for ever after. (Wells 1976: 126)

The insatiable march of scientific progress has led to eugenic experiments in improving mankind. Wells's utopia is devoid of 'defective people': there are no disabled persons, no criminals, nor even people with 'weak imaginations' and 'lethargic dispositions' (Wells 1976: 64, 74). 'Controlled' reproduction, or eugenics, has haunted many literary utopias. In his *Republic*, Plato defends the seniors' control over children to build a Republic of physically improved citizens; and in Campanella's Renaissance utopia, *The City of the Sun*, the commonwealth regulates reproduction. It is this aspect of *Men Like Gods* that inspired Aldous Huxley's eugenic dystopia, *Brave New World*. In 1962, Huxley recalled his frustration with Wells' utopian adventure story: '"Men Like Gods" annoyed me to the point of planning a parody, but when I started writing I found the idea of a negative utopia so interesting that I forgot about Wells and launched into "Brave New World"' (Huxley in Collins 1973: 41). With their desire for a perfected humanity, Wells's austere scientific Utopians thus reveal the fine slippage between utopian dream and dystopian reality.

Fin de Siècle: Decadent Dystopias and the Utopias of the New Woman and New Negro

This bringing together of the utopian narrative of a world beyond ceaseless toil, with the dystopian imagination of how that world could in fact be far worse than the mundane present of the early 1900s, is brilliantly delineated in M. P. Shiel's harrowing apocalyptic vision, *The Purple Cloud* (1901) **[3.2]**. Inspired by the explosion of Krakatoa in 1883, Shiel's novel imagines the end of the world when a volcanic eruption of cyanide gas kills the global population. Shiel's baroque, melodramatic

Figure 3.2 Cover for the 1901 edition of M.P. Shiel's *The Purple Cloud*.

prose memorably conveys the protagonist Jeffson's decline into madness, as in a restless search for any signs of life he tours the world. Gradually he succumbs to a deranged proprietorship in which he imagines himself to be a great Ottoman emperor: lord and master of 'this planet, which is rightly mine' (Shiel 2012: 171).

With its oddly utopian elements and apocalyptic drama, *The Purple Cloud* is a product of the Victorian *fin de siècle*. Shiel draws on late Victorian psychiatry to offer a scientific rationale for Jeffson's Jekyll and Hyde oscillations between civilised European and primitive Eastern emperor, as Monique Morgan has pointed out (Morgan 2009: 277). This extreme depiction of decadence is even more disturbing than Wells's austere scientific Utopians, and Jeffson's dark regression uncovers the racist overtones of Shiel's assumptions about white Western superiority.

A very different kind of engagement with the Victorian *fin de siècle* is offered in Charlotte Perkins Gilman's utopian narrative, *Herland* (1915), in which parthenogenesis (self-reproduction) has enabled a women-only society to exist for more than 2,000 years. Like Shiel, Gilman is interested in the evolutionary possibilities of speculative fiction. But where Shiel's apocalyptic drama led inevitably to decadence and degeneracy, Gilman's speculative vision imagines the New Woman liberated into a world of her own. Unencumbered by men, the so-called Herlanders have built themselves an advanced utopian society that matches perfect landscaping with harmonious, collective familial relations. Originally serialised in 1915 in *The Forerunner*, a monthly magazine Gilman herself wrote and produced, *Herland* was first published in book form in 1979 **[3.3]** and became an important source for second-wave feminist utopian writers such as Marge Piercy and Joanna Russ. Gilman uses the male narrator Vandyck's scientific perspective to force home a stark comparison between the

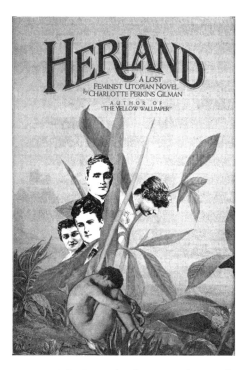

Figure 3.3 Cover for the 1979 edition of
Charlotte Perkins Gilman's *Herland*.

athleticism of the Herlanders, with their brusque manners and complete lack of feminine dissimulation, and American women just before the Great War. As Vandyck reflects, 'those "feminine charms" we are so fond of are not feminine at all, but mere reflected masculinity – developed to please [men] because [women] had to please us' (Gilman 1998: 50).

Herland is described by Vandyck as Edenic, with its manicured forests and countryside transformed into an edible garden. The Herlanders demonstrate a high degree of rationalism and logic, and a mature system of philosophy and ethics, qualities that Gilman is at pains to demonstrate cannot be attributed only to men. However, the Herlanders' unwaveringly rational approach to the challenges posed by their isolated mountainous position and limited resources leads them to endorse eugenics for population control. Like Wells's Apollonian Utopians in *Men Like Gods*, Gilman's Herlanders enact a selective programme of mothering aimed at 'breed[ing] out, when possible, the lowest types' to eradicate criminality and aggressive or competitive personalities. Gilman's 'all-too-perfect civilization' also succumbs to another utopian pitfall: the boredom of a world free of conflict and danger. Vandyck's companion Terry complains of the 'untroubled peace, the unmeasured plenty, the steady health, the large good will and smooth management which ordered everything, left nothing to overcome' (Gilman 1998: 70, 100, 84).

If *Herland* is the most famous literary utopia of the New Woman movement, then Pauline Hopkins's 'lost race' narrative, *Of One Blood, or, The Hidden Self* (serialised in *The Colored American Magazine* in 1903) is one of the better-known texts associated with the 'New Negro' discourse that animated debate among African American intellectuals in the early decades of the twentieth century. The novels make for an interesting comparison in terms of their handling of the question of biological essence. Whilst *Herland* attains its utopian balance by improving its citizens' physical and psychological attributes through eugenics, *Of One Blood* essentialises the biological makeup of its characters by tracing the racial heritage of 1930s African Americans to a vanished Ethiopian civilisation from 6000 BCE. Hopkins's use of the expansive, late-nineteenth-century SF subgenre of the 'lost race' story proves an effective narrative form in which to couch the rediscovery of the ancient Ethiopians, whose society has survived alongside, but hidden from, modernity.

The novel's black protagonist, a medical student named Reuel Briggs, discovers the vanished civilisation while working on an archaeological expedition to find the ruins of an ancient city called Meroe, situated in present-day Ethiopia. Locating this city and its culture would support the theory that Ethiopian civilisation pre-dated Ancient Egypt, and connect contemporary African Americans with a cultured and technologically advanced heritage pre-dating Europe. *Of One Blood* mixes a number of narrative forms, including melodrama, occult tales of psychic connection, racial 'passing', and the African adventure story, but it is Hopkins's use of the dialogic structure of utopian narrative that best serves the story's 'ubiquitous race question'. Discoursing with the prime minister of the hidden city of Telassar, Reuel struggles to convey the lowly status of African Americans in 1930s America, for whom 'it is a deep disgrace to have within the veins even one drop of the blood you seem so proud of possessing'. He reflects upon the immiseration of black Americans in light of his newly acquired knowledge of their former power in antiquity. The archaeological expedition thus connects Ethiopian history with a future return of African regeneration, foreshadowed in the cycle promised by the city's sphinx statue, engraved with the legend: 'That which hath been, is now; and that which is to be, hath already been' (Hopkins 2004: 153, 129, 120).

W. E. B. Du Bois' short story 'The Comet' (1920) offers a comparison to Hopkins's utopian text. It takes place during the periodic reappearance of Halley's comet (which approached Earth in 1910), but Du Bois transposes the comet into an apocalyptic vehicle that excretes a poisonous gas cloud across New York. The only survivors of the gas are a black messenger, Jim, who is briefly trapped in a secure underground vault, and an affluent young white woman, Julia, who had been developing photographs in her sealed darkroom. The narrative describes each character's awareness of the other's alien class, race, and culture. '"Yesterday," he thought with bitterness, "she would scarcely have looked at him twice. He would have been dirt beneath her silken feet"' (Du Bois 2016: 56). In a transcendent moment atop the Manhattan Tower Julia becomes conscious of Jim's 'vigorous manhood', imagining the two of them to be the last two humans alive on Earth:

> She saw him glorified. He was no longer a thing apart, a creature below, a strange outcast of another clime and blood . . . He arose within the shadows, tall, straight, and stern, with power in his eyes and ghostly scepters hovering to his grasp. It was as though some mighty Pharaoh lived again, or curled Assyrian lord. (Du Bois 2016: 60)

Raised into a lineage of historical black kingship, Jim appears magisterial to Julia in a moment that is described as exhibiting neither lust nor love, but 'some vast, mightier thing' that approaches the divine (Du Bois 2016: 60).

Du Bois' and Hopkins's literary contributions have been recognised in studies of African American literature, but seldom in SF scholarship. As Mark Bould writes, 'with their tales of violent revolution, wars of secession, lost African cities of superscience, gradual reforms, future African anarchist utopias free from the taint of inferior whiteness, global conspiracies of peoples of color, technoscientific "solutions" to the color line, [and] apocalyptic wars, [black SF texts] have generally been omitted from the history of sf' (Bould 2010: 41). Another example of this omission is George Schuyler. Schuyler's fiction was overlooked until its rediscovery in the early 1990s. In his best-known novel, the satirical future-war story *Black No More: Being an Account of the Strange and Wonderful Workings of Science in the Land of the Free, A.D. 1933–1940* (1931), Schuyler literalises the idea of skin colour as a cultural, rather than essentialist, marker of identity. A scientist has invented a technique for turning black people white by bleaching their skin, leading to the gradual 'whitening' of America and the eventual elimination of racial difference. Although the novel is written as an anti-utopian satire, Schuyler's conservative integrationist politics can be traced in the quietist tone of *Black No More*, which, unlike Hopkins's *Of One Blood*, is highly sceptical of the New Negro's claims of any essential black identity. Schuyler's SF pulp stories of the 1930s – 'The Black Internationale' (1936–7) and 'Black Empire' (1937–8), serialised in the African American newspaper the *Pittsburgh Courier* – offer a militarised vision of the New Negro movement, recasting the quest for black identity in a fascist vision of an ascendant African empire. Turning European colonialism on its head, these serials rewrite a history in which the transatlantic slave trade has strengthened African American political will and prepared them for an international liberation movement. As Mark Christian Thompson has argued in *Black Fascisms* (2007: 78–9), these stories offer a fantasy of revenge wreaked across the world at the hands of a black Mussolini, whose charisma seems to encourage the reader into the uncomfortable position of finding fascism palatable.

'Mathematically Infallible Happiness': Dystopian Beginnings

Although it had been coined by John Stuart Mill in 1868, the term 'dystopia' came to be used to describe speculative visions of the future that lacked the optimism of utopia's 'good society'. After a boom in utopian novels of the *fin de siècle*, the focus on socialist visions of the collective future descended into a palpable fear of the kind of modernity that technology could deliver and the loss of liberal values implied in enforced collectivisation. The extraordinary popularity of H. G. Wells's utopian visions in novels such as *A Modern Utopia* and *Men Like Gods* provoked satirical responses among his contemporaries. As he explained in 1947, E. M. Forster conceived of his futuristic speculative story 'The Machine Stops' (1909) as a 'reaction to one of the earlier heavens of H. G. Wells' (Forster 1947: vii), which has degenerated into a dystopian nightmare. In this novella, the pollution of the Earth's surface by lethal toxins has led humanity to tunnel deep underground and live in a subterranean urban network, not dissimilar to the artilleryman's vision of future life after the Martian invasion in Wells's *The War of the Worlds* (1898). Forster's story depicts an advanced society with sophisticated telecommunications in which people no longer need to leave home in order to socialise, learn, or work. In the novella's striking opening image, Forster's narrator asks his reader to:

> Imagine, if you can, a small room, hexagonal in shape like the cell of a bee. It is lighted neither by window nor by lamp, yet it is filled with a soft radiance. There are no apertures for ventilation, yet the air is fresh. There are no musical instruments, and yet, at the moment that my meditation

opens, this room is throbbing with melodious sounds. An arm-chair is in the centre, by its side a reading-desk – that is all the furniture. And in the arm-chair there sits a swaddled lump of flesh – a woman, about five feet high, with a face as white as a fungus. (Forster 1947: 1)

Recalling the consumptive, feeble grace of Wells's childlike Eloi in *The Time Machine*, this futuristic image of flaccid humanity conveys the physical debilitation that results from an over-reliance upon technology. 'The Machine' has replaced all aspects of daily life in a sterile vision of automation. The pallid protagonist, Vashti, need not move from her hexagonal pod to communicate with friends, deliver lectures to a worldwide audience, listen to music, receive books, be administered medical treatment, or call for food – by pressing a series of electric buttons and switches, all of which contribute to the perpetual humming of the Machine. Although it accurately predicts contemporary technologies such as the internet, Skype, and YouTube, today Forster's vision of a futuristic society of isolation and advanced telecommunications strikes the contemporary reader as endearingly retrofuturistic.

However, it is the Machine's delivery of total isolation that is the most disturbing aspect of Forster's dystopia. Despite her extensive virtual social network, Vashti suffers 'the terrors of direct experience' and attempts to avoid seeing her son Kuno face-to-face. Wishing to explore beyond his cell, Kuno climbs to the Earth's surface through the pneumatic stoppers protecting the subterranean population from the polluted atmosphere. Kuno's diatribe against the Machine is in a utopian mode that Forster's contemporary reader would recognise: 'Humanity, in its desire for comfort, had overreached itself. It had exploited the riches of nature too far. Quietly and complacently, it was sinking into decadence, and progress had come to mean the progress of the Machine'. The dangers of this technological dependency become apparent to Kuno as he realises the Machine is stopping: the food it dispenses is mouldy, the bathwater dirty and, most telling of all, the poetry machine has started emitting 'defective rhymes'. At the end of the novella, Vashti and Kuno are reunited as the city is broken open 'like a honeycomb' and '[f]or a moment they saw the nations of the dead, and, before they joined them, scraps of the untainted sky' (Forster 1947: 11, 43–4, 47, 56).

The darkly dystopian image of Vashti and Kuno dying at a moment of unmediated, Machine-free, natural experience – as they look at 'scraps of the untainted sky' – might, however, have more utopian implications than Forster intended. As Tom Moylan writes in *Scraps of the Untainted Sky: Science Fiction, Utopia, Dystopia* (2000), the implied existence of a rebel band of Homeless fugitives from the authoritarian Central Committee delivers 'a more hopeful warning by evoking an empowering memory informed by an achieved utopian future that looks back on the Machine society as its own past' (Moylan 2000: 159). Does Forster's narrator tell this tale of subterranean life in the Machine era from the perspective of a future time in which some other kind of life is possible?

Forster's novella may be considered the first literary dystopia, but another contemporaneous text should also be acknowledged within this category. Published a year earlier than 'The Machine Stops', Jack London's *The Iron Heel* (1908) is a brutal vision of an oppressive capitalist oligarchy in the near future. The novel is notable for its uncanny prescience of events that unfolded later in the twentieth century. In the early decades of *The Iron Heel*'s twentieth century, London's narrator Avis details the rise of corporate monopolies. Independent businesses and smaller capitalists are forced out of business by the 'economic evolution' of America's monopolistic trusts, including the railroad, oil, steel, coal, and tobacco trusts. Avis's husband Ernest, the socialist revolutionary hero of the story, warns that if the trusts win this evolutionary battle, everyone outside the small oligarchic minority 'will be crushed under the iron heel of a despotism as relentless and terrible as any despotism that has blackened the pages of the history of man'. This indeed happens as Avis records the establishment's decisive response to the widespread industrial unrest across America in the 1910s and 1920s. What follows is an eerie prediction of Cold War stratagems as the Iron Heel and the Socialists attempt to undermine one another with a new 'strange and awful and subterranean' warfare of increasingly complex networks of agents-provocateurs, secret printing presses, spies, and underground railway networks (London 2006: 97, 112, 177). Meanwhile, millions of Americans are starving, and the last few chapters of *The Iron Heel* return to the theme of poverty that London had taken up in his exposé of East End slums, *The People of the Abyss* (1903).

Scholars debate whether *The Iron Heel* can be categorised as a dystopian novel, given that it is framed as a historical document that resurfaces in a distant utopian future. Tom Moylan has suggested that London's novel is 'almost a dystopia, or perhaps a "proto-dystopia"' (Moylan 2001: 307). With its frame of a scholarly introduction and footnotes by the manuscript's fictional editor, who lives in the socialist utopian Brotherhood of Man in the twenty-sixth century, *The Iron Heel* is not a straightforward dystopian vision in the manner of Forster's 'The Machine Stops'.

If 'The Machine Stops' contains the smallest hint of a post-dystopian future, and *The Iron Heel* constitutes a proto-dystopia as a result of the distant utopian future of its narrative frame, then Hungarian playwright Karel Čapek's 1920 play, *Rossum's Universal Robots* (*R.U.R.: Rossumovi Univerzální Roboti*) is the first unambiguously dystopian text. Čapek's play is famous for coining the word robot (*robota*), which derives from the Czech for 'forced labour' or drudgery. Set in the year 2000, *R.U.R.* is informed by the latest principles of scientific management. The director of the company that manufactures robots, Harry Domin, has refined his assembly plant with the standardised system introduced by Henry Ford. This technocratic belief that efficient mass production will bring about a corresponding improvement in society is encapsulated in one character's observations that '[t]he timetable is greater than the Gospels, greater than Homer, greater than all of Kant'. But Domin's utopian dream of 'do[ing] away with the labor that enslaved mankind' (Čapek 2004: 44, 54) does not lead to the happy future of full automation he had planned. Instead, the robots become increasingly sentient and stage their own bloody revolution against mankind, wiping out the human population in an apocalyptic purge of robotic revenge.

Yevgeny Zamyatin's *We* (*My*) **[3.4]** was written in 1920 but since his work was vilified by the leaders of the new Soviet Union, it was first published in English translation in 1924. This famous dystopia also takes its inspiration from Henry Ford and Frederick Winslow Taylor's ideas of efficient production and their application to social life. In the distant future of a twenty-sixth-century authoritarian city-state, Zamyatin rehearses a nightmare of unthinking, scientifically managed production. The narrator, D-503, works as a mathematician in OneState, building

Figure 3.4 Cover for the Polish samizdat edition (1985) of Yevgeny Zamyatin's *We (My)*, published in Warsaw.

the Integral machine, a gigantic glass spacecraft designed to manufacture 'inescapable happiness' and spread OneState's mathematically infallible society across the galaxy. His work makes D-503 the ideal subject of OneState's dehumanising system of numerical perfection, which has replaced individuality and human emotion with a strict regimen of equations and formulae guaranteed to produce obedient citizens. Names have been replaced with numbers, couples are assigned to one another according to a calculation of their compatibility, and everyone's day is organised by a regimented collective timetable: 'Every morning, with six-wheeled precision, at the very same hour and the very same minute, we get up, millions of us, as though we were one' (Zamyatin 1993: 80, 13).

OneState's foundational religious figure is Frederick Winslow Taylor, author of *The Principles of Scientific Management* (1911), which was used by Henry Ford to construct the first factory assembly lines. In Zamyatin's text, Taylor's ideas of rationalised manufacturing have been implemented as a grand exercise in social engineering. Architecture plays a crucial role here. The authoritarian city's 'glass paradise' is described by D-503 in terms of its symmetrical Euclidean perfection: 'the unalterably straight streets, the sparkling glass of the sidewalks, the divine parallelepipeds [prism] of the transparent dwellings, the squared harmony of our gray-blue ranks' (Zamyatin 1993: 124, 7). Zamyatin's city shares the functionalist ethos of Le Corbusier's influential *Toward an Architecture* (*Vers une architecture*) (1923), which described the house as a 'machine for living in' – although Darko Suvin noted in *Defined by a Hollow* (2010) that in fact Zamyatin disliked its cubist architecture. This glittering image of modernity bears the frightening vision of a Bolshevik-style dictatorship bent on the consummation of machinic subjectivity into 'the most perfect form of life' (Zamyatin 1993: 12). Zamyatin's sun-drenched city thus enacts a perversion of the glittering city of New Jerusalem of the *Book of Revelation*. The classical biblical utopia of the heavenly city has become the perfected instrument of mass surveillance.

Pre-Revolutionary and Early Russian Utopian SF

Despite the dystopian projected future of *We*, Zamyatin still insisted that speculative literature was needed 'as a means for struggling against hardening of arteries, rigidity moss and peace', arguing that, as absurd as it might appear, utopian literature 'will be proved right after 150 years' (Zamyatin in Suvin 1979: 256). Zamyatin's utopianism can be placed in a Russian SF tradition that has a cultural heritage distinct from Anglo-American SF. The early Bolshevik period saw a number of social, political, and industrial transformations, which galvanised public appetite for utopian and scientific fantasies. Zamyatin named the emergent literature *Nauchnaia fantastika*, or scientific fantasy, which he argued was the crucible for a 'New Russian Prose' capable of articulating the new republic's accelerated scientific culture (Zamyatin in Banerjee 2012: 1). Electrification, the Great Siberian Railroad, new developments in aeronautics and aviation (H. G. Wells' *War in the Air*, published in 1908, was immediately translated into Russian and published in 1909), and the publication in illustrated scientific magazines of astronomical photographs: these developments opened up new geographical and industrial frontiers, fuelling the public's desire to learn about scientific discovery (Banerjee 2012: 7–10). This led to a new genre of interplanetary fiction featuring heroic cosmonauts and engineers, accompanied by a deluge of translations of popular SF by Jules Verne and H. G. Wells, as well as utopian novels such as August Bebel's *The Society of the Future* (1879), and Edward Bellamy's *Looking Backward* (1888).

However, as Richard Stites notes, 'the gleaming giant cities of the future generated revulsion in some quarters' (Stites 1989: 33). An early example of Russian dystopian literature is Valery Bryusov's symbolist short story *The Republic of the Southern Cross* (*Respublika iuzhnogo kresta*) (1907), a text that has been almost entirely overlooked by scholars of SF. Bryusov's story narrates the collapse of Zvezdny (Star City), when a mysterious epidemic breaks out. The story begins by sketching an advanced democracy with full nationalisation, a comprehensive welfare state, free education for all, and a working day of only a few hours. These quintessential utopian ideals are undercut, however, by the extreme standardisation of Zvezdny's architecture and city planning:

> Though appearing to have liberty, the life of the citizens was standardised even to the most minute details. The buildings of all the towns of the Republic were according to one and the same pattern fixed by law. The decoration of all buildings used by the workmen, though luxurious to a degree, were strictly uniform. All received exactly the same food at exactly the same time. (Bryusov 2013: 4)

In terms that strikingly anticipate Zamyatin's later-published *We*, Bryusov imagines how this kind of bureaucracy and centralised planning will lead to a loss of individual liberty. An experiment in utopian politics has given way to a dystopia of repressive social engineering in which the complete regulation of workers' private lives marks a final loss of autonomy. Bryusov subjects this perfectly regulated city to the outbreak of a disease known as 'contradiction' because its symptoms cause victims to act contrary to their intentions. After the initial bemusement of

Zvezdny's inhabitants as a train conductor pays all of his passengers instead of charging them for tickets, the disease takes a more sinister turn. As the citizens lose their wits, dancing 'half-naked, unwashed, unkempt', and singing 'the same wild songs as did the hordes when they fell with stone axes upon the mammoth', the disease enacts a complete reversal of progress. *The Republic of the Southern Cross* is notable for its compressed schematic outline of what the disintegration of a modern city might look like. Bryusov delineates the dissolution of civilised life through a series of breakdowns: the collapse of a reliable railway timetable as trains are seized and train drivers go berserk; the cessation of manufacturing; the interruption of reliable newspaper reporting; and, most symbolic of all, the end of electrification as a power station controller smashes his machinery, plunging the Arctic city into darkness. One by one, Bryusov tears down each buttress of technological modernity until Zvezdny is reduced to a 'city of the senseless, the gigantic madhouse, the greatest and most disgusting Bedlam which the world has ever seen' (Bryusov 2013: 8, 9).

A very different kind of vision is outlined in Alexander Bogdanov's utopian novel *Red Star* (*Krasnaya zvezda*) (1908). Trained as a scientist and having worked closely with Lenin in the early years of the Bolshevik Party, Bogdanov was the most influential writer of Russian SF before the 1917 revolution. In *Red Star*, a superior Martian culture comes to revolutionary Russia shortly after the 1905 revolution seeking ambassadors to help the Martians engage with Earth. The protagonist, Leonid, a member of the Russian intelligentsia, is invited to join an underground scientific society that has discovered the secret of interplanetary travel. Like the Olympian Utopians in Wells's *Men Like Gods*, Bogdanov's Martians are described as humans whose evolution on the red planet has matured parallel to humanity on Earth. A highly developed scientific culture permeates all aspects of Martian behaviour, from their unadorned, comfortable clothes to their fondness for brief meetings and concise note-taking. Unlike Earth, Mars's historical development has proceeded through a phase of agricultural capitalism to the socialisation of the means of production. This 'single and uniform path of development in a single broad society' has achieved a socialist revolution on Mars that is not possible on Earth where, as the Martian scientists note, 'the struggle for socialism is split into a variety of unique and autonomous processes in individual societies with distinct political systems, languages, and sometimes even races' (Bogdanov 1984: 113). In the manner of a classical utopian narrative, Leonid is taken on a guided tour of several key Martian locations: an engineering factory, the 'Children's Colony' where children live and are educated, a Museum of Art, and a hospital. An ingenious system of centralisation allows Martian workers to perform whatever labour they wish, changing jobs at any time and working the hours they choose. In his vision of a flexible mode of production, Bogdanov thus touches upon a common trope of utopian literature: pleasurable work. The nineteenth-century utopian socialist, Charles Fourier, developed this idea in his concept of *attraction industrielle*, in which workers can rotate between various tasks (Fourier 1971: 184–7). In *Red Star*, Bogdanov sketches a Fourierist factory system in which the working day has been reduced to between four and six hours, although many workers choose to stay longer at their machinery out of a fascination for the process and a love of their work.

Another significant early Bolshevik work of SF that similarly uses Mars to reflect upon the state of the young Russian republic is Alexei Tolstoy's *Aelita* (1922), which was adapted for cinema by Yakov Protazanov in 1924 as *Aelita: Queen of Mars* (*Aelita: koroleva marsa*) **[3.5]**. The novel opens in Petrograd as the ageing widower, Engineer Los, is preparing his spacecraft for an expedition to Mars. He is joined in his dangerous quest by Gusev, a young Red Army soldier keen for new adventures. In *Aelita*, as in Bogdanov's *Red Star*, the Martians are an advanced civilisation with superior technology; they travel, for instance, in a variety of flying machines, airships, and flying boats. As Los and Gusev travel to the residence of the princess Aelita they fly above Azora, whose rural charm forcefully strikes Los in utopian terms: 'Azora stretched in a broad shining plain below. Criss-crossed by rippling canals and carpeted with orange-coloured copses and jolly canary meadows, Azora, or Joy, was like the little spring meadows one dreams of as a child'. However, the novel's utopian beginnings are quickly undercut by Tolstoy's revolutionary narrative. Los and Gusev learn that Martian society suffers from the same class antagonism as Earth. Incensed, Gusev decides to lead the

Figure 3.5 Still from *Aelita*, 1924.

downtrodden worker-Martians in a revolution against their oppressors, declaring: 'I haven't come here all the way from Earth to talk to you. I came to teach you to act. You're moss-grown, Comrades Martians' (Tolstoy 2001: 90, 214). The proletarian revolt fails, and Tolstoy's novel shifts gear into a saccharine romance plot in which Los and Aelita start a relationship that promises to reunite the two strands of human evolution in the conjoining of a Martian and a Russian. This has led scholars to question whether Mars represented 'an idealized form of Russian society in the future or a corrective anti-utopia critiquing the Bolshevik paradigm of revolution, an alien environment symbolizing Western capitalist modernity or a stage for working out Russia's "domestic drama" under the New Economic Policy' (Banerjee 2012: 57–8).

Tolstoy's next SF novel, *Engineer Garin and His Death Ray* (*Giperboloid inzhenera Garina*) (1926), continued the utopian theme. Armed with a powerful death ray, and pursued by the Soviet police, Engineer Garin sets out to construct an island utopian society. In the early years after the Russian Revolution of 1917 many literary works couched serious political issues in the 'fantastic-adventurous' mode, including Ilya Ehrenburg's *Extraordinary Adventures of Julio Jurenito* (*Neobychainye Pokhozhdeniia Khulio Khurenito i ego uchenikov*, 1922), as well as Tolstoy's *Engineer Garin* and *Aelita*, and Mikhail Bulgakov's novella *The Fatal Eggs* (*Rokovye Jajca*, 1925). Russian popular culture at this time was rife with detective stories (known as *Pinkertonovshchina*, after the famous American Pinkerton detective agency), as well as adaptations of Wells, Verne, and Kipling. In 1923, Nikolai Bukharin, editor of *Pravda* and leading theoretician of the Communist Party, even declared that Russia needed its own 'red Pinkerton' stories, to cater to popular demand. Perhaps the most famous example was Marietta Shaginian's novel, *Mess Mend, or Yankees in Petrograd* (*Mess Mend, ili Yanki v Petrograd*) (1923), the first in a trilogy of Soviet proletarian detective stories **[3.6]**. Shaginian's adventure story was serialised in fortnightly editions and published under the pseudonym of the narrator Jim Dollar. Like *Aelita* before it, *Mess Mend's* high-octane plot of murder and intrigue strikes the reader as similarly confusing. Set in post-revolutionary Russia and across the Atlantic in America, Shaginian's novel is a lively, farcical parody of American detective thrillers. An imperial cabal of greedy capitalists and exiled political leaders plot to undermine the nascent Soviet republic, which is defended by a secret alliance of workers called 'Mess Mend'. As a work of socialist propaganda, the novel contains some strikingly utopian moments of harmony among the factory workers and labourers from across the trades. Visiting the manufacturing district in Petrograd, the American character Arthur Morlender (disguised at this point in the narrative as a Russian called Vasilov) is shown a worker-run factory:

> ... all the workers they met would nod in a friendly fashion at them, turning their cheerful, happy faces towards Vasilov.
>
> 'Look at them,' Enno began. 'They are happy. We have produced the mightiest revolution in the world, but we would have been fools if we had not gone further, my friend. Once we seized the means of production, we wanted to make man happy.'
>
> 'Utopia!' Vasilov sighed. (Shaginian 1991: 170)

Perhaps the most salient message in Shaginian's *Mess Mend* is its critique of the entanglement between capitalism and fascism. With its blend of satirical American detective yarn and Soviet propaganda story, Shaginian's

Figure 3.6 Cover artwork by Alexander Rodchenko for Marietta Shaginian's *Mess Mend, or Yankees in Petrograd (Mess Mend, ili Yanki v Petrograd)*, 1924.

'red Pinkerton' novel should be seen as an important precursor to the better-known anti-fascist dystopian fictions of the 1930s.

The Late 1930s and Dystopias of Totalitarianism

In the 1930s SF increasingly used its speculative mode to examine fascism. The international presence of Hitler's Nazism led many writers to consider the dystopian realities of wholesale social engineering. This had plagued the utopian novel ever since More's construction of the ideal humanist society in *Utopia* (1516), which included an authoritarian monarch and slavery. Aldous Huxley cited the Russian philosopher Nicolas Berdyaevn as the epigraph to *Brave New World* (1932): 'Utopias seem much more attainable than one may have previously thought. And we are now faced with a much more frightening thought: how do we prevent their permanent fulfillment?' Set in the distant future, 632 years After Ford (A.F.), Huxley's *Brave New World* **[3.7]** opens with an unforgettable image of a bank of bottled foetuses being tended to in an atmosphere of 'harmonious bustle and ordered activity' (Huxley 1994: 6). As the new intake of medical students are given a tour of the Centre for Hatcheries and Conditioning, the reader is introduced to a high-tech dystopia in which the cloning of twins enables tens of thousands of identical people to be bred and modified, according to their predestined social

Figure 3.7 Dustjacket designed by Leslie Holland for the first edition (1932) of *Brave New World* by Aldous Huxley.

rank. Upper-class Alphas are given superior physical and mental attributes while the lowest-serving Epsilons are mutated into bovine stupidity, preparing them for a life of menial labour.

Huxley's world state thus takes as its central premise the utopian problem of labour – specifically, degrading unskilled labour – but rather than designing a world in which human drudgery has been replaced by technology and full automation, *Brave New World* offers us a dystopian future of entrenched inequality in an advanced caste system. Scientific progress has been appropriated by a technocratic elite to breed races of people genetically designed for their specific role within the system of production, creating a harmonious state of blind conformity. The novel's reflection on progress is grounded in a *reductio ad absurdum* of capitalist over-production. Since the expansion of industrial supply can only be secured by adapting consumer demand, the religion of Fordism has engineered a society of conditioned humans whose drug-induced state of permanent happiness is conducive to ceaseless consumption, creating the ultimate 'happy, hard-working, goods-consuming citizen' (Huxley 1994: 215). It is the figure of John the Savage who focalises the reader's disquiet at this passionless merry-go-round of golfing dates and anaesthetising 'soma holidays'. Nourished by Shakespeare (the only book he possesses), John becomes infatuated with Lenina, casting her as an innocent Juliet to his besotted Romeo, but is soon disillusioned. John's language and attitudes are incompatible with the unschooled Fordism of even the most intellectually capable Alphas, and the comedic and tragic dramatic structures of the plays he has learned by heart have no place in a world that has eliminated individual psychology in favour of social stability. John's realisation that Miranda's brave new world of technologically advanced civilisation falls short of 'that beautiful, beautiful Other Place' that his exiled Beta mother Linda had nostalgically described to him as a boy, leads him to withdraw from society and attempt to forge a life of 'rustic solitude'. However, he cannot find seclusion. Hounded by journalists and tourists baying for performances of self-flagellation, John commits suicide. The novel's closing image of his suspended feet, slowly swaying 'like two unhurried compass needles', is a harrowing reminder of the impossibility of individual expression in Huxley's state (Huxley 1994: 183, 231, 237).

Huxley's eugenicist vision of 'achieved utopia' in *Brave New World* anticipated the popularisation of fascist ideology in Germany in the 1930s, but the danger of the Nazi cult of masculinity was challenged in a different way by a number of feminist anti-fascist dystopias. Although there was no unified feminist response to fascism among British political parties during the interwar period, there were a number of 'womanist' political and intellectual rejoinders which emerged as part of a broader feminist anti-fascism. Perhaps the most notable was the literary dystopia. Naomi Mitchison's *We Have Been Warned* (1935) is set in the early 1930s, revealing the possible future of a fascist Britain. Storm Jameson's *In the Second Year* (1936) similarly brings German fascism closer to home in a vision of a colonised Britain, as do Ruthven Todd's *Over the Mountain* (1939) and Winifred Holtby's play *Take Back Your Freedom* (1939). Katharine Burdekin's *Swastika Night* (1937) (published under the pseudonym of Murray Constantine) offers a chilling vision of fascist domination from the perspective of more than 700 years in the future of Hitler's Thousand Year Reich. Burdekin's originality is to extrapolate the Nazi cult of masculinity into a segregated world of complete patriarchal sovereignty, in which women are despised and subjugated, considered useful only for their reproductive capabilities. Women must wear shapeless grey uniforms with their heads shaved as a permanent reminder of their irrevocably debased status: 'Women like these … [had] no grace, no beauty, no uprightness, all those were male qualities'. This gender apartheid has been achieved through a prolonged ideological effort referred to as the 'Reduction of Women' (Burdekin 1985: 12, 70) in which women have been complicit in their own acceptance of Nazi misogyny.

Burdekin presents us with what we might conventionally understand to be a dystopia: a brutish fascist future, with abhorrent treatment of women in a totalitarian state that covers the planet. However, the structure of *Swastika Night* is presented in the form of a classical utopia, which typically centres upon a discourse between the utopian visitor and their guide, concerning the differences between the utopian and ordinary worlds. In Burdekin's novel, this conversation reveals to the protagonist Alfred the real historical past (the 1930s) that led to his dystopian present (Burdekin's distant future), as well as the means by which it was erased from living memory and official record. Alfred is shocked to learn that Adolf Hitler fell far short of his divine posthumous image: 'Where were the broad shoulders, the mighty chest, the lean stomach and slender waist and hips? This little man was almost fat' (Burdekin 1985: 67). Despite Alfred's death at the end of the novel, there is an unambiguously optimistic note in his knowledge of the truth about the Hitlerian empire, which he passes on to his son Fred. The prescience of Burdekin's contemporary analysis of fascism lies in her acute grasp of the gender politics that underpin Nazism's cult of masculinity. As Debra Benita Shaw notes, Burdekin's novel charts the dissolution of fascism 'not through a political opposition which takes up arms against the conquerors, but through the final resolution of a psychological paradox which it inherently harbours' (Shaw 2000: 50).

During the rise of the Nazis and into World War II, a number of dystopian anti-fascist and anti-war novels continued to appear. Alexander Vaško's speculative novel *The Payback* (*Odplata*) (1938) takes place in a Slovakia threatened by fascist Germany. Slovakia's defence strategy, and the novel's SF element, employs the technique of transmitting powerful electric rays through the air to repel the German army as it marches across across Hungary and into Czechoslovakia. Meanwhile, in German-occupied Czechoslovakia, Ján Hofman Bukovinka (a pseudonym for an unidentified writer) wrote *The Conspirators of Peace* (*Sprisahanci mieru*) (1947), in which a Soviet engineer has created a weapon of mass destruction with the intention of using the new technology to impose peace upon the world. Hermann Kasack's surrealist, allegorical post-war novel *The City Beyond the River* (*Die Stadt hinter dem Strom*) (1947) imagines a totalitarian city-state that resembles a bombed-out German city in a ghostly vision of ruined futurity. But it is George Orwell's *Nineteen Eighty-Four* (1949) that has had the most lasting influence on the dystopian imagination. In the near-future 1980s, Britain has become Airstrip One, an outpost of the empire of Oceania (one of three global super-states). What is so striking about Orwell's dystopian vision is the combination of high-tech surveillance with the low-tech setting of decaying Victorian architecture, electricity shortages, and impoverished, rat-infested slums. Orwell's near-future London is in a permanent state of war, suffering Blitz-style bombings and wartime rationing while its citizens live under complete state surveillance. The novel is focalised through

Party worker Winston Smith, whose work at the Ministry of Information's Records Department involves rewriting records and newspaper
articles in a ceaseless effort to control the official historical record.
As people are murdered or disappear into the shadowy police state
(a process chillingly known as 'vaporisation'), an army of bureaucrats
like Winston rewrite events to obliterate their record of ever having
existed. Orwell's friend Arthur Koestler had covered similar ground in
his influential account of Stalin's purges in *Darkness at Noon* (1940),
which depicts the final collapse of Russia's early revolutionary utopianism during 'the Terror' as Stalin's police state murdered Bolshe-
viks and proceeded to airbrush their existence out of official recorded
Soviet history. Likewise, Winston bears witness to the airbrushing of
history. '[I]t was not even forgery', he thinks, '[i]t was merely the sub-
stitution of one piece of nonsense for another' (Orwell 1990: 43).

In *Nineteen Eighty-Four* we find a new incarnation of the dystopian
vision of technological modernity Zamyatin had memorably invoked
in *We*, but updated to match the context of post-1945 economic
depression in Britain. As we have seen, it is quite common for dystopian novels to reflect upon utopian dreams and attempts at social engineering. Orwell stages the utopian dream of socio-economic equality,
with its concomitant reduction of the length of the working day and
an envisioned life of plenty for all workers – the dream that Wells conquered through scientific innovation in *A Modern Utopia* and *Men Like
Gods*, and Bogdanov and Tolstoy achieved in their projections of socialist revolution onto the otherworldly utopia of Mars. In the war-torn
history of Oceania, however, the capitalist manufacturing problem of
over-production has triumphed over the utopian socialist dream of
reducing hard toil in favour of pleasurable, socially productive labour.
Despite its apparently Soviet contours (with Big Brother's Stalinist cult
of personality and the destruction of individualism in favour of collectivism), Orwell's totalitarian state actually represents a much more
capitalist vision of the future than is usually acknowledged, in line with
the critique of capitalism found in the earlier utopias of Wells, Bogdanov, and Tolstoy. Orwell himself had insisted that *Nineteen Eighty-Four*
had been written '*against* totalitarianism and *for* democratic Socialism, as
I understand it' (Orwell 1970: 28). Thus, as Winston reads in Goldstein's
text-within-the-text, the 'idea of an earthly paradise in which men

should live together in a state of brotherhood, without laws and without brute labour . . . had been discredited at exactly the moment when it became realisable' (Orwell 1990: 212–13). Slumped into his corner table at the Chestnut Tree Café in a gin-fuelled stupor Winston finally discovers his love for Big Brother at the end of the novel. Just like his mentor Aldous Huxley's *Brave New World*, Orwell's *Nineteen Eighty-Four* ends with an inescapable image of utter despair. Or does it? As Margaret Atwood notes, Orwell's Appendix on Newspeak 'is written in standard English, in the third person, and in the past tense, which can only mean that the regime has fallen, and that language and individuality have survived. For whoever has written the essay on Newspeak, the world of 1984 is over' (Atwood 2005: 337). Like London's *The Iron Heel*, Orwell's *Nineteen Eighty-Four* relies on a futuristic frame of reference to contain its dystopian world within a past that has been survived and redeemed.

As Winston's surrender at the end of *Nineteen Eighty-Four* shows us, the resonant power of dystopian novels lies in their fraught relationship with utopian dreaming. Zamyatin's *We*, Huxley's *Brave New World*, and Orwell's *Nineteen Eighty-Four* thus force the reader, as Erica Gottlieb suggests, to consider 'how an originally utopian promise was abused, betrayed, or, ironically, fulfilled so as to create tragic consequences for humanity' (Gottlieb 2001: 8).

References

Atwood, Margaret (2005), 'George Orwell: Some Personal Connections' in *Curious Pursuits: Occasional Writing 1970–2005*, London: Virago, pp. 333–40.

Banerjee, Anindita (2012), *We Modern People: Science Fiction and the Making of Russian Modernity.* Middletown, CT: Wesleyan University Press.

Bogdanov, Alexander (1984), *Red Star: The First Bolshevik Utopia* [1908], ed. Loren R. Graham and Richard Stites, trans. Charles Rougle. Indianapolis, IN: Indiana University Press.

Bould, Mark (2010), 'Revolutionary African-American Sf Before Black Power Sf', *Extrapolation* 51: 1, pp. 40–68.

Bryusov, Valery Yakovlevich (2013), *The Republic of the Southern Cross and Other Stories* [1907], (London: Constable, 1918), pp. 3–10.

Burdekin, Katherine (1985), *Swastika Night* [1937]. New York: The Feminist Press.

Busch, Justin E. A. (2009), *The Utopian Vision of H. G. Wells*. Jefferson, NC: McFarland & Co.

Campanella, Tommaso (1981), *The City of the Sun: A Poetical Dialogue* [1602], trans. Daniel J. Donno. Berkeley, CA: University of California Press.

Čapek, Karel (2004), *Rossum's Universal Robots* [1921], trans. Claudia Novack. London: Penguin Classics.

Cioran, Samuel D. (1991), 'Introduction' to Marietta Shaginian, *Mess-Mend: Yankees in Petrograd*, trans. Samuel D. Cioran. Ann Arbor, MI: Ardis.

Collins, Christopher (1973), *Evgenij Zamjatin: An Interpretive Study*. The Hague: Mouton.

Du Bois, W. E. B. (2016), 'The Comet' [1920], in *The Big Book of Science Fiction*, ed. Ann and Jeff VanderMeer. New York: Vintage Books, pp. 53–61.

Forster, E. M. (1947), 'Introduction', in *Collected Short Stories*. London: Sidgwick and Jackson.

———— (2011), *The Machine Stops and Other Stories*. London: Penguin Classics.

Fourier, Charles (1971), *Harmonian Man: Selected Writings of Charles Fourier*, ed. Mark Poster, trans. Susan Hanson. New York: Doubleday.

Gilman, Charlotte Perkins (1998), *Herland* [1915], ed. Kathy Casey. London: Dover.

Gottlieb, Erica (2001), *Dystopian Fiction East and West: Universe of Terror and Trial*. Montreal: McGill-Queen's University Press.

Gottlieb, Julie (2010), 'Varieties of Feminist Responses to Fascism in Inter-War Britain', in *Varieties of Anti-Fascism: Britain in the Inter-War Period*, ed. Nigel Copsey and Andrzej Olechnowicz. Basingstoke: Palgrave, pp. 101–18.

Hopkins, Pauline (2004), *Of One Blood, or, The Hidden Self* [1903]. New York: Washington Square Press.

Huxley, Aldous (1994), *Brave New World* [1932]. London: Flamingo.

Le Corbusier (2007), *Toward an Architecture*, trans. John Goodman, 2nd edition. Los Angeles: Getty Publications.

London, Jack (2006), *The Iron Heel* [1908], ed. Jonathan Auerbach. London: Penguin Classics.

Mitchison, Naomi (1934), *The Home and a Changing Civilisation*. London: John Lane/The Bodley Head.

———— (2012) *We Have Been Warned* [1935]. Kilkerran: Kennedy & Boyd.

Morgan, Monique R. (2009), 'Madness, Unreliable Narration, and Genre in *The Purple Cloud*', *Science Fiction Studies* 36: 2, pp. 266–83.

Moylan, Tom (2000), *Scraps of the Untainted Sky: Science Fiction, Utopia, Dystopia.* Boulder, CO: Westview.

Orwell, George (1970), *The Collected Essays, Journalism and Letters of George Orwell, Vol. 1*, ed. Sonia Orwell and Ian Angus. Harmondsworth: Penguin/Secker & Warburg.

———— (1990), *Nineteen Eighty-Four* [1949]. London: Penguin.

Plato, *The Republic*, ed. G. R. F. Ferrari, trans. Tom Griffith (2000). Cambridge: Cambridge University Press.

Scharnhorst, Gary (2000), 'Historicizing Gilman: A Bibliographer's View', in *The Mixed Legacy of Charlotte Perkins Gilman*, ed. Catherine J. Golden and Joanna Schneider Zangrando. Newark, DE: University of Delaware Press, pp. 65–73.

Schuyler, George S. (1993), *Black Empire* [1937–8], ed. Robert A. Hill and R. Kent Rasmussen. Boston, MA: Northeastern University Press.

Shaginian, Marietta (1991), *Mess-Mend: Yankees in Petrograd* [1923], trans. Samuel D. Cioran. Ann Arbor, MI: Ardis.

Shaw, Debra Benita (2000), '*Swastika Night*: Katharine Burdekin and the Psychology of Scapegoating', in *Women, Science and Fiction: The Frankenstein Inheritance.* Basingstoke: Palgrave, pp. 42–64.

Shiel, M. P. (2012), *The Purple Cloud* [1901], ed. John Sutherland. London: Penguin Classics.

Suvin, Darko (1979), 'Russian SF and its Utopian Tradition', in *Metamorphoses of Science Fiction: On the Poetics and History of a Literary Genre.* New Haven, CT: Yale University Press, pp. 243–69.

———— (2010), *Defined by a Hollow: Essays on Utopia, Science Fiction, and Political Epistemology.* Oxford: Peter Lang.

Stites, Richard (1989), *Revolutionary Dreams: Utopian Vision and Experimental Life in the Russian Revolution.* Oxford: Oxford University Press.

———— (1992), *Russian Popular Culture: Entertainment and Society Since 1900.* Cambridge: Cambridge University Press.

Thompson, Mark Christian (2007), *Black Fascisms: African American Literature and Culture between the Wars.* Charlottesville, VA: University of Virginia Press.

Tolstoy, Alexei (1987), *Engineer Garin and His Death Ray* [1926], trans. George Hanna. Moscow: Raduga Publishers.

———— (2001), *Aelita* [1922], trans. anonymous. Amsterdam: Fredonia Books.

Wells, H. G. (1976), *Men Like Gods* [1923]. London: Sphere Books.

———— (1982), 'Utopias' [transcript of ABC radio broadcast, 19 January 1939], *Science Fiction Studies*, 9: 2, pp. 117–21.

———— (2005), *A Modern Utopia* [1905], ed. Gregory Claeys. London: Penguin Classics.

———— (2016), *Experiment in Autobiography: Discoveries and Conclusions of a Very Ordinary Brain (since 1866)*. London: H. G. Wells Library.

Zamyatin, Yevgeny (1993), *We* [1921], trans. Clarence Brown. London: Penguin Classics.

Zarnay, Jozef (1996), 'Science Fiction from a Dusty Shelf: A Short History of the Fantastic in Slovak Literature to 1948', trans. Cyril Simsa, *Science Fiction Studies* 23: 1, pp. 27–36.

What to Read Next

Alexander Bogdanov, *Red Star: The First Bolshevik Utopia*, edited by Loren R. Graham and Richard Stites, translated by Charles Rougle (Indianapolis: IN: Indiana University Press, 1984).

Katherine Burdekin, *Swastika Night* (New York: The Feminist Press, 1985).

Charlotte Perkins Gilman, *The Yellow Wall-Paper, Herland, and Selected Writings,* edited by Denise Knight (London: Penguin, 2009).

Pauline Hopkins, *Of One Blood, or, The Hidden Self* (New York: Washington Square Press, 2004).

H. G. Wells, *A Modern Utopia*, edited by Gregory Claeys (London: Penguin Classics, 2005).

Yevgeny Zamyatin, *We*, translated by Clarence Brown (London: Penguin Classics, 1993).

Chapter 4

Pulp SF and its Others, 1918–39

Mark Bould

The story of interwar anglophone SF can be located between the long slow decline of the British scientific romance and the fabrication of a distinctive pulp genre in America, usually dated from the first issue of Hugo Gernsback's *Amazing Stories* in April 1926.

The scientific romance emerged in the 1880s as an imaginative response to a rapidly changing world. Lord Kelvin's physics and Charles Lyell's geology vastly increased estimates of the Earth's age. Charles Darwin's theory of natural selection firmly located humans as just another species of animal. Misapplied by Herbert Spencer to the social order and in Max Nordau's jeremiad *Degeneration*, evolution was used to reinforce class, race, and gender hierarchies in the service of empire through the threat of species decline and the fall of civilisation. Scientific romance also often articulated the development of monopoly capitalism, including Britain's shifting position in a period of intensified competition between European colonial powers. Until World War I, it was dominated by such authors as J. D. Beresford, Arthur Conan Doyle, George Griffith, William Hope Hodgson, William Le Queux, M. P. Shiel, and, above all, H. G. Wells.

In the wake of the war, scientific romance's imaginary voyages, utopian and eschatological fantasies, and technological and biological speculations often took a darker turn. For example, in Conan Doyle's *The Land of Mist* (1926), the fiery Professor Challenger, who first erupted in *The Lost World* (1912), no longer pursues dinosaurs or battles pre-hominid apes but succumbs to spiritualism (as did Conan Doyle himself after the death of his son during the war). Challenger could still offer a booming flourish in 'When the World Screamed' (1928), but although his claim that the Earth is a living entity is proven correct, the planet's response to his deep exploratory drilling project is a cry of pain. Even Wells turned to religion in *The Undying Fire* (1919), an updated version of Job, and its non-fiction precursor, *God the Invisible King* (1917), albeit religion of an idiosyncratic rationalised sort, based not on a deity but in human psychology, and which he soon renounced. H. Rider Haggard, whose colonial adventure fiction from *King Solomon's Mines* (1885) onward inspired countless scientific romances, merged the two forms in *When the World Shook* (1919). An ancient being, who destroyed terrestrial civilisation 250,000 years ago, is awoken from suspended animation. Following a psychic tour of the contemporary world, including the battlefields of Belgium, he is inclined to destroy it once again.

The interwar scientific romance, however, was not dominated by the late careers of such writers, but by an emerging generation who consciously responded to them. For example, Aldous Huxley's dystopian *Brave New World* (1932) is as much a satire on Wells's utopian fiction as on contemporary social trends, and Olaf Stapledon's speculations on future human history and evolution in *Last and First Men* (1930) and on the magnitude and diversity of the cosmos in *Star Maker* (1937) are critical extensions of Wells's work. Furthermore, as World War I receded, many authors wrestled with the hope, disappointment, and/or threat of the Russian Revolution, the emergence of Stalinist tyranny, the looming end of European empires, the social and economic consequences of the Depression, the rise of fascism abroad and at home, and with other foreshadowings of the next world war.

American pulp SF drew on international and American models. Gernsback's first *Amazing Stories* editorial construed Jules Verne, H. G. Wells, Edgar Allan Poe, and Edward Bellamy as the forebears and

Figure 4.1 Cover for *Amazing Stories*,
April 1926.

models of the new 'scientifiction' he would publish **[4.1]**. Ironically, although Gernsback also mentions the occasional stories published in his non-fiction pulps *Radio News* and *Science and Invention*, he overlooked the kind of precursor fiction that would dominate the early SF pulps. Action-oriented SF featuring boy inventors, engineers, and other adventurers in exotic locations – the past, the future, far-flung terrestrial locations, other worlds – appeared in dime novels from the late 1860s onwards, in the first general fiction pulps such as *The Argosy* (from 1896) and *All-Story* (from 1905), and in the fantasy and horror pulp magazine *Weird Tales* (from 1923). Preferring to invoke authors with a little more cultural capital, and thus (misleadingly) to distinguish his product from that of potential competitors, Gernsback chose not to mention Edgar Rice Burroughs, Ray Cummings, George Allan England, Murray Leinster, H. P. Lovecraft, or Abraham Merritt, although he would go on to publish reprints and new stories by them alongside his reprints of Poe, Verne, and Wells.

Gernsback advocated a form of SF that combined scientific accuracy, prophetic vision, and thrilling romance, but was often hard-pushed to find such material. The general fiction pulps, which throughout the 1920s and 1930s published more SF than the specialist genre pulps, had higher rates of pay, and thus Gernsback often had to rely on reprints and translations while waiting for new writers to emerge.

In 1929, Gernsback lost control of *Amazing* to a rival, but following the bankruptcy suit promptly launched *Science Wonder Stories* and *Air Wonder Stories* to publish what he now called 'science fiction'. These magazines merged within a matter of months, and *Wonder Stories*, under editor David Lasser, briefly became the leading SF pulp. The only other competitor was *Astounding Stories of Super-Science*, founded in 1930, which was dominated by action-adventure SF. Its publisher, William Clayton, went out of business in 1933 and the title was bought by Street & Smith. Under F. Orlin Tremaine, a more thoughtful and ambitious editor, *Astounding* soon led the field. This position was cemented after John W. Campbell took over as editor in 1937, bringing with him a significant refinement of Gernsback's vision for the genre that would be embraced, more or less, by such British SF writers as Arthur C. Clarke and Eric Frank Russell after World War II, albeit while retaining something of a scientific romance sensibility.

The interwar scientific romance has typically been neglected by recent histories of SF, such as Brian Aldiss's *Billion Year Spree* (1973), Roger Luckhurst's *Science Fiction* (2005), Adam Roberts's *The History of Science Fiction* (2006) and Mark Bould and Sherryl Vint's *The Routledge Concise History of Science Fiction* (2011). These volumes restrict their discussion to a few luminaries – Huxley, Stapledon, C. S. Lewis – who might be situated alongside such European modernists as Franz Kafka, Karel Čapek, Yevgeny Zamyatin, and Mikhail Bulgakov. At the same time, their emphasis on the American pulps tends to start in 1926 and pay little attention to the fiction actually published in the magazines over the next decade (much of which remains unreprinted) beyond the space operas of E. E. 'Doc' Smith. Instead, they focus on isolated works which can, retrospectively, be seen to lay the groundwork for

Campbell's editorial revolution and the so-called Golden Age he inaugurated. This chapter will attempt a revision of the way this history is told, paying greater attention to both the scientific romance and pulp fiction, extending the period of the latter back into the decade before *Amazing Stories*, and pointing to some noteworthy non-anglophone SF in passing.

In the Aftermath of War

In *The Seventh Bowl* (1930), Neil Bell, writing as 'Miles', notes with weary resignation that 'The Treaty, signed at Versailles in 1919, that had ended the Great War and was to end all wars, merely made a renewal of that conflict inevitable' (Miles 1930: 19). This despairing note is not uncommon in the scientific romance. John Gloag's *To-Morrow's Yesterday* (1932) is presented as the transcript of a film using a secret new 3D technology. In the film, the future inhabitants of the Earth, descended from cats, travel back three million years in time to witness various scenes that might explain how human civilisation came to destroy itself (Lao She's dystopian 1933 critique of Chinese culture and bureaucracy, *Maocheng Ji/Cat Country*, also depends upon a species of intelligent cat). As with World War I, a complex interweaving of treaties and alliances propels nations into war, but with far more advanced weapons. Within hours, the world is in ruins. Jumping forward 400 years, the film shows the one man who exhibits any sense of scientific enquiry being killed in a fight over a woman by the chief of 'the Richmond Tribe, the third largest tribe in Britain' (Miles 1930: 85). Ten thousand years later, the sound of tom-toms fills the air as the last Britons descend into superstitious savagery, worshipping the memory of their machines. The novel ends with the audience leaving the cinema: a newspaper ominously declares a European crisis and a national state of emergency, and the 'midnight . . . sky [is] barred with searchlights' (Miles 1930: 120).

In war poet Edward Shanks's *The People of the Ruins* (1920), Jeremy Tuft wakes from accidental suspended animation 150 years into the future. The world has been destroyed (by, it is implied, a worker's uprising) and the Speaker, as England's ruler is named, gives the temporally displaced war veteran shelter, but compels him to wage war. In Cicely

Hamilton's *Theodore Savage* (1922), civilisation is brought to its knees when the League of Nations fails to stave off an international crisis that escalates into war. There are no conventional battlefields. Instead, cities are swiftly rendered uninhabitable, driving their inhabitants out into a countryside where crops have also been targeted. Civil organisation breaks down. Starvation and brutality set in. Savage eventually joins an effectively neolithic tribe, accepting their religious injunctions against science and technology. He survives into old age, the last person to remember the world that had been. After his death, he becomes a legendary figure, 'a personification of the Great Disaster', a 'Merlin, Frankenstein and Adam; the fool who tasted of forbidden fruit, the magician whose arts had brought ruin on a world, the devil-artisan whose unholy skill had created monsters that destroyed him' (Hamilton 2013: 187). John Collier's *Tom's A-Cold* (1933) is set in 1995, where the collapsed civilisation is barely even remembered. A small, isolated community, struggling to survive, abducts women from a similar community so as to reproduce and expand and thus be better able to fend off the seemingly inevitable expansion of a third, larger community. It is a tale of rivalry, tribal succession, and of preparations for war. There is no prospect for change or redemption; civilisation will not be restored. The only future is one of mere survival, of perpetual narrow horizons, and the always-looming prospect of further decline.

A more elegiac note is struck in *The World's End* (1937) by Storm Jameson, writing as William Lamb. After opening scenes of jaded bourgeois life in fashionable London – all empty chatter, tolerated infidelities, and vague forebodings of war – Richard Blake decides to break up with his mistress and, to his wife's dismay, abandon the capital. He drives off alone into the countryside in search of personal renewal on the very night that the world suffers titanic geological upheavals and a global inundation. He survives on an outcrop of moorland and grows old in a world in which humans persist but the species has no future. *The World's End* can be understood as a riposte to Sydney Fowler Wright's well-received *Deluge* (1927). Wright embraces the flood that sweeps away the modern world as a positive thing, since it enables the re-establishment of a feudal patriarchal 'natural' order in which bourgeois men can enjoy multiple female partners and the unquestioning obedience of the working classes.

It is perhaps unsurprising that this reactionary triumphalist primitivism, so much more in tune with the dominant mood of pulp fiction, saw the book become a bestseller in America and, in 1933, a special effects-laden Hollywood movie.

Race and Colonialism

While Gloag's *To-Morrow's Yesterday* notes in passing, and with a certain dismay, that soon after the outbreak of war 'The southern counties from Devon to Kent [were] occupied by Senegalese divisions of French Colonial troops' (Gloag 1946: 79), race is a much more pronounced factor for other authors. P. Anderson Graham's *The Collapse of Homo Sapiens* (1923) is presented as letters given to their editor by a mysterious acquaintance. They tell of a mystically inclined young man who encounters an alien entity that projects him two centuries into the future, where London lies in ruins. What remains of white humanity has regressed into cannibalistic bestiality, except for a tiny enclave on the Thames, barely holding on. The protagonist discovers that Britain and the West, weakened by the evils of trades unionism and terrified of Bolshevik-inspired revolution, failed to take seriously rumours of 'a colossal alliance ... of yellow men, brown men and black men, who aimed at nothing less than ousting the white races from the[ir] superior position' (Graham 1923: 64). Having, 'by some mysterious accident', 'mastered the secrets of the west – the mechanical and chemical devices by which the western sphere had for long maintained its superiority', the 'coloured races' launched a successful 'war of extermination' (Graham 1923: 151). While historians 'agreed that the German devastation of the Somme valley was the most awful outrage of its kind in modern history ... it was nothing to the completeness with which the coloured army ... laid England waste' (Graham 1923: 263).

In contrast, when the frontline soldiers of Théo Varlet and André Blandin's bawdy *La Belle Valence / Timeslip Troopers* (1923) discover an improved version of Wells's time machine and transport themselves from the trenches to fourteenth-century Valencia, they ally themselves with the Moors, the era's 'true custodians' of civilisation, against the Catholic Inquisition, and attempt to establish scientific modernity

(Varlet and Blandin 2012: 107). As with Mark Twain's *A Connecticut Yankee in King Arthur's Court* (1889), it all ends in bloodshed and history rolls on unchanged. It would not be until L. Sprague de Camp's *Lest Darkness Fall* (1939) that this kind of venture would succeed in establishing an alternative history to that of our own world. Martin Padway, cast back to Rome in the year 535, makes copper brandy stills and borrows Arabic numerals so he can introduce double-entry book-keeping before moving on to printing presses and semaphore telegraphy. His career as an arms manufacturer is less successful, so he becomes involved in political and dynastic machinations, ultimately averting the Dark Ages.

Graham's layering of voices in *The Collapse of Homo Sapiens* suggests that the author might be more ambivalent than some of his characters about race. Yet it is nothing like the overtly scathing critique of colonialism by the Czech Karel Čapek's *Válka s Mloky/War with the Newts* (1936). Three American SF novels from the same period are also unusual in their foregrounding of race, and take an obviously anti-colonial stance. In W. E. B. DuBois's *Dark Princess: A Romance* (1928), the African American protagonist Matthew Towns, thwarted in his ambition to become a doctor because he is forbidden to take a required obstetrics course in a white hospital, exiles himself to Europe. There, he falls in love with Kautilya, an Indian princess who is a member of 'a great committee of the darker peoples; of those who suffer under the arrogance and tyranny of the white world' (DuBois 1995: 16). Towns must persuade this secretive coalition of Indians, Chinese, Japanese, Arabs, and Egyptians that African Americans have a role to play in their global revolution. The novel ends with the Great Central Committee of Yellow, Brown, and Black finalising their plans: in 1952, after another fifteen years of preparation, 'the Dark World goes free – whether in Peace and fostering Friendship with all men, or in Blood and Storm – it is for Them – the Pale Masters of today – to say' (DuBois 1995: 296). George S. Schuyler's *Black No More* (1932) features a process which, 'by electrical nutrition and glandular control', can turn black people white (Schuyler 1998: 1). A savagely misanthropic comedy ensues as both black and white people put themselves through increasingly absurd contortions to either maintain, or subvert, the colour line. The novel ends with the discovery that those who have undergone the treatment are now lighter-skinned than 'white' people, which means the formerly black people now darken their skin so as to be taken for white, while white people darken their skin so as to not be too white and thus mistaken for formerly black people. Schuyler's *Black Empire* – originally serialised pseudonymously as 'The Black Internationale' (1936–7) and 'Black Empire' (1937–8) in the *Pittsburgh Courier*, a major African American newspaper – is rather more sanguinary. It depicts the conspiratorial scheme of a ruthless genius, Dr Henry Belsidus, to liberate Africa from white capitalist-imperialism. To achieve this, he triggers a second American civil war and a war in Europe, and introduces a panoply of SF technologies, including huge subterranean complexes, hydroponics, solar power, faxes, closed circuit and broadcast television, photoelectric cells, frozen food, artificial oases, short-wave radiation cures, underground airfields, planes capable of flying 350 miles per hour at 50,000 feet, aerial bombardment of military and civilian targets, thermite bombs, chemical and biological warfare, ray guns, and other superweapons. Ultimately, the Sahara is greened and a hypermodern pan-African empire is established.

Anti-Fascist, Left-Wing, and Feminist SF

While *Black Empire* can be understood as, in part, a furious response to the Italian invasion of Ethiopia, SF from isolationist America rarely addressed the rise of European fascism or the impending war. One exception is Sinclair Lewis's *It Can't Happen Here* (1935), which depicts the political ascendancy of populist politician Berzelius 'Buzz' Windrip, loosely based on Louisiana governor Huey Long. Posing as a champion of traditional American values, Windrip is elected President. He introduces a form of corporatist totalitarianism, sidelines Congress, overrides states' rights, criminalises dissent, establishes concentration camps, and unleashes the terroristic, paramilitary Minute Men to enforce his will. The majority of Americans approve of these measures, but a resistance movement develops and a series of coups weaken the fascist grip on power. The novel ends with the new civil war unresolved.

Written in the closing months of the Great War, Milo Hastings's *Children of 'Kultur'* (1919), later retitled *The City of Endless Night*, is one of the few pulp fictions to address any of these concerns. In the twenty-first century, Germany – finally defeated after a second world war – has contracted to just Berlin, a vast, armoured, impregnable, and almost entirely subterranean city-state. In this rabidly racist autocracy, there is a rigid eugenic hierarchy and strict regimentation. The state controls everything, from the food supply to information to reproduction, reducing women to either prostitutes for the pleasure of the upper classes or brood mares to bear strong and docile workers. Family life and private property have been eradicated, and the individual is utterly subordinated to the will of the state. The novel presents an eerily prescient vision of Berlin under the Nazis.

Nat Schachner, the author of over a hundred pulp stories in the 1930s that have never been collected, repeatedly circled around issues of race and the threat of fascism. 'In 20,000 A.D.!' (1930), co-written with Arthur Leo Zagat, depicts a future world divided between the small, balloon-headed Masters and the giant, four-armed black Robots, who are not machines but an organic slave race (in this, he follows Čapek's 1920 play *R.U.R.*, which coined the word 'robot' to describe its organic artificial people). Any commentary on race is undermined by the depiction of the Robots as slow-witted dupes of the Master who is urging revolution upon them – so that he can displace a rival Master rather than change anything. In 'The Robot Technocrat' (1933), set twenty years further into the Great Depression, America is divided into rival political parties, ranging across the spectrum from Extreme Communist through Patriots and Fascists to Monarchists, including the Nationalists, led by Adolph Hiller. When a machine is developed that is able to predict the different kinds of future each party would produce, and after Hiller is killed trying to eliminate all his rivals, the surviving party leaders surrender their aspirations and cede all power to the machine's technocratic governance, following the anti-democratic logic of many advocates of the Technocracy movement in the 1930s (see Segal). 'Ancestral Voices' (1933) satirises notions of racial purity. The scientist Pennypacker, proud of his Norman heritage, travels back in time to the sacking of Aquileia, and kills one of the Hun invaders, instantaneously wiping out all of his would-have-been descendants, including Pennypacker himself. Among the others who disappear in the vignettes accompanying the main narrative are a racist Mitteleuropean dictator called Hellwig, and a pair of heavyweight boxers based on the German Max Schmeling and the Jewish Max Baer. In 'He From Procyon' (1934), a visiting alien implants a device in the brains of six characters that enables them to control the will of others. Jordan, a minor official with fascist leanings, broadcasts his power, enslaving millions and becoming the dictator of America.

The power of media propaganda is also central to Miles J. Breuer's 'The Gostaks and the Doshes' (1930). The protagonist slips into a parallel – and slightly less technologically advanced – world, but his semi-bucolic existence is disrupted when people start insisting that 'the gostak distims the doshes'. His inability to make any sense of this phrase, while all around him it whips people into violent nationalist frenzy and pushes nations towards war, prompts him to refuse the newly instituted draft and face summary execution. Often recalled, inaccurately, as an anti-Nazi story about Josef Goebbels, its bleak vision of the power of propaganda is all the more chilling because it requires no magical alien intervention and is overtly set in a supposed democracy – and is undoubtedly informed by the twenty months Breuer spent in the US medical corps in France during World War I.

The relative scarcity of such work should not be seen to imply a lack of political engagement among pulp readers and writers. David Lasser, who edited the *Wonder Stories* magazines from 1930 to 1933, was undoubtedly responsible for their occasionally progressive content since he was also a Socialist Party organiser and an activist in the unemployed movement – activities for which Gernsback eventually fired him. Harl Vincent published around seventy action-oriented stories in the first decade of the pulps, in which traces of a leftist politics are evident, although it is not always clear whether this is merely a side-effect of reusing certain generic material already familiar from Wells and from Fritz Lang's film *Metropolis* (1927). For example, 'Barton's Island' (1929), 'Gray Denim' (1930), and 'Power' (1932) feature dystopias of class divisions between a hedonistic ruling class and a downtrodden proletariat, in which democracy is merely a cover story for plutocratic power.

Lilith Lorraine's 'Into the 28th Century' (1930) depicts a feminist socialist democracy that encourages racial inter-marriage. In her 'The Brain of the Planet' (1929), a scientist broadcasts mind-control waves that force people into altruistic behaviour; once this establishes class and gender equality, he destroys the machine, leaving humankind immeasurably improved. M. F. Rupert's 'Via the Hewitt Ray' (1930) features Lucile, an accomplished aviatrix who, aided by her scientist friend Marion, goes in search of her inventor father. He is stranded in another dimension populated by three distinct groups: barely human savages; a matriarchy which keeps intelligent men alive for reproductive purposes (and attractive men for non-reproductive sexual pleasure); and a group of hyper-rational but physically degenerate men who, in their war against the women, unleash terrible creatures from another dimension. Lucile rescues her father, ensures matriarchal victory, and returns home with a man she can turn into a suitable mate, albeit by performing a more conventional femininity herself. Leslie F. Stone's 'Men with Wings' (1929) **[4.2]** is set in a future which practises free love and where property has been abolished, and in the sequel, 'Women with Wings' (1930),

Figure 4.2 Illustration for Leslie F. Stone's *Men with Wings* from the July 1929 issue of *Air Wonder Stories*.

interplanetary, interspecies miscegenation is presented as the obvious solution when childbirth becomes fatal to Earthwomen and the Venusian matriarchy find their menfolk underperforming. A woman successfully passes as a man in Stone's 'Out of the Void' (1930) and genders are comically role-reversed in 'The Conquest of Gola' (1931). Her 'The Hell Planet' (1932) mounts a pointed critique of colonial adventure narratives. It is scathing about the treatment of indigenous Venusians *and* prospectors and frontiersmen by the system that happily sacrifices them both. 'Friend Island' (1918) by Gertrude Barrows, writing as Francis Stevens, recounts a tall tale told in a gender-role-reversed twenty-second-century future. An 'Ancient Mariness' regales a man daring enough to venture into one of the 'water-front . . . tea shops frequented by able sailoresses of the poorer type' (Stevens 2004: 192). Many years earlier, she was stranded alone on a beautiful island which she slowly comes to realise is sentient, female, and caring, if a little jealous and overprotective, and christens her Anita. Their relationship is idyllic until the return of a male castaway who fled the island; his foul language, unfit for feminine ears, soon prompts Anita to erupt. The queer overtones of this unusual female friendship are echoed in Stevens's 'Serapion' (1920), a tale of psychic phenomena in which the protagonist is possessed by the spirit of his dead uncle.

Perhaps most famous among the leftists working in the pulps is a group of New York-based fans who, seeing SF's potential for social critique, formed the Committee for the Political Advancement of Science Fiction in 1937 and the Futurian Science Literary Society in 1938. Several of the group were members of the Young Communist League, and collectively they evolved a broadly Marxist position that embraced – and democratised – many of the ideas of the increasingly conservative Technocracy movement. However, although the group included many who would go on to become significant writers, magazine and book editors, critics, and agents – Isaac Asimov, James Blish, Virginia Kidd, Damon Knight, Cyril Kornbluth, Robert A. Lowndes, Judith Merril, Frederik Pohl, Donald Wollheim – they were all at the start of their careers; their impact on the shape of SF would not begin to be felt until the 1940s, although they would remain influential until at least the 1970s (see Knight).

One of the more unusual leftist uses of SF in the period was in Upton Sinclair's 'End Poverty in California' campaign, intended to seize the Democratic nomination for Governor of the state. In a sixty-four-page pamphlet, *I, Governor of California, and How I Ended Poverty* (1933), he recounts, from a point in the near future, how his campaign enabled him to transform California's ailing economy by instituting a form of state socialism. Although he was in reality defeated – a tale recounted in *I, Candidate for Governor: And How I Got Licked* (1935) – he did also contribute a similar pamphlet, *We, People of America, and How We Ended Poverty* (1934), to campaigners in the national election.

A similar tack was taken in Britain with G. R. Mitchison's *The First Workers' Government* (1934). A history book purportedly written around 1980, it outlines the first few years of a majority Labour government elected in 1936, which uses existing institutions to transform Britain's failing capitalist economy into a socialist one without the need for revolution. Focused almost entirely on the legislation and organisational structures necessary to rapidly achieve such a goal, it even includes a twenty-five-page draft of the 'Emergency Powers (Financial) Act, 1936' that underpins the accomplishments of the worker's government. Barbara Wootton, one of the Labour party's key economists, also turned to SF in *London's Burning* (1936). Unlike Mitchison, she offers no policy suggestions, instead depicting, through a benevolent, middle-class liberal businessman and his family, the unavoidable collapse of Britain unless something substantial and significant is done to address the chaos and depredations of the capitalist economy and thus forestall violent revolution.

Unsurprisingly, anti-fascist SF was more prominent in the scientific romance than the pulps. Sometimes such novels are inattentive in their conflation of fascism, Nazism, socialism, Bolshevism, and Stalinism, while others see fascism as merely a particular manifestation of a broader mechanist culture; and often they are marked by peculiar ambivalences. Probably the most striking example from France is Claude Farrère's *Les condamnés a mort* (*Useless Hands*) (1920), in which a hierarchical social Darwinist America is divided into a ruling class, a tier of managers, and a brutalised proletariat. When the workers' demands for a shorter working day and better pay are ignored, they call for a general strike, only to find themselves replaced with machines. They attack the factories, but are wiped out with a lethal ray. The author's sympathies seem to lie with the workers but the novel effectively, if despairingly, counsels resignation to their lot.

In Edmund Snell's *Kontrol* (1928), the scientist Guriev, working for a secret organisation, transplants genius-level brains into physically superior bodies and, using hypnotic techniques, erases their former identities, thus creating an army of strong, smart human automata. On an island in the East Indies, he has established a fascistic colony in which this race of subordinated supermen slave to create the super-science weapons that will enable the Soviet Union to conquer the world. Mind control is also central to Joseph O'Neill's *Land Under England* (1935), in which a subterranean civilisation is dominated by a shared consciousness, eradicating the notion of individualism and rendering dissent impossible; but once the protagonist escapes this horrific society, he seems drawn to its freedom from conflict. This terror of loss of selfhood and individual will, common in dystopian visions of the period, finds its most brilliant treatment in Polish Stanisław Ignacy Witkiewicz's *Nienasycenie / Insatiability* (1930).

J. Leslie Mitchell's *Three Go Back* (1932) transports an arms manufacturer, a pacifist, and a woman whose beloved was killed in the Great War back into prehistoric times, where the values of the two men are tested and the social harmony of a nonetheless arduous Stone Age life is celebrated. In *Gay Hunter* (1934), Mitchell reworks this formula, pitching a female protagonist and two men into a future in which humankind has reverted to the kind of Stone Age existence enjoyed in the earlier novel. While the men – both British fascists – set out to subdue the inhabitants and rebuild the world, the eponymous heroine discovers that it was centuries of chemical and atomic warfare between rival fascists that destroyed civilisation. With the aid of the locals, she defeats the threat posed by her erstwhile companions. Andrew Marvell's *Minimum Man* (1938) features supermen, this time a newly evolved race of tiny people who play a key role in overthrowing fascist dictatorship; the point of the novel, however, seems to be that if fascism can emerge from human politics, then it is time for humankind to pass from the Earth, to make way for a more mature and intelligent, and less emotional,

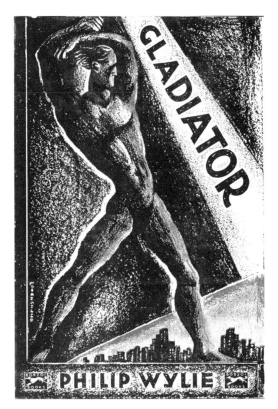

Figure 4.3 Cover for Philip Wylie's
Gladiator, 1930.

successor species. That there is no place in our world for the avatars of
humanity's evolutionary successor species is underscored in such British
superman narratives as Muriel Jaeger's *The Man with Six Senses* (1927)
and Olaf Stapledon's *Odd John* (1935), while in the US Philip Wylie's
The Savage Gentleman (1932) and *Gladiator* (1930) **[4.3]** influenced the
development of such pulp characters and comic book superheroes as
Lester Dent's Doc Savage (from 1939) and Jerry Siegel and Joe Shuster's
Superman (from 1938).

As the storm clouds gathered, H. G. Wells's *The Holy Terror* (1939)
tried, somewhat satirically, to understand what drives revolutionaries and
creates dictators. It begins in the 1920s, with the birth of Rud Whitlow,
and follows his eventual rise to global power as a surprisingly charismatic

revolutionary leader. His efforts to build a utopia on Earth are ultimately undermined by the ego that earned him his nursery moniker, and he must be assassinated before his paranoia destroys all that he has built. It remains unclear the extent to which Wells has Lenin, Stalin, or even Franklin Roosevelt in mind (he had met all of them), or whether he was trying to make sense of Hitler's ascendancy on the eve of war.

Three novels by women display none of these ambiguities. Storm Jameson's *In the Second Year* (1936), set in a fascist Britain just five years in the future, re-enacts events from the second year of Hitler's chancellorship, culminating in the equivalent of the Night of the Long Knives. Prime Minister Hillier, partly at the behest of Colonel Hebden (based on Hermann Goering), head of the Special Guard (the Gestapo), turns against his childhood friend, Richard Sacker (Ernst Röhm), head of the National Volunteer Guard (the Sturmabteilung), which had helped propel Hillier to power, and also executes General Smith (Kurt von Schleicher, the last President of the Weimar Republic). This is no mere *roman à clef*, though. In part a hard-headed attempt to analyse the appeal of fascism in Britain, just as support for Oswald Mosley's British Union of Fascists was starting to decline, and in part an indictment of Labour politicians such as Hugh Dalton who participated with Conservatives and Liberals in Ramsay MacDonald's coalition government, its primary focus is on the everyday choices, compromises, and inertias by which terrible things are allowed to happen, and on the heroism even the smallest acts of resistance can require. Jameson's *Then We Shall Hear Singing* (1942) is set in an occupied central European country in which a Nazi doctor performs experimental lobotomies on villagers in order to make them forget such ideas as nation, democracy, and equality. Foolishly, he assumes old women can pose no threat, and so they go untreated, but it is their ability to remember and to remind that seeds the anti-Nazi resistance.

Swastika Night (1937), by Katharine Burdekin (writing as Murray Constantine), depicts a future 700 years after the Nazi victory. The world is divided into two spheres, the other dominated by fascist Japan, with which there is little contact. The strict social hierarchy is headed by the Knights, an aristocratic elite, who govern ordinary Germans and, below them, the subjugated peoples of other nations. Women are segregated in compounds, regarded as mere animal stock and the common property of men, fit for breeding with and raising daughters but not sons, who are taken from them in infancy. Homosexuality is tolerated as inevitable among young men, but longer-term attachments are discouraged. Christianity has been all but eradicated, replaced by the worship of a deified Hitler. Alongside its extended conversations about how this world came to be, the novel features a slender narrative about the passing-on from one generation to another of secret, suppressed knowledge: that Hitler was not a blond giant but a short, brown-haired mortal; that the non-German states were not primitive tribes in need of civilisation but just as advanced as Germany; and that women are fully human and were once regarded as such.

Planetary Romance, Weird Fiction, Space Opera, and the Campbell Revolution

One of the major currents feeding into SF was the colonial adventure fiction pioneered by H. Rider Haggard's *King Solomon's Mines* (1885) and *She* (1886–7), which was full of lost worlds, lost tribes, lost races, lost remnants of ancient European cultures (or Atlantis), and often included super-science and parapsychological elements. In the interwar US, this influence is most evident in Edgar Rice Burroughs's Pellucidar and Caspak series, beginning respectively with *At the Earth's Core* (1914), and *The Land that Time Forgot* (1918). In the former, David Innes and Abner Perry's 'iron mole' tunnels 250 miles (400 kilometres) down through the planet's core to its hollow interior, which is populated by sundry species and tribes of ape-men, gorilla-men, cavemen, and flying reptiles – a set-up ideal for conquest and exploitation. In the latter, the conflation of evolution with colonial myths of progress – which typically treated peoples of colour as primitives somehow locked in an earlier stage of species evolution and of civilisation, the peak of which is to be found in white Europe – is mapped onto the geography of a lost Pacific island. Eggs laid in a river by a higher species of human develop into fish, some of which become amphibians, then reptiles, then mammals, then hominid apes, and so on, until the few that survive and successfully travel upstream become fully fledged humans.

Burroughs's planetary romances, such as the Barsoom series (1912–43), beginning with *Under the Moons of Mars* (1912), transplant such colonial views and racial logics to extra-terrestrial locations. Over the course of the first three novels, Confederate veteran John Carter finds himself inexplicably transported to a Mars populated by various decadent, barbarous, and colour-coded species and races, falls in love with and marries a princess who he saves multiple times from the threat of rape, kills hundreds of people in sword fights, saves the planet from global asphyxiation, unites warring tribes, and is awarded by universal acclaim the highest rank on the planet, Jeddak of Jeddaks. There are a further eight volumes. Often incoherent, laborious, and repetitive, especially in their serial captures and escapes, they also contain moments of almost surreal invention. For example, in *The Chessmen of Mars* (1922) **[4.4]**, Carter's half-Martian daughter Tara discovers a pair of symbiotic species: the rykors, which look like decapitated corpses, and the kaldanes,

Figure 4.4 Cover art by J. Allen St John for Edgar Rice Burroughs's *The Chessmen of Mars*, 1922.

who are so intellectually evolved that their bodies have withered away to crab-like pincers. Barely able to move, the kaldanes forced the inter-breeding of local animals with humanoid Martians to create the rykors as mounts for them to ride around on, controlling them by manipulating their nervous systems.

Burroughs's success led to a proliferation of planetary romances, including Ray Cummings's *The Girl in the Golden Atom* (1919), J. U. Giesy's *Palos of the Dog Star Pack* (1921), and Ralph Milne Farley's *The Radio Man* (1924), respectively set in a subatomic world, on a planet orbiting Sirius, and on Venus. Each spawned sequels. Simultaneously, colonial adventure fiction also played a major role in the development of weird fiction, which mixed Gothic and SF elements to produce a sense of uncanny dread, in stories such as Jack London's 'The Red One' (1918), and Francis Stevens's 'The Nightmare' (1917) and 'Sunfire' (1923). The key American weird fiction writers of the period, however, are A. Merritt and H. P. Lovecraft.

In Merritt's 'The People of the Pit' (*All-Story* 1918), a pair of explorers in the Yukon see strange lights dancing around a curious, five-peaked mountain, and then discover a dying man who tells them of his descent into a nearby abyss. Far below the ground, he found an ancient city inhabited by beings of light that forced him to participate in a peculiar, degrading ritual. He managed to escape, but the ordeal costs him his life. In 'The Moon Pool' (1918), the botanist Goodwin encounters an old friend, Throckmartin, who is the sole survivor of an ill-fated expedition to a remote Micronesian island that accidentally unleashed 'the Dweller' from a subterranean chamber. Another being of light, roughly humanoid but with tentacles, it took each member of the expedition, including Throckmartin's wife. He intends to equip a rescue party and return to the island but that very night the Dweller catches up with him. In 'The Conquest of the Moon Pool' (1919), a longer sequel prompted by the original story's popular success, Goodwin leads an expedition to the island. Soon they find themselves deep underground in the last surviving fragment of the ancient continent of Lemuria, which sank beneath the waves millennia ago. This picks up on many mystical and occult accounts of the lost continent of Lemuria circulating at the time – an equivalent myth to the Greek story of Atlantis, but in the Indian Ocean.

In Merritt's text, Muria is a technologically advanced but decadent feudal civilisation, with the usual tensions between royalty and priesthood,
and an ethnically distinct underclass. While the Dweller is worshipped
as the Shining One, there are those who remain loyal to the Silent Ones,
or Taithu, the survivors of the ancient reptilian civilisation who created
the Dweller, not expecting it to turn to evil. The expedition, in addition to triggering a civil war between these factions, encounter a pair
of beautiful priestesses – one wicked and libidinous, the other demure
and virtuous – who vie over one of their number. In 1919, Merritt
combined the two stories into a single novel – though the join remains
obvious – which Gernsback reprinted as a serial in *Amazing* in 1927.
Goodwin reappeared as the protagonist of 'The Metal Monster' (1920),
in which an expedition in central Asia discovers not only another lost
civilisation but also an alien race of what at first appear to be geometri-
cal metal beings; these various spheres and tetrahedra turn out to be
mere casings for a magnetic lifeform that distributes itself among them.

The connected stories that have subsequently become known as Lovecraft's 'Cthulhu mythos' – including 'The Colour Out of Space' (1927),
'The Call of Cthulhu' (1928), 'The Dunwich Horror' (1929), 'The Whis-
perer in Darkness' (1931), 'The Dreams in the Witch-House' (1933), 'The
Shadow Out of Time' (1936), 'The Haunter of the Dark' (1936) and 'The
Thing on the Doorstep' (1937) – emphasise the utter insignificance of
humankind by suggesting the vast physical and temporal scale of the cosmos and of the dangerous proximity of other dimensions from which
unspeakable horrors might emerge. Typically, these stories take place in
remote New England locales, shunned by modernity, where settler families have declined into decrepitude and idiocy, perhaps through incest,
perhaps through miscegenation. Indescribable horrors, vast and indifferent, visit strange maladies and madness on isolated farms. They leave
peculiar traces that tend to dissipate in sunlight. Destruction and death
trail in their wake.

At the Mountains of Madness (1936) **[4.5]**, which Lovecraft consciously
built on Edgar Allan Poe's enigmatic and inconclusive *The Narrative of
Arthur Gordon Pym* (1837), is set in the Antarctic, and ultimately gives a
more coherent account of the kind of events at which the other mythos
stories only hint. Five years earlier, an expedition led by the narrator,

Figure 4.5 Illustration for 'At the Mountains of Madness' by H. P. Lovecraft, from *Astounding* magazine, February 1936.

Dyer, discovered a cave containing the unfossilised remains of an apparently ancient species, winged marine creatures that are three-quarters animal and one-quarter vegetable. Most of the expedition was wiped out by these Old Ones. Dyer then discovered an ancient city, whose peculiar geometry indicates some connection with the murderous beings, and pieces together the hitherto unknown history of prehistoric Earth. The Old Ones are colonisers from another solar system who ruled the Earth for hundreds of millions of years. They waged victorious wars against races of cephalopods and fungoid arthropods, but then fell foul of their own creation – the shoggoth, a mindless protoplasmic lifeform that evolved intelligence and revolted against their telepathic control. Dyer barely escaped the shoggoth that the surviving Old Ones unwittingly awoke; his sole companion, who looked back at the city as they flew to safety, was driven mad by whatever it was he saw. Dyer feels compelled to give a full account in order to warn an incautious humankind of the horror that awaits them.

Despite its popularity with many SF readers of the time, the weird fiction tradition exemplified by Merritt and Lovecraft has subsequently been marginalised or dismissed by SF fandom and criticism. Darko Suvin, for example, influentially dismissed Lovecraft as practising 'a sub-literature of mystification', arguing that the 'commercial lumping of it into the same category as SF is ... a grave disservice and rampantly socio-pathological phenomenon' (Suvin 1979: 9). Nonetheless, even such signature forms of 1930s pulp SF as the planetary romance and space opera are frequently under the influence of the weird.

For example, C. L. Moore brought a strong sense of weirdness to a dozen stories featuring the adventures of Northwest Smith, a seemingly hard-boiled adventurer 'whose name is known and respected in every dive and wild outpost on a dozen wild planets' (Moore 2007: 17). In 'Shambleau' (1933), Smith rescues an innocent-seeming girl from a Martian mob, only to discover that she comes from the species that inspired the myth of the Medusa. He falls into languorous, feverish dreams and as she telepathically feasts upon him, he becomes aware of a vast and forgotten history in which ancient humans long ago ventured into space. Later stories in the series also point to cosmic gulfs and indescribable horrors. Curiously, despite Smith's reputation and the way Moore draws on westerns and other kinds of adventure fiction, he is frequently a passive, even feminised figure. At the end of 'Shambleau', for example, he must be rescued – and not by a human but a Venusian.

Similarly, Clark Ashton Smith, whose 'The City of Singing Flame' (1931) and 'Beyond the Singing Flame' (1931) are marked more by wonder than dread, brought a weird sensibility to more obviously science-fictional stories such as 'The Immortals of Mercury' (1932). On an expedition to Mercury, Cliff Howard is abducted by natives who intend to eat him, and rescued by an ancient subterranean civilisation of immortals, who intend to kill him (and use his protoplasm to fashion armour that enables them to survive the planet's heat). At the moment of execution, he breaks free and flees, but rather than escaping, returning to his ship and wreaking revenge, as one might expect of a colonial adventure narrative transplanted onto another world, he descends deeper into Mercury's interior. He wanders through caverns full of strange flora and fauna. He eventually finds his way back through a gateway, and emerges onto the surface of the planet to find himself on the side of the planet that (according to the science of the time) faces perpetually away from the sun.

Stanley G. Weinbaum's 'A Martian Odyssey' (1934) and 'Valley of Dreams' (1934) are indicative of a rather different trend emerging in the pulps. The former focuses on the 800-mile trek that Jarvis, a crashed explorer, must take across the surface of a Mars that is, more or less, scientifically accurate for the period (while also sporting canals and other such traces of outdated speculation and earlier fictional versions of the planet). He encounters various species: Tweel, an ostrich-like creature who becomes an ally even though communication between them is almost impossible; a predatory plant that telepathically lures its prey; an animal that, oblivious to other life-forms, just goes on steadfastly building increasingly large pyramids out of the silicon bricks it excretes; and a species whose sole purpose seems to be dumping rock and vegetable matter into a grinding machine. In the sequel, a decoration on an ancient ruin show that Martians visited Earth long ago and became Egypt's deities. Weinbaum creates a sense of the incommunicably ancient and alien, and of humankind's contingency, but the alien species, however horrific or indifferent they might be, are in the end merely plants and animals. There is nothing ontologically weird about the age of the universe or how it dwarfs humanity; this is fact, not a source of horror. With Tweel, it is possible to recognise the sentience of an Other and the potential to share values and objectives despite the difference.

A similar transition can be observed in the space opera of the period. Edmond Hamilton's lively *Interstellar Patrol* stories for *Weird Tales* (1929–34) are written in an oddly incantatory prose that occasionally pauses to reflect on the vast, inconsolable bleakness of space, of a 'cosmic gloom', an 'infinite darkness and stillness' that is 'soul-shaking in its deepness and extent' (Hamilton 2009: 61). These escalating stories present a not-exactly-consistent vision of a future of space-faring humans and alien species – 'the strange brain-men of Algol ... the birdlike people of Sirius', 'fur-covered and slow-moving beings from the planets of dying Betelgeuse... invertebrate insect-men from the races of Procyon; strange, dark-winged bat-folk from the weird worlds of Deneb' (Hamilton 2009: 55, 94) and so on. These beings defend our galaxy against the threat posed by other, even more alien aliens, typically from another galaxy and usually depicted as monstrous. In 'The Star-Stealers' (1929), the threat is posed by 'upright cone[s] of black flesh' each 'supported by a dozen or more smooth long tentacles ...supple boneless octopus-arms', who share 'no single point of resemblance to anything human, nothing which the appalled intelligence could seize upon as familiar' (Hamilton 2009: 72). In 'The Comet-Drivers' the menace is 'liquid-creatures! ... each but a pool of thick black liquid, flowing viscously about, in each of which pools floated two round, white blank disks, great white pupil-less eyes' and which sometimes flow 'together into a single liquid mass, a great black pool in which floated all their eyes, their liquid bodies mingling together!' (Hamilton 2009: 312). Despite the hideous otherness and galaxy-threatening nature of such creatures, Hamilton takes pains to depict them not as evil so much as compelled to take desperate measures to save themselves from some form of cosmic destruction.

More melodramatic and yet somehow more pedestrian, E. E. 'Doc' Smith's trilogy of *The Skylark of Space* (1928), *Skylark Three* (1930) and *Skylark of Valeron* (1935) begins as an inventor tale but rapidly plunges into the depths of interstellar space and alien wars. Smith's more substantial contribution to the development of space opera came in the seven-volume *Lensman* saga, starting with *Galactic Patrol* (1939–40). Hamilton's stories are notionally all set in the same future but events from one are not recalled in the next; in contrast, the *Skylark* novels follow the same characters and the *Lensman* stories set such more or less continuing adventures against a galactic history of warring, if not exactly Lovecraftian, elder species. John W. Campbell's *Arcot, Morey and Wade* stories (1930–32), which follow a *Skylark*-style arc, are much more determinedly focused on engineering. In long expository passages, science, pseudoscience and speculation blend together, producing a painstaking rhetoric of persuasion, a particular register of plausibility.

In a similar vein, 'Who Goes There?' (1938), Campbell's story about a shapeshifting alien's attempt to take over an Antarctic research station (and the basis for two films, Christian Nyby's 1951 *The Thing from Another World*, and John Carpenter's 1982 *The Thing*), is best understood as a riposte to Lovecraft's *At the Mountains of Madness* and a manifesto for the new kind of SF he would champion and develop when appointed editor of *Astounding* in 1937. There, he drew together a stable of new and established authors (including Isaac Asimov, L. Sprague de Camp, Lester del Rey, Robert A. Heinlein, L. Ron Hubbard, Henry Kuttner, C. L. Moore, Clifford D. Simak, Theodore Sturgeon, A. E. Van Vogt, and Jack Williamson) and promulgated a mode of SF with a greater focus on scientific plausibility, consistent world-building, and less laboured, more evocative – and thus digestible – exposition.

Conclusion

Other varieties of SF continued to thrive in the pulps and in other media, including radio and comics, but Campbellian SF rapidly became normalised during the war years. In Britain, after the long-anticipated World War II, the scientific romance persisted in a minor key, transformed by the influence of the American magazine tradition. It was also rather derailed by the 1950s 'mushroom' boom of cheap genre paperbacks in Britain, such as the colourful but crude SF of Vargo Statten (a pseudonym of John Russell Fearn, who had been publishing, often competently and sometimes pseudonymously, in the pulps, particularly *Astounding*, since 1933). John Wyndham, who had also appeared in the pulps, particularly *Wonder Stories*, since 1931, adopted a different approach, fashioning a distinctively middle-brow British voice for such novels as *The Day of the Triffids* (1951). In contrast, Arthur C. Clarke from his 1946 debut oriented his work to American markets, while retaining something of the scale and tone of Wells and Stapledon.

Thoroughly sublated, the scientific romance nonetheless persists in the often distinctive flavour of British SF, in contemporary authors as different as Gwyneth Jones and Stephen Baxter, but is perhaps most obvious nowadays in one-off SF novels by authors better known for other kinds of fiction, such as P. D. James's *The Children of Men* (1992) and Kazuo Ishiguro's *Never Let Me Go* (2005).

References

Aldiss, Brian (1973), *Billion Year Spree: The History of Science Fiction.* London: Weidenfeld & Nicolson.

Ashley, Mike (2000), *The Time Machine: The Story of the Science-Fiction Pulp Magazines from the Beginning to 1950.* Liverpool: Liverpool University Press.

Bould, Mark, and Sherryl Vint (2011), *The Routledge Concise History of Science Fiction.* London: Routledge.

DuBois, W. E. B. (1995), *Dark Princess*. [1928] Jackson: University Press of Mississippi.

Gloag, John (1946), *To-Morrow's Yesterday. First One and Twenty.* London: George Allen & Unwin.

Graham, P. Anderson (1923), *The Collapse of Homo Sapiens*. London: G. P. Putnam.

Hamilton, Cicely (2013), *Theodore Savage*. [1922] Boston: HiLo Books.

Hamilton, Edmond (2009), *The Star-Stealers: The Complete Tales of the Interstellar Patrol*. [1929] Royal Oak: Haffner.

Knight, Damon (1977), *The Futurians: The Story of the Science Fiction 'Family' of the 30s that Produced Today's Top SF Writers and Editors*. New York: Day.

Luckhurst, Roger (2005), *Science Fiction*. Cambridge: Polity.

'Miles' (1930), *The Seventh Bowl*. London: Eric Partridge.

Moore, C. L. (2007), 'Shambleau' [1933], in *Northwest of Earth*. Seattle: Paizo, pp. 17–48.

Ramaswamy, Sumathi (2004), *The Lost Land of Lemuria: Fabulous Geographies, Catastrophic Histories*. Berkeley: University of California Press.

Rieder, John (2008), *Colonialism and the Emergence of Science Fiction*. Middletown: Wesleyan.

Roberts, Adam (2006), *The History of Science Fiction*. Basingstoke: Palgrave Macmillan.

Schuyler, George S. (1998), *Black No More*. [1932] London: The X Press.

Segal, Howard P. (1985), *Technological Utopianism in American Culture*. Chicago: University of Chicago Press.

Stableford, Brian (1985), *Scientific Romance in Britain, 1890–1950*. London: Fourth Estate.

Stevens, Francis (2004), 'Friend Island' [1918], in *The Nightmare and Other Tales of Dark Fantasy*, ed. Gary Hoppenstand. Lincoln: University of Nebraska Press, pp. 193–203.

Suvin, Darko (1979), *Metamorphoses of Science Fiction: On the Poetics and History of a Literary Genre*. New Haven, CT: Yale University Press.

Varlet, Théo, and André Blandin (2012), *Timeslip Troopers* [1923], trans. Brian Stableford. Encino: Black Coat Press.

What to Read Next

Murray Constantine (Katharine Burdekin), *Swastika Night* (London: Gollancz, 2016).

Damon Knight, ed., *Science Fiction of the Thirties* (New York: Bobbs-Merrill, 1976).

H. P. Lovecraft, *At the Mountains of Madness* (New York: Modern Library, 2005).

George S. Schuyler, *Black No More* (New York: Modern Library 1999).

Olaf Stapledon, *Starmaker* (London: Gollancz, 1999).

Lisa Yaszek and Patrick B. Sharp, eds, *Sisters of Tomorrow: The First Women of Science Fiction* (Middletown: Wesleyan University Press, 2016).

Chapter 5

After the War, 1945–65

Malisa Kurtz

The 1940s have long been heralded as the Golden Age of SF, but many like to argue that the post-war period and the boom in the 1950s was the genre's *true* Golden Age. Big changes were underway in the genre at this time. Whereas pulp SF had attracted smaller fan communities, post-war SF expanded rapidly, drawing new audiences as a result of changes in the genre's editorship, publishing, and narrative forms. SF veterans such as Isaac Asimov, Robert Heinlein, and A. E. Van Vogt continued to publish after the decline of the pulps, but they were joined by a new generation including Ray Bradbury, Arthur C. Clarke, Philip K. Dick, and Judith Merril. This rise in new talent significantly altered the direction of SF's literary and thematic interests. Furthermore, though pulp era SF was primarily influenced by the editorial hand of John Campbell, as the last chapter explored, by the 1950s new editors such as Anthony Boucher, Horace Gold, and Merril pushed the genre in new directions. For many, SF finally 'matured' in the 1950s, reaching new literary heights that helped position the genre as a central platform for cutting-edge social critique.

This chapter is divided into five sections, each highlighting a major development that occurred in the genre between 1945 and 1965. It is important to note that these changes did not occur in isolation; change in one area of the genre inevitably affected other areas. For instance, while SF was published around the world in the 1950s, American SF dominated the marketplace. Accordingly, this also influences the genre's central themes during the post-war period when American SF was primarily concerned with visions of nuclear war, Cold War competition, and the effects of consumer culture. American economic and cultural dominance extended to media production, and though science fiction film and television are not discussed in this chapter, the expansion of SF media also played an important role in the genre's growth during the 1950s and 1960s. Certain television shows based on comic and pulp figures such as *Buck Rogers* (1950–51) and *Flash Gordon* (1954–5) had short production spans, but others such as *The Twilight Zone* (1959–64) are still significant works in the genre today. During the 1950s and 1960s, then, SF also shifted away from its niche beginnings to become a part of popular culture at large.

The Publishing Boom and Bust

One of the most significant changes experienced in the genre at the end of World War II was the rapid expansion of SF magazine and paperback publishing, especially in the US. Edward James argues that because of the country's post-war economic and cultural dominance, SF during this time is generally recognised as an American product (James 1994: 54). Indeed, post-war prosperity led to the establishment of several new publishers in the field, reaching a peak in 1953 when thirty-seven magazines were in circulation. New magazines subsequently expanded the genre's boundaries, changing both SF's form and content. Pulp magazines, for example, were supplanted by digest-sized magazines, and the bright, garish covers of the pulps replaced with the more subdued, sophisticated covers of publications such as *Galaxy*. Other periodicals such as *Magazine of Fantasy and Science Fiction (F&SF)* **[5.1]** prioritised literary quality and sophistication in the genre over adherence to generic norms. While *Galaxy* and *F&SF* became celebrated and long-lasting publications, SF's magazine boom ended fairly quickly as publishers folded in an over-saturated market and by 1955 only eleven magazines remained in circulation. Paperback publishing, however, continued to

Figure 5.1 Cover for Winter/Spring 1950 issue of *Fantasy & Science Fiction* magazine.

flourish as books such as Heinlein's *Stranger in A Strange Land* (1961) and Frank Herbert's *Dune* (1965) became bestsellers in both genre and mainstream markets.

As a result of the post-war cultural boom, American SF was reprinted around in the world in countries such as France, Italy, Mexico, and Sweden. In France, *Galaxie* and *Fiction* appeared in 1953, initially as translations of American counterparts *Galaxy* and *F&SF*. *Galaxie* ceased publication in 1959, but *Fiction* soon became a leading SF magazine in the 1950s and 1960s under the editorial guidance of Alain Dorémieux. Dorémieux published translations as well as French SF by authors such as Philippe Curval and Daniel Walther. In Britain, magazine publishing was much smaller, though *New Worlds* and *Science Fantasy* became celebrated publications. While there was magazine publishing across Europe, book publishing was more prolific than SF periodicals. This difference in publishing markets inevitably had an impact upon SF themes across different countries – for example, in Britain disaster novels were heavily influenced by the legacy of H .G. Wells's scientific romances, while in the US the genre's pulp magazine history affected narrative theme and tone.

Out of the several magazines that emerged in the 1950s, *Galaxy* and *F&SF* are arguably the most influential in the genre. *F&SF* was first published in 1949 under editors Anthony Boucher and Jesse Francis McComas, who played vital roles in shaping the publication. Boucher in particular reinforced the need for SF that was more literary and 'mature' than the early pulps, and his work at *F&SF* helped develop the genre's increasing respectability. In addition to its emphasis on literary quality, *F&SF*'s format also played a critical role in presenting SF as a more sophisticated genre – *F&SF* eliminated the interior illustrations and bright, kitschy covers of the early magazines, replacing the pulp format with a digest-sized publication.

Just as new publication formats were altering the face of SF, new authors were also reshaping the genre's thematic interests as they increasingly utilised SF conventions for political allegory and satire. In contrast to the technological orientation of early pulps such as *Astounding*, stories published in *Galaxy* and *F&SF* used SF to critique the era's socio-political conservatism while warning of potential dystopian futures. *Galaxy* in particular became well known for its 'social science fiction'; that is, SF that concentrated on questions about ethics, philosophy, and social change. From its very first issue the magazine claimed it was different from the 'western'-style SF that transplanted frontier adventures into outer space. 'You'll never see it in *Galaxy*,' the magazine's back cover claimed on the first issue in October 1950; instead, 'What you will find in *Galaxy* is the finest science fiction . . . authentic, plausible, thoughtful . . . written by authors who do not automatically switch over from crime waves to Earth invasions.' *Galaxy* was edited by Horace Gold, an already experienced SF writer and editor, who successfully managed the publication from its beginning in 1950 until he retired from *Galaxy* in 1961. In its first few years alone, Gold's magazine published some of SF's most renowned stories including Ray Bradbury's 'The Fireman' (1951), Heinlein's 'The Puppet Masters' (1951), Alfred Bester's 'The Demolished Man' (1952), and Theodore Sturgeon's 'Baby is Three' (1952), later to become part of *More Than Human* (1953).

While magazine publishing eventually dwindled by the late 1950s, SF paperback publishing continued to flourish around the world. Now-familiar genre publishers such as Ace Books, Bantam Books, and Ballantine Books released their first SF texts between 1951 and 1952, solidifying SF's place in the paperback market. Authors such as Bradbury, Dick, Frederik Pohl, and Kurt Vonnegut published fix-ups from previously serialised works as well as new novels. Bantam, for instance, released Bradbury's collection *The Martian Chronicles* in 1951, which consisted of both new and previously published short stories, and Pohl and C. M. Kornbluth's 'Gravy Planets' was republished in 1952 by Ballantine Books as *The Space Merchants*. Like the format changes that occurred in SF magazine publishing, innovative techniques were also created by book publishers to expand their markets. In 1952 Donald Wollheim, long-time SF editor at Ace Books, launched 'Ace Doubles', books that were two novels bound together, back to back **[5.2 and 5.3]**; the reader had only to flip a book upside down and turn it over in

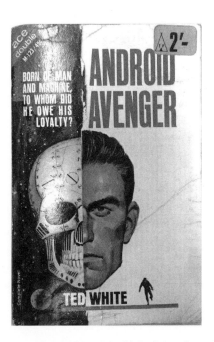

Figure 5.2 One cover for the 'Ace Double' edition featuring Ted White's *Android Avenger*, 1965.

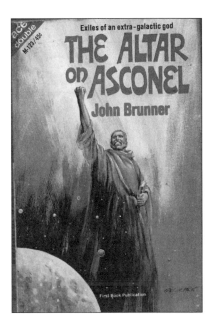

Figure 5.3 Other cover of the 'Ace Double' edition featuring John Brunner's *The Altar on Asconel*, 1965.

order to read the second novel. Both Ace Books and Ballantine Books published SF on a regular basis throughout the 1950s and 1960s, and Ace Books is still a prolific SF publisher to this day, claiming to be 'the oldest continuously operating science fiction publisher in the United States' (*ACE* 2016).

Hard Science Fiction

Though the 1950s would see science fiction open its door to new authors and new perspectives on the genre, much SF during this decade was still primarily influenced by the pulps of the 1940s and by Campbell's editorial work at *Astounding*. Campbell often promoted SF that would later align with the notion of 'hard' science fiction. These stories emphasised scientific plausibility and technical application, or as James Gunn puts it, 'Hard science fiction, like science, took as its first premise that the universe could be understood by an organized application of observation and thought' (Gunn 2005: 87). The term itself actually developed in the late 1950s when P. Schuyler Miller first used it in his 1957 review of Campbell's *Islands of Space* (1957), Murray Leinster's *Colonial Survey* (1957), and Hal Clement's *Cycle of Fire* (1957). Miller writes that *Islands of Space* is 'very characteristic of the best "hard" science fiction of its day', and that, '[a]ll three [novels] seem to me to be examples of what some readers mean when they say they want "real" *science* fiction' (Miller 1957: 142–3). Though the meaning of the term has since altered slightly, many fans still consider 'real' SF to be works that follow the scientific rationalism of hard SF. The division between hard SF and New Wave SF (which focused less on science and more on literary experiment, as explored in Chapter 6) becomes particularly pronounced in the mid-1960s, but the roots of such division were already established in the 1950s. Authors who became associated with the technical orientation of hard SF during this time include, for example, Arthur C. Clarke (*A Fall of Moondust* 1961), James Blish (*Surface Tension* 1952), and Poul Anderson ('Kyrie' 1968).

Stories that exemplify hard SF abound in the 1950s, including most famously Clement's *Mission of Gravity* (1954) and Tom Godwin's 'The Cold Equations' (1954). Both texts require their characters to follow specific scientific principles and logic. *Mission of Gravity*, for instance, carefully applies the laws of gravity and centrifugal force to an alien planet. The novel's expository passages on the applications of physics are examples of what is colloquially known as 'infodumps', or long forays into technical explanation, in the genre. Though 'The Cold Equations' does not succumb to the infodumps common in hard SF, it does present a moral dilemma which can only be resolved through the application of scientific rationalisation. Godwin's story takes place aboard an Emergency Dispatch Ship headed to supply an outer planet with much-needed medicine. When a stowaway (Marilyn) is discovered aboard, the ship's pilot (Barton) is forced to explain that she must be jettisoned as the ship does not have enough fuel to complete its flight. The flight is headed to save the lives of six other men, and Marilyn's excess weight compromises the mission. For Barton, then, 'there could be no alternative' except to 'coldly, deliberately, take the life of a [wo]man' (Godwin 1998: 449). Despite the story's refusal to succumb to easy sentimentality and its ability to follow through with the 'logical' decision to eject Marilyn, scholars such as Mark Bould and Sherryl Vint note that celebrating such rationalism also 'adamantly ignore[s] the story's systematic repression of all the human decisions that created the problem in the first place' (Bould and Vint 2011: 85). In other words, Godwin's story intentionally constructs a scenario in which there are no emergency fuel supplies and no alternatives to the supposedly 'rational' decision of ejecting Marilyn.

Hard SF proliferates throughout the 1950s, and SF's 'Big Three' – Isaac Asimov, Arthur C. Clarke, and Robert Heinlein – frequently published in this subgenre. Though Asimov, Clarke, and Heinlein do explore 'social' issues in their work, their stories typically portray a strong commitment to the scientific spirit. In fact, Asimov's Three Laws of Robotics best exemplify this, as the Laws function as scientific principles (even if they are fictional) that each of Asimov's Robot stories must carefully follow. Hence in murder mysteries such as *The Caves of Steel* (1953) and *The Naked Sun* (1956) where robots are prime suspects, readers must figure out how a murder could have been committed when the First Law of Robotics states that a robot cannot harm a human being. Both novels eventually reveal that the killing was committed by a human who manipulated unknowing robots into performing the act. Asimov's Laws have become central features of SF texts containing robots and artificial intelligence, and part of the narrative pleasure in such stories is derived from the reader's attempt to work through the logic of the imposed Laws of Robotics in the plot.

Social Science Fiction

Alongside hard SF, post-war SF also developed a cycle of 'social science fiction', or stories that were more concerned with philosophical speculation, ethics, and exploring the human condition than they were with scientific accuracy or prediction. In his 1953 article 'Social Science Fiction' Isaac Asimov identified three main types of SF plot, centring on: gadget; adventure; or social science fiction. Asimov suggested that social science fiction focused on the social impact of technologies, but continued to argue that all SF must retain the scientific spirit. My own definition of social science fiction expands on Asimov to include stories that use SF tropes but are not concerned with adhering to the premises of modern science.

In social SF, astute critiques of consumerism, industrial life, militarism, and Cold War paranoia replace the technological utopianism of the early pulps. *Galaxy* and *F&SF* were leading magazines in this area, publishing social science fiction from authors such as Bradbury, Dick, Harlan Ellison, Damon Knight, and Robert Silverberg. While American-based magazines dominated the global market, it is important to note that social science fiction was also being produced around the world. Authors such as John Wyndham, Stanisław Lem, and Arkady and Boris Strugatsky published SF that explored the human condition and social progress into the future. During the 1950s and 1960s, then, SF around the world was expanding in directions very different from the early adventure tales of *Astounding*.

From its beginning in 1950 *Galaxy*'s stories focused primarily on social issues and speculation, and historically it has been identified as the leading publication for social science fiction. For example, Bradbury's 'The Fireman' (1951) **[5.4]** – later to become the basis of *Fahrenheit 451* – was first published in *Galaxy*. 'The Fireman' is set in a future where books are banned because they offer contradictory opinions instead of conforming to the ideals of this future society. Many readers consider 'The Fireman' a critique of Cold War paranoia, and in particular, Senator Joseph McCarthy's practice of exposing 'subversive' thought for its apparently Communist sympathies. Because of its status as a relatively marginal pulp genre, SF was one of the few spaces where stories such as Bradbury's were free to pursue critiques of McCarthyism and the political conservatism of the US. As Judith Merril points out, in the 1950s 'science fiction became, for a time, virtually the only vehicle of political dissent' (Merril 1971: 74).

Along with authors such as Heinlein and Vonnegut, Bradbury frequently published social science fiction in non-SF magazines such as *Collier's Weekly* and *The Saturday Evening Post*. 'The Pedestrian' (1951), for instance, was published in *The Reporter*, and much like 'The Fireman' the story is typical of Bradbury's critiques of mass media and conformity. 'The Pedestrian' depicts a future where people are so consumed by mass

Figure 5.4 Cover for *Galaxy* science fiction
magazine, February 1951.

media that magazines and books are defunct, and people are punished
for expressions of individualism. The story follows Leonard Mead, an
out-of-work writer, who is out for a night stroll when he is arrested for
his 'abnormal behaviour'. The patrol car which arrests Leonard considers
walking at night unusual as everyone else is inside their homes watch-
ing television. Leonard is taken to the Psychiatric Centre for Research
on Regressive Tendencies for his failure to comply with the habits of
modern life. Both 'The Fireman' and 'The Pedestrian' are reflections on
the political and cultural conservatism which defined much of the 1950s,
a decade that also saw the establishment of the House Un-American
Activities Committee and its stifling of creative talent.

Harlan Ellison's breakthrough story '"Repent, Harlequin!" Said the
Ticktockman', also published in *Galaxy* (1965), responds to such cultural

conservatism by depicting a dystopian future where any form of free expression, creativity, or dissent is punished by the shortening of one's lifespan. The story opens with an excerpt from Thoreau's 'Civil Disobedience' (1849) beginning with the line, 'The mass of men serve the state thus, not as men mainly, but as machines with their bodies' (Ellison 2010: 368). Indeed, Ellison's story portrays a future society which functions like a well-oiled machine – citizens follow rigid schedules, perform their work with precision, and are monitored for their efficiency by 'The Ones Who Kept The Machine Functioning Smoothly' and the notorious 'Ticktockman'. However, this social order is soon disrupted by Everett C. Marm, or the 'Harlequin', whose absurd and erratic behaviour causes mass chaos. Everett is eventually punished for his transgressions by the Ticktockman who 'reprograms' him, 'just like what they did to Winston Smith in *Nineteen Eighty-Four*' (Ellison 2010: 368). Ellison's story, like George Orwell's *Nineteen Eighty-Four*, exemplifies how authors used SF's central tropes – mechanical futures, technological development, dystopian/utopian settings – as a means to critique the socio-political conservatism of the 1950s and 1960s.

One of the most well-known examples of satirical SF published in *Galaxy* is Frederik Pohl and C. M. Kornbluth's 'Gravy Planets' (first serialised in 1952 and later published in book form as *The Space Merchants*). Pohl and Kornbluth's story is a scathing critique of corporate greed and consumer culture amidst the expansion of the middle class in mid-century America. The narrative centres on Mitch Courtenay, an advertising man who is tasked with selling the idea of life on Venus (an arid, destitute land) to the people of an over-populated America. Corporations control the US government and public through invasive advertising, products deliberately designed to be addictive, and a life of hyper-consumption bound by debt. Like Asimov's *The Caves of Steel* (also serialised in *Galaxy*), *The Space Merchants* imagines a world where overpopulation and consumerism have depleted Earth's resources, and the only way to escape impending disaster is by colonising other planets. The idea that escape from Earth's environmental disasters might be found in space is inevitably a sign of the times – with the threat of nuclear war looming in the 1950s, dreams of space travel and colonisation dominate the SF imagination.

Like *The Space Merchants*, Philip K. Dick's stories during this time are also exemplars of the way in which social science fiction critiqued post-war consumerism. 'Foster, You're Dead' (1955), for example, highlights how catastrophe and war are lucrative markets. Dick's story follows Mike Foster, a young boy whose family does not have a bomb shelter because his father, Bob Foster, believes that the threat of war is a marketing scheme designed to propagate rampant consumerism. Bob perceptively recognises that 'the way to sell something was [to] create anxiety in people' (Dick 2013: 171) and that war in fact becomes a perfect platform for selling commodities to families concerned with the safety of their children. The war, Bob says, is '[t]he perfect sales-pitch' where '[b]uy or die—[is the] new slogan' (Dick 2013: 171). The threat of nuclear war looms over every aspect of life in the narrative, from the disaster drills at Mike's school to the commodity fetishism which drives families to continually purchase the latest bomb shelters. This commodity fetishism also manifests in Mike's desperate longing for a bomb shelter – he truly believes the shelter makes him 'incredibly powerful' and 'complete and entire' (Dick 2013: 169). Mike's momentary 'freedom' from anxiety therefore also reveals the consumerist ideology which equates purchasing power with the power for self-determination.

Emerging from the context of the post-war boom and the expansion of suburban America in the 1950s, Dick's story is an insightful critique of the relationship between consumerism and patriotism. Just as advertising and government work hand-in-hand in *The Space Merchants*, US companies during and after the war equated patriotism with domestic spending. Suburban life in the 1950s therefore not only supported economic growth, but also symbolised the 'freedoms' of consumer choice and the potential for ordinary citizens to buy status, social standing, and prestige. Dick's short stories frequently address the impact of consumer culture on social and psychological development, themes he explores in tales such as 'We Can Remember It for You Wholesale' (1966) – the basis for the film *Total Recall* (1990) – where even our memories and identities are constructed through the products we buy. Similarly, 'Some Kinds of Life' (1953), 'Sales Pitch' (1954), 'Nanny' (1955), and later, most famously, *Ubik* (1969) all consider how the pervasive reach of capitalism has reshaped the individual psyche, family life, and ultimately our social fabric.

Like the social science fiction published in *Galaxy*, SF in Europe during the 1950s also used the genre as a platform for exploring questions about the nature of human relationships and social development. Stanisław Lem's work, for example, examines the limits of human knowledge and the provisionality of science in novels such as *Solaris* (1961), *The Cyberiad* (1965), and *His Master's Voice* (1968). Though Lem's *Summa Technologiae* (1964) is a work of non-fiction, it is a visionary book that deserves mention, as in it Lem reflects on the future of technology and the evolutionary future of mankind, philosophical questions he continually poses throughout his fiction books. His novels, for example, are often about breakdowns in communication or the failure to truly understand the difference of the 'Other'. Both *Solaris* and *His Master's Voice* are first-contact narratives that use the premise of the alien Other in SF to posit epistemological questions about how we really come to know, or comprehend, the world around us. While these novels do not directly address the political context of the Cold War, they do pose questions about the ethics of scientific and military research.

In the Soviet Union, Ivan Yefremov's ground-breaking *Andromeda Nebula* (1957) **[5.5]** ushered in a phase of social SF as Soviet writers increasingly used the genre as a space for allegory, freedom of expression, and political critique after the cultural thaw between East and West after the death of Stalin. *Andromeda* depicts a utopian Communist future in which Earth has made contact with extra-terrestrial civilisations across the galaxy. The book follows several characters including, a Director of the Outer Stations, a group of astronauts, and multiple scientists whose interplanetary adventures serve as critiques of contemporary culture. For example, in the first major plot line of the book, Yefremov explores the dangers of atomic energy. In this storyline, the spaceship *Tantra* is sent to investigate 'Zirda', a planet which has gone mysteriously silent in their interplanetary communications. When *Tantra* arrives, the crew discover that 'Zirda had perished from an accumulation of harmful radiations following numerous careless experiments and the reckless use of dangerous forms of nuclear energy instead of wisely continuing the search for other, less harmful sources' (Yefremov 1959: 24). Other Soviet authors – including most famously Arkady and Boris Strugatsky, who

Figure 5.5 Cover for the first English-language edition of Ivan Yefremov's
Andromeda, 1959.

began writing together from the 1950s and are best known for *Roadside
Picnic* (1972) – followed Yefremov's lead in turning to SF as a medium
for philosophical, political, and social critique.

Atomic War(nings) and Future Disaster

Andromeda Nebula is only one example of how SF during the 1950s and
1960s reflects on the dangers of unfettered scientific advance. During
this time, a particular strain of social science fiction emerged which
critically examined the cost of scientific progress through post-apocalyptic scenarios and representations of nuclear disaster. For example,
novels such as Leigh Brackett's *The Long Tomorrow* (1955) and Walter M.
Miller's *A Canticle for Leibowitz* (1959) explore the value of scientific
progress in the aftermath of nuclear war. Additionally, disaster narratives

often served as warnings about the consequences of nuclear energy in stories such as Theodore Sturgeon's 'Thunder and Roses' (1947), which depicts a future devastated by the mutually assured destruction enabled through nuclear weapons. Similarly, Merril's 'That Only a Mother' (*Astounding* 1948) and *Shadow on the Hearth* (1950) explore the violent disruption of family life after war, and Wilson Tucker's *The Long Loud Silence* (1952) is a bleak and somewhat cynical story about the struggle to survive in a post-apocalyptic wasteland of eroding morals. Similarly, in Britain disaster narratives such as John Wyndham's *The Day of the Triffids* (1951) and John Christopher's *The Death of Grass* (1956) focus on the disintegration of middle-class values and the struggle to survive amidst catastrophe.

Kurt Vonnegut's work is exemplary of social science fiction, and although he often distanced himself from the genre, Vonnegut's novels frequently use SF conventions to critique the social consequences of scientific development and modern industrial life. In *Player Piano* (1952), for example, Dr Paul Proteus undergoes a transition from embracing the 'the divine right of machines, efficiency, and organization' (Vonnegut 2006: 301) – embodied in the Fordist production line that famously used Frederick Taylor's time and motion studies – to questioning the human cost of such technological development. In this future, workers are no longer needed as the scientific elite have developed more efficient, automated manufacturing systems. Only managers and engineers are required to perform the most valuable work. Ordinary blue-collar workers and those without technical knowledge, then, are considered 'useless', and live without the means for work or access to political power. In *Cat's Cradle* (1963), Vonnegut extends his critique of scientific development to consider the dangers of separating science from social responsibility. The novel follows the Hoenikker family who possess a new scientific development known as 'ice-nine', a substance that can freeze any object upon touch. While ice-nine is initially developed out of scientific curiosity, it is soon used for disastrous ends. Ice-nine clearly functions as an allegory for nuclear physics and *Cat's Cradle* as a satire of the nuclear arms race during the Cold War. Vonnegut's novel, however, is only one example of the many stories which functioned as arms race allegories in SF at the time.

In England, John Wyndham's *The Day of the Triffids* and John Christopher's *The Death of Grass* do not directly address the threat of nuclear war, but they do exemplify the preoccupation with post-apocalyptic scenarios that characterised much of the cultural imagination during the 1950s and 1960s. In *The Day of the Triffids* **[5.6]** disaster arises after an assumed weapons attack blinds almost everyone who watched the weapon/meteor event. Only a few sighted people remain, including protagonist Bill Masen. Bill eventually finds a small group of other sighted survivors, and the novel follows their struggle to survive the ensuing chaos as they attempt to navigate competing moral positions and eventually establish new colonies. In a similar vein, *The Death of Grass* considers a post-apocalyptic future when a virus destroys global grain production, creating mass chaos and famine. Christopher's novel

Figure 5.6 Cover for the Penguin paperback edition of John Wyndham's *The Day of the Triffids*.

follows John Custance, Roger Buckley, and their respective families as they attempt to reach John's brother and the safety of his rural farmland.

Notably, in both *The Day of the Triffids* and Christopher's *The Death of Grass* the apocalyptic event itself is less significant than the social changes which occur in the face of disaster – namely, the slow erosion of all that is familiar, including the security of middle-class values. Critic Brian Aldiss considers *The Day of the Triffids* an example of Britain's 'cosy catastrophes', in which the 'hero should have a pretty good time . . . while everyone else is dying off' (Aldiss and Windgrove 1973: 294), but Wyndham's novel is in fact a more intimate exploration of how disaster affects the individual. Rather than focusing on grand, historical overviews of apocalypse, as works such as *A Canticle for Leibowitz* do, *The Day of the Triffids* and *The Death of Grass* both focus on social collapse at an individual level, examining the moral challenges one faces when forced to compete for survival. Both novels are thus more subtle explorations of nuclear war that focus on individual, psychological trauma instead of political commentary.

British post-apocalyptic narratives boomed in the 1950s and 1960s, and are part of a larger cycle of disaster narratives descending from early SF, such as H. G. Wells's *The War of the Worlds* (1898). Along with Christopher and Wyndham, J. G. Ballard and Arthur C. Clarke also follow in this tradition. Some of Ballard's most famous post-apocalyptic novels – including *The Drowned World* (1962) and *The Burning World* (1964) – focus on crumbling social structures and psychological trauma in the face of man-made and natural disasters. Similarly, Clarke's *Childhood's End* (1953) depicts a post-apocalyptic scenario in which Earth is invaded by a mysterious alien species. Unlike the majority of post-apocalyptic novels during this time, however, Clarke's novel rewrites the alien invasion trope and SF's imagination of disaster by depicting a future in which the Cold War ends peacefully because of the arrival of aliens. When an alien species known as the Overlords lands on Earth, they stop an impending nuclear attack, end social prejudices, and attempt to prepare mankind for a new evolutionary future. Indeed, *Childhood's End* imagines a post-Cold War scenario, but instead of depicting a society that must reconstruct itself after war, Clarke's epic history imagines a completely alien future and the transcendence of humanity as we know it.

Like *Childhood's End* and *The Martian Chronicles*, Miller's post-apocalyptic novel *A Canticle for Leibowitz* has garnered much critical acclaim since its publication. Miller's novel, originally published as three short stories in *Fantasy and Science Fiction* between 1955 and 1957, is an expansive future history that follows multiple generations as civilisation attempts to rebuild itself after a global nuclear war. In this future, most scientific knowledge has been destroyed in retaliation against the scientific progress which first led to nuclear war. However, through the 'Albertian Order of Leibowitz', a monastic establishment dedicated to preserving human knowledge, scientific progress eventually develops once again, only to lead to another nuclear war and vast environmental destruction. *A Canticle for Leibowitz* thus considers the cyclical nature of history and the rise and fall of civilisations.

While this section briefly explored British disaster narratives in contrast to post-apocalyptic tales from American authors, I want to be careful to avoid reinserting divisions between British and American SF. Specifically, I want to avoid the division which sometimes occurs in historical overviews of SF that distinguish between the 'low' mass culture of pulp magazines and the more serious 'high' literature of European SF. While different national contexts and publication histories do affect the genre's development to an extent, American SF and European SF in the 1950s mutually informed each other. Clarke and Wyndham, for instance, frequently published work in the American pulps. Furthermore, authors publishing outside SF at this time also had a notable impact on the genre's imagination of disaster. For instance, Nevil Shute's *On the Beach* (1957), Pat Frank's *Alas, Babylon* (1959), and Mordecai Roshwald's *Level 7* (1959) all present deeply personal, detailed accounts of the consequences of nuclear war. Post-apocalyptic narratives working directly in SF and outside of the genre proliferated in the 1950s and 1960s, and ultimately this section can only offer a brief glimpse into a greater subgenre.

Women's SF as Critique

Just as authors such as Bradbury, Ellison, and Vonnegut used SF as a platform for social critique, women during the post-war period also used the genre as a space for political dissent, both challenging gender expectations and rewriting social norms. Though SF during the Golden Age of the pulps was a predominantly male field, women were publishing in the genre long before the 1950s. Authors such as C. L. Moore, Clare Winger Harris, and Lilith Lorraine regularly published in the early pulps, paving the way for women in SF after the war. Furthermore, as SF markets rapidly expanded in the 1950s, it also welcomed a number of women writing within related genres such as fantasy and slipstream (a term coined by Bruce Sterling to describe texts that mix genre elements with more 'mainstream' literary fiction). Lisa Yaszek notes that 'nearly 300 women began publishing in the SF community after World War II' (Yaszek 2008: 3), and several of these authors would become leading voices in the genre's development.

Where pulp SF focused predominantly on male scientists and protagonists, authors such as Judith Merril consistently put women's lives at the centre of SF stories, thereby challenging narratives that excluded women from technoscientific culture. *Shadow on the Hearth* **[5.7]**, for example, focuses on Gladys Mitchell, a typical suburban housewife who attempts to hold her family together in the aftermath of a nuclear attack. Importantly, *Shadow on the Hearth* foregrounds women's lives while considering larger socio-political critiques. As Merril writes, '*Shadow on the Hearth* was a very political novel. It was written for political reasons, and one of the central characters was a physicist who understood about atomic warfare and what it meant' (Merril and Pohl-Weary 2002: 100). While stories such as *Shadow on the Hearth* bring domestic settings into SF, other SF works foreground protagonists who are professional women or scientists. Merril's 'Daughters of Earth' (1952) and 'Dead Center' (1954), Kate Wilhelm's 'No Light in the Window' (1963), and Naomi Mitchison's *Memoirs of a Spacewoman* (1962) all focus on professional women working in space travel. Women's SF, then, was also a part of greater developments in social science fiction, as authors used the genre to challenge the assumptions of patriarchal science and explore changing gender expectations.

Though Merril is most well known for her editorial work, Merril's early writings are insightful critiques of SF's norms. 'Dead Center', for example, presents a compelling counterpart to the patriarchal science of Godwin's 'The Cold Equations'. Where Godwin's story glosses over the moral assumptions behind its 'laws', Merril's story considers

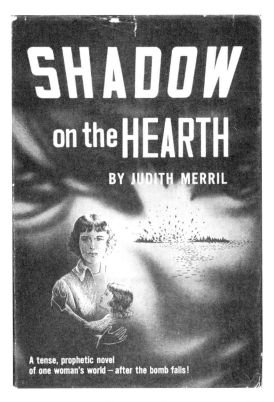

Figure 5.7 Cover for the Doubleday Books first edition of Judith Merril's *Shadow of the Hearth*, 1950.

how scientific progress is deeply affected by, and entrenched in, particular social systems. The story follows the Kruger family: Ruth Kruger, an established engineer; her husband Jock, a rocket pilot; and their young son Toby. When Jock's latest space flight malfunctions, he is left stranded on the dark side of the Moon, and Ruth must work on a rescue mission to save him. Merril's story alternates between the perspective of all three characters, eventually revealing that Toby is scared his mother's absence at work means she is abandoning him like his father. Merril's story repeatedly refers to the 'human factors' (Merril 1960: 127) that complicate Jock's mission, and while the phrase refers specifically to the complications that arise during space flight, it also implicitly gestures towards the human cost of scientific development.

Merril's story confronts the patriarchal frameworks in science on a number of fronts. First, Jock's mission goes awry because Ruth is replaced by another rocket engineer, Andy Argent, whose design malfunctions. When Ruth is finally chosen to lead the rescue mission, she must balance her return to work with her parental duties, a fact that her employer, Rocket Corps, repeatedly ignores. Ruth feels guilty for leaving Toby alone so often, but she also feels guilty for her failures at work and for not challenging Argent's rocket designs when she suspected something was wrong. Ruth is essentially punished for her desire to have both a family and a career; as she says, 'It's different for a woman' who must juggle career and gendered expectations (Merril 1960: 130). Under a patriarchal social system which fails to acknowledge that women remain primary caretakers, professional women such as Ruth are forced to handle the pressures of demanding careers and the expectations of traditional gender roles.

Importantly, Merril's stories refuse to homogenise the diversity of women's lived experiences, and while Ruth is a talented scientist, other characters, like *Shadow on the Hearth*'s Gladys, are homemakers. Merril's characters represent women with diverse desires, perspectives, skills, and ways of living. 'Daughters of Earth', for example, follows six generations of women who embrace space colonisation and travel in very different ways. Joan exemplifies scientific ambition and she eventually heads to Pluto in order to establish a new colony. Joan's mother, Martha, however, is the typical domestic mother who remains planet-bound. While Martha prefers to remain on Earth, she is also proud, excited, and nervous for Joan's adventures, and in this way shares some of Joan's excitement for space. As Dianne Newell and Victoria Lamont argue, 'Merril's female space pioneers are neither superwoman adventurers nor tragic figures of sacrifice; rather, they are complex characters with conflicting desires for both the safety and familiarity of home and the unknown possibilities of space' (Newell and Lamont 2009: 58–9).

Like Merril's work, Pamela Zoline's 'The Heat Death of the Universe' (1967) is an example of the highly experimental and ground-breaking work published by women in SF. I include her story from the late 1960s as a seminal piece of women's SF and as a gesture towards the proliferation of innovative SF that would follow. Specifically, Zoline's story is representative of the literary experimentation and radical social critique in New Wave SF. 'The Heat Death of the Universe' follows Sarah Boyle, a housewife whose day begins to slowly fall apart. The story draws on the second law of thermodynamics, which states that entropy increases to a maximum in closed systems. As the story explains, 'It has been held that the Universe constitutes a thermodynamically closed system, and if this were true it would mean that a time must finally come when the Universe "unwinds" itself . . . This state is referred to as the "heat death of the Universe"' (Zoline 2010: 420). Using this scientific premise, Zoline's story portrays entropy in relation to domestic life; in other words, Sarah is trapped in the closed system of domesticity that consumes all her energy and eventually leaves her feeling empty and unfulfilled. The story begins with Sarah as a 'vivacious and intelligent young wife and mother' (Zoline 2010: 418), and it ends with Sarah's 'unwinding'. Tired, crying, and confused, she finds her world falling apart, and like the eggs that she throws around in frustration, Sarah 'begin[s] to fall away slowly, slowly' (Zoline 2010: 429). Zoline's innovative story expands the boundaries of SF by using generic conventions (applying physics to the narrative logic of the story) in order to critique gender roles and expectations.

In addition to Merril, Mitchison, and Zoline, there are a number of other women whose work in the late 1950s and early 1960s helped shape SF's development. Leigh Brackett, for instance, was a prolific writer in the field from 1940 until her death in 1978. One of her most critically acclaimed works is the post-apocalyptic novel *The Long Tomorrow*. Additionally, Joanna Russ and Ursula K. Le Guin increasingly published in the 1960s, with works such as 'Nor Custom Stale' (1959) by Russ, and the novels *Rocannon's World* (1966), and *Planet of Exile* (1966) by Le Guin. Authors who are now predominantly associated with fantasy and slipstream fiction also published prolifically during this period, including Andre Norton, Anne McCaffrey, Marion Zimmer Bradley, and Carol Emshwiller. Furthermore, Merril was reshaping the genre through her editorial work in her 'Year's Best' anthologies, which ran from 1956 to 1967, and later through her New Wave anthology *England Swings SF* (1968). While this chapter can only address a few of the important women who shaped the genre, it is clear that the 1950s

and 1960s represent a time of great change in SF as the genre welcomed
new readers, achieved new literary heights, and broached new subjects
with increasing socio-political awareness.

The Times They Are A-Changin'

Despite the rise of social science fiction in the 1950s, SF during this
time typically failed to address the historical realities of the civil rights
movements or the continued violence against people of colour around
the world. In the mid-fifties, new voices in fandom eventually forced
the genre to examine its racial diversity, but these conversations were
often naïve attempts to position SF as a post-racial space. This naivety is
most clearly exemplified in the figure of popular fan writer Carl Joshua
Brandon. Amidst ongoing desegregation movements in America,
Brandon stated in his writings that he was black. However, Brandon was
ultimately revealed to be the fictional creation of white authors Terry
Carr and Peter Graham. Carr and Graham created Brandon intending
to demonstrate that race was inconsequential in the genre, but all they
did was reveal SF's deep lack of diversity. Hence the unfortunate situation in which, in order to discuss race in the genre, two white authors
had to appropriate the identity of an African American man, revealing
that SF was still primarily dominated by white, male authors and fans.

Outside of fandom, when SF did address race such texts often
assumed post-racial futures or portrayed race metaphorically through
the figure of the alien, robot, or non-human Other. Heinlein's *Starship Troopers* (1959), for example, takes place in a future which claims
to be a 'democracy unlimited by race, color, creed, birth, wealth, sex,
or conviction' (Heinlein 1987: 194). It is narrated by a soldier only
very belatedly revealed to be of Filipino origin in an attempt to confront readers' assumptions, but the novel's extreme violence against an
alien species called the 'Bugs' reveals an underlying xenophobia and
racial intolerance that persists in this future. Heinlein's novel is only one
example of how SF can embrace a form of multi-culturalism while hid-
ing its own colonialist attitude. In contrast to *Starship Troopers*'s symbolic
racial violence, Bradbury's *The Martian Chronicles* overtly draws parallels
between SF's colonial imagination and the history of colonisation in

North America. In stories such as '—And the Moon be Still as Bright' Bradbury explicitly compares the extinction of Martian Natives to the violent dispossession endured by Native Americans in the US. A few of the stories in Bradbury's collection – including 'Way in the Middle of the Air' – also focus specifically on the lives of African Americans who flee from racism by boarding rocket ships headed to Mars.

By the mid-1960s SF would begin to challenge racist representations more openly and to consider the importance of cultural difference in its narratives. *Black Man's Burden* (1961) by Mack (Dallas McCord) Reynolds, for instance, directly addresses issues regarding racial intolerance and colonialism, though it ultimately reproduces problematic stereotypes about 'primitive' African societies. There is a whole group of utopian, science-fictionally tinged writings that leads up to revolutionary movements like the Black Panthers in the 1960s and 1970s. Samuel R. Delany's work in the late 1960s also began to rewrite SF's colonial gaze. Delany's early works are typical space narratives in many ways, but his stories take a decidedly different tone from works by Asimov, Clarke, or Heinlein. For instance, in a rare move at the time, *The Einstein Intersection* (1967) takes the perspective of the alien Other and forces readers to assume the position of a character typically marginalised in SF. However, Delany's writings were in many ways still novel to the genre, as evidenced by Delany's anecdote about his attempt to publish *Nova* (1968) with John Campbell. Delany notes Campbell ultimately rejected the novel on the premise that readers might not be able to relate to a black character (Delany 1998).

Conclusion

Science fiction published from 1945 to 1964 sits between two of the genre's most well-known historical moments: the Golden Age of SF pulps in the 1940s and the emergence of the New Wave in the 1960s. The 1950s and early 1960s, then, are often seen as a lull in the genre's development. However, this transitional period was in fact an exciting time in SF as the genre reflected on the rapidly changing atmosphere of global politics and technoculture. SF publishing boomed in the midst of post-war prosperity, expanding to reach new audiences and welcoming new authors whose works represent some of the most popular SF stories to date. Bradbury's stories, for example, are taught in high schools around the world; Dick's work continues to be adapted for television and film; and Lem is still one of the most critically acclaimed SF authors. Additionally, by the early 1960s SF was prepared for the increasingly experimental works of authors such as Ballard, Delany, Russ, Thomas M. Disch, and Brian Aldiss. Without positing a certain timeframe as representative of the genre's 'true Golden Age', then, we might at least say that post-war SF exemplifies the genre's truly innovative potential for social critique, ethical reflection, and philosophical speculation.

References

ACE. (2016), Penguin Random House. Available from: http://www. penguin.com/meet/publishers/ace/. Accessed 5 October 2016.

Aldiss, Brian, and David Wingrove (1973), *Trillion Year Spree*. London: House of Stratus.

Ashley, Mike (2005), *Transformations: The Story of the Science-Fiction Magazine from 1950 to 1970*. Liverpool: Liverpool University Press.

Asimov, Isaac (1979), 'Social Science Fiction' [1953], in *Modern Science Fiction: Its Meaning and Its Future*, ed. Reginald Bretnor, 2nd edn. Chicago: Advent, pp. 157–96.

Bould, Mark (2010), 'Revolutionary African-American SF Before Black Power', *Extrapolation* 51: 1, pp. 53–81.

Bould, Mark, and Sherryl Vint (2011), *The Routledge Concise History of Science Fiction*. New York: Routledge.

Csicsery-Ronay Jr, Istvan (2004), 'Science Fiction and the Thaw', *Science Fiction Studies*, 31: 3 (November), pp. 337–44.

Delany, Samuel R. (1998), 'Racism and Science Fiction', *The New York Review of Science Fiction* 120 (August), http://www.nyrsf.com/racism-and-science-fiction-.html. Accessed 8 February 2017.

Dick, Philip K. (2013), 'Foster, You're Dead' [1955], in *Selected Stories of Philip K. Dick*. Intro. by Jonathan Lethem. New York: Houghton Mifflin Harcourt, pp. 157–76.

Ellison, Harlan (2010), '"Repent, Harlequin!" Said the Ticktockman', [1965] in *The Wesleyan Anthology of Science Fiction*, ed. Arthur B. Evans,

Istvan Csicsery-Ronay Jr., Joan Gordon, Veronica Hollinger, Rob Latham, and Carol McGuirk. Middletown: Wesleyan University Press, pp. 367–78.

Godwin, Tom (1998), 'The Cold Equations' [1954], in *The Science Fiction Hall of Fame: Volume 1, 1929–1964*, ed. Robert Silverberg. New York: Orb, pp. 449–71.

Gunn, James (2005), 'The Readers of Hard Science Fiction' in *Speculations on Speculation: Theories of Science Fiction*, ed. James E. Gunn and Matthew Candelaria. Toronto: The Scarecrow Press, pp. 81–94.

Heinlein, Robert (1987), *Starship Troopers* [1959]. New York: Penguin.

James, Edward (1994), *Science Fiction in the Twentieth Century*. Oxford: Oxford University Press.

Merril, Judith (1960), *Out of Bounds*. New York: Pyramid.

———— (1971), 'What do you mean: Science? Fiction?' [1966] in *SF: The Other Side of Realism*, ed. Thomas Clareson. Bowling Green: Bowling Green University Press, pp. 53–95.

Merril, Judith, and Emily Pohl-Weary (2002), *Better to Have Loved: The Life of Judith Merril*. Toronto: Between the Lines.

Miller, P. Schuyler (1957), 'The Reference Library', *Astounding Science Fiction*, 60: 3 (November), pp. 142–3.

Newell, Dianne, and Victoria Lamont (2009), 'Daughter of Earth: Judith Merril and the Intersections of Gender, Science Fiction, and Frontier Mythology', *Science Fiction Studies* 36: 1 (March), pp. 48–66.

Silverberg, Robert (2010), 'Science Fiction in the Fifties: The Real Golden Age', in *Nebula Awards Showcase 2010*, ed. Brett Fawcett. New York: Roc, pp. 163–72.

Vonnegut, Kurt (2006), *Player Piano* [1952]. New York, NY: The Dial Press.

Yaszek, Lisa (2008), *Galactic Suburbia: Recovering Women's Science Fiction*. Columbus, OH: The Ohio State University Press.

Yefremov, Ivan (1959), *Andromeda Nebula: A Space Age Tale*, trans. George Hanna. Moscow: Foreign Lang. Publ. House.

Zoline, Pamela (2010), 'The Heat Death of the Universe' [1967], in *The Wesleyan Anthology of Science Fiction*, ed. Arthur B. Evans, Istvan Csicsery-Ronay Jr, Joan Gordon, Veronica Hollinger, Rob Latham, and Carol McGuirk. Middletown: Wesleyan University Press, pp. 415–29.

What to Read Next

J. G. Ballard, *The Drowned World* [1962] (London: Fourth Estate, 2014).
Arthur C. Clarke, *Childhood's End* [1953] (London: Pan, 2010).
Philip K. Dick, *The Man in the High Castle* [1963] (London: Penguin, 2015).
Ursula K. Le Guin, *Rocannon's World* [1966], reprinted in *Worlds of Exile and Illusion: Rocannon's World, Planet of Exile, City of Illusions* (London: Orb, 1997).
Walter Miller, *A Canticle for Leibowitz* [1959] (London: Orbit, 1997).
Theodore Sturgeon, *More Than Human* [1953] (London: Gollancz, 2000).

Chapter 6

The New Wave 'Revolution', 1960–76

Rob Latham

The consensus in SF history is that the 1960s were an epochal moment in the genre, marking a radical break with the pulp tradition of technophilic adventure stories and ushering in an array of dystopian themes and avant-garde styles of writing. According to Damien Broderick, this shift was prompted by 'a reaction against genre exhaustion' on the part of a younger cohort of authors and editors. 'By the early sixties,' he asserts, 'much sf had become complacent, recycling with minor modification a small number of tropes and ideas'; as a result, renegade talents began to push the genre in new directions, towards a 'disruptive, existentially fraught and formally daring' mode of SF (Broderick 2003: 49–50). Like many critics, Roger Luckhurst sees this shift as aligned with 'the generational dissent of the young against the Establishment' that marked the cultural politics of the decade, with the new SF 'strongly resistant to the cybernetic languages of capitalist efficiency' and distrustful of 'the shiny promises of technological modernity' (Luckhurst 2005: 141, 143). The SF that emerged during the 1960s, generally referred to as the 'New Wave', was thus boldly experimental and militantly political, in ways that represented a sharp break with previous writing in the field.

This consensus is, in its broad contours, accurate, but it also tends – as does any critical viewpoint that emphasises rupture at the expense of continuity – to exaggerate the alleged exhaustion of old-style SF and overstate the revolutionary nature of the New Wave movement. More importantly, it also ignores major changes in the genre's infrastructure during the 1950s that paved the way for the New Wave's innovations. The 1960s avant-garde did not arrive out of nowhere but emerged from – and depended deeply upon – a series of institutional transformations in the production, distribution, and consumption of SF, developments that were genuinely radical (that is, 'foundational') in their implications and effects.

Markets and Mastery

The most significant of these transformations was the blossoming of a hardcover and paperback book market. For the first few decades of its existence in the United States, SF was exclusively a magazine culture, spurred and shepherded by a small cadre of editors, the most influential being John W. Campbell, Jr at *Astounding Stories*. Doubleday and Co. became, in 1950, the first major publishing house to launch a hardcover SF line, and two years later, the first SF-only imprint, Ballantine Books, debuted. By the end of the decade, most major publishers were regularly featuring SF titles. At the same time, the American magazine market – once exceptionally diverse – was rapidly contracting: by the mid-1950s, all of the pulps had folded or converted to digest format, with only six titles – from a peak of twenty-three – surviving into the new decade. The consequences of this transformation were profound, and would be felt fully only during the 1960s and 1970s, as the New Wave rose and spread.

One significant effect of the wide-scale conversion to book format was that writers no longer had to tailor their work for serialisation, punctuating long stories with episodic cliffhangers, but could instead plan fully fledged novels with their own integral structure. Many of the texts marketed as novels during the early 1950s – for example, Ray Bradbury's *The Martian Chronicles*, Isaac Asimov's *I, Robot*, A. E. Van Vogt's *The Voyage of the Space Beagle* (all 1950) – were, in fact, repackaged 'fix-ups' of material previously published in the magazines. By the mid-1950s, however, there was a thriving trade in paperback originals, with many budding talents (such as Poul Anderson, Philip K. Dick, Jack Vance) generating a host of new titles and thus building a readership outside the traditional magazine setting. Books were not only distributed more widely than the pulps, but were also promoted as the fruits of individual creators rather than as collective products: the names of authors, rather than the titles of periodicals, were the main 'brands'. As Evan Brier has shown, it was this branding function that allowed Bradbury to emerge, by the mid-1950s, as both *the* representative SF writer and as a uniquely gifted figure who transcended the genre altogether (Brier 2010: 45–73).

By the end of the decade, writers could begin to imagine careers that were not beholden to the small handful of editors – Campbell at *Astounding*, Horace Gold at *Galaxy*, Anthony Boucher at *The Magazine of Fantasy and Science Fiction* – who had once controlled the flow of output into the marketplace. Maverick talents such as Philip José Farmer and Theodore Sturgeon had long chafed at the constraints imposed by these gatekeepers, in particular their routine excision of hot-button content, especially politically controversial or sexually suggestive material. According to Farmer, Campbell and Gold invariably rejected 'any story which contains a society based on different sex mores' because they found the topic 'personally disgusting and disturbing' (quoted in Cogswell 1992: 139–40). Book editors were, in general, less bound by such taboos: Farmer's delirious novel *Flesh*, about an orgiastic fertility cult, and Sturgeon's searching pansexual utopia *Venus Plus X*, were released as paperback originals in 1960. This trend towards greater openness gained pace after a series of major obscenity trials liberalised publication standards in the US and UK, further weakening the grip of editorial monitors.

As a result, SF authors began to see themselves, for perhaps the first time, as autonomous artists fully in control of their subject matter and mode of expression. In the early 1950s, Bradbury – along with Robert A. Heinlein and a few others – had broken out of the pulp ghetto into prestigious 'slick' venues such as *Collier's* and *The Saturday Evening Post*, while Kurt Vonnegut, with his well-received novels *Player Piano* (1952) and *The Sirens of Titan* (1959), had shown that it was possible to forge a successful career without being invidiously marginalised as a 'category' writer. Further subverting such pigeonholing tendencies, Judith Merril, in her annual series of 'Year's Best' anthologies, regularly mingled genre efforts with mainstream fabulations by the likes of Eugène Ionesco, John Steinbeck, and Isaac Bashevis Singer. Throughout the decade, Merril consistently pushed for higher literary standards within the field, advocating for a more expansive aesthetic of 'speculative fiction' and co-founding – along with James Blish and Damon Knight – the Milford Writers' Workshop, where peer-to-peer feedback germinated fresh ideas and promoted professional solidarity. Ambitious authors willing to tackle compelling issues of social moment began to reach a wide readership, and novels such as Walter M. Miller's *A Canticle for Leibowitz* (1959) and Heinlein's *Stranger in a Strange Land* (1961) – with their complex depiction of the tension between spiritual and secular values – became surprise bestsellers. At the dawn of the 1960s SF stood poised to achieve a cultural visibility, a commercial success, and a literary acclaim of which the pulp era could only have dreamed, as I have discussed more fully in a chapter in the *The Routledge Companion to Science Fiction* (2009).

But the pulp tradition would not be so readily effaced. Despite the growing sophistication of theme and style that characterised the best 1950s SF, the vast bulk of work produced and marketed as science fiction during the decade remained fairly straightforward – if not formulaic – tales of space adventure. In fact, several of the new paperback outlets simply picked up where the old pulps had left off, with the prolific Ace Books specialising in 'doubles': two fast-paced, colourful novels bound back-to-back. Moreover, every attempt to expand the borders of the field brought a sharp counter-reaction: many authors and fans resented the crossover success of Bradbury and Vonnegut, seeing them as turncoats in their embrace of mainstream respectability, and the advent of writers' workshops prompted dark mutterings about a nefarious 'Milford Mafia' whose influence was deeply pernicious. According to Golden Age stalwart Lester del Rey, the 'consensus of taste' enforced at Milford inculcated a reverence for style over content, a grave trend in a field traditionally defined by its big ideas (del Rey 1980: 223).

By the early 1960s, the genre had begun to sort itself into two main camps: a rising cohort of authors and fans who embraced the heady freedoms afforded by the book market, looking forward to a day when the borders segregating SF from mainstream fiction would finally collapse; and a sizeable rump of old-school devotees, who cherished the legacy of the pulps and scorned the empty blandishments of what they derisively dubbed 'mundane' literature. This background is crucial to understanding the development of SF during the subsequent decade, since it shows not only that the conditions that made the New Wave possible – a diversification of markets and, hence, of styles of writing – were laid during the 1950s, but also that the combustible issues that would soon come to define the genre – in particular, the furious clash between SF traditionalists and avant-gardists – had already begun to smoulder. All that was needed was a spark that would set the whole field alight.

Exploring Strange *New Worlds*

That spark came in the spring of 1964, when a young author named Michael Moorcock took over the helm of *New Worlds* magazine, the premier British publication in the field. Founded in 1946, *New Worlds* modelled itself on Campbell's *Astounding*, and under original editor John Carnell, it published competent, scientifically literate adventure stories and think pieces. In 1950, Carnell launched a sister publication, *Science Fantasy*, whose more eclectic contents included, starting in 1961, a series of brooding sword-and-sorcery tales, penned by Moorcock, featuring the world-weary sorcerer Elric of Melniboné. When Carnell decided to step down, he offered Moorcock his choice of editorial assignments and was surprised when the young man chose the rather more conservative *New Worlds*. But Moorcock's decision was a canny one since all he really wanted was the title, with its suggestions of novelty and exotic reconnoitring. For some time, he had hoped to publish an entirely different sort of magazine, one that 'would attempt a cross-fertilization of popular sf, science and the work of the literary and artistic avant-garde' (Moorcock 1983: 11). His goal, on the one hand, was to unsettle the complacency of genre SF by compelling it to confront the technical advances of Modernism, including impressionistic and fragmented narrative styles, while on the other hand revitalising experimental writing – which he saw as too precious and involuted – by infusing it with the raw energy of science-fictional ideas.

At Moorcock's urging, Carnell had published, in the penultimate issue under his editorship, a pioneering story by J. G. Ballard, 'The Terminal Beach' (1963), which fit this new agenda precisely. A haunting montage of high-tech imagery chronicling the psychic dissolution of an atom-age anti-hero, the story divided British fandom, with some readers embracing its bold surrealism while others lambasted it as dull and obscurantist. Ballard had for some time been pushing the boundaries with enigmatic and lyrical tales such as 'The Voices of Time' (1960), and his 1962 novel *The Drowned World* had perversely celebrated planetary disaster rather than seeking solutions, as traditional SF treatments would have dictated. In 1962, Ballard published a guest editorial in *New Worlds* – 'Which Way to Inner Space?' – whose perspectives converged with Moorcock's: bemoaning the genre's lack of 'experimental enthusiasm', he called on SF authors to abandon the sterile wastelands of outer space in favour of a deep dive into the unconscious, returning with a range of 'private symbologies' rendered in 'oblique narrative style[s]' (Ballard 1996, 197–8). Ballard's favourite SF author, so he claimed, was William S. Burroughs, an American avant-gardist whose meandering 'cut-up' texts sketched out hallucinatory fantasies of alien eroticism. The first issue of *New Worlds* under Moorcock's direction featured Ballard's panegyrical profile of Burroughs, along with a militant editorial by Moorcock entitled 'A New Literature for the Space Age', which promised readers a cutting-edge SF that was 'unconventional in every sense' (Moorcock 1964: 3).

Hampered initially by budgetary constraints and a pocketbook format, Moorcock's *New Worlds* eventually hit its stride, especially after a 1967 grant from the Arts Council permitted a redesign into a large-scale glossy replete with striking page layouts and trippy photo collages **[6.1]**. In 1966, the magazine began running Ballard's series of 'condensed novels', clearly inspired by Burroughs, which sought to expose the libidinous fantasies lurking balefully beneath the post-war image culture of advertisement and celebrity; eventually gathered into the author's 1970 book *The Atrocity Exhibition*, these were probably the most wildly experimental works ever published in a science fiction magazine. But they were joined by many other path-breaking efforts, undertaken both by younger authors eager to test their artistic mettle

Figure 6.1 Cover by Mal Dean for *New Worlds* issue 191 edited by Langdon Jones, New Worlds Publishing, June 1969.

and by older hands inspired by the chance to move in fresh directions. Of the latter cohort, Brian W. Aldiss's tales of the 'Acid Head Wars' were undoubtedly the most arresting, chronicling – in a pixilated style inspired equally by late Joyce and LSD – the adventures of an ambiguous messiah in a fragmented Europe of the future.

Works such as these were clearly responding to Moorcock's call, in a 1965 editorial, for forms of SF that would be 'relevant to the world of Now' because they 'reflect[ed] the mood of the sixties' (Moorcock 1965: 25, 2). Pamela Zoline's 'The Heat Death of the Universe' (1967), for example, drew upon the budding feminist movement in its caustic satire of a suburban housewife who is persistently foiled and finally maddened by entropy, while John Sladek's 'Masterton and the Clerks' (1967) offered a scathing Kafkaesque take on the inanities of modern bureaucracy. Two novel-length serials featured in the magazine during 1967 and 1968 were likewise spawned out of contemporary contexts: Thomas M. Disch's darkly ironic *Camp Concentration* depicted a dystopian near future in which a metastasised Vietnam War has led to the brutal suppression of dissent; and Norman Spinrad's *Bug Jack Barron*, narrated in the hip lingo of the counterculture, arraigned the contemporary mass media using tools borrowed from Marshall McLuhan and Abbie Hoffman.

If Moorcock's goal in publishing such work was to spark debate, he succeeded beyond his wildest dreams. Indeed, Spinrad's novel, with its frank, slangy eroticism, led to a denunciation, in Parliament, of the Arts Ministry for funding such 'filth', and major British distributors refused to stock the magazine for fear of inviting obscenity charges, a storm colourfully recalled by Moorcock much later in a retrospective *New Worlds* anthology (1983). Controversy dogged and hobbled the magazine during the six years of Moorcock's editorship, and constant money woes led the burned-out editor to hand the reins to younger associates while he churned out reams of hackwork to pay the bills. Still, he had wanted a revolution and he got one: during the mid-to-late 1960s, *New Worlds* became, throughout the anglophone world, an inspiration for insurgents seeking to revitalise the genre, if not burn it down entirely. In the US, Judith Merril took up the cause, championing Ballard in particular as a uniquely brilliant visionary, and editing the appallingly titled *England Swings SF: Stories of Speculative Fiction* (1968), which culled its contents from *New Worlds*. Moorcock himself, starting in 1967, crafted a series of anthologies for the US market that repackaged work from the magazine, and the major serials by Aldiss, Delany, and Spinrad were released as books in short order. Their impact was galvanising.

Significantly, it was in reprint form – that is, *as books* – that this fiction had its full effect, especially since *New Worlds* lacked an American distributor. Indeed, under Moorcock, the magazine saw its subscription base dry up, as old-guard readers, repelled by the new contents, deserted the struggling enterprise in droves, while even its most avid fans grew frustrated with the capricious shifts in publication schedule. Most SF readers encountered the potent speculations of Ballard and the others in hardcover and paperback form, thus confirming the new centrality of the book market. That said, it is indisputable that Moorcock's bold encouragement of experiment helped spur book editors to expand their sense of what constituted acceptable SF. Spinrad has testified that *Bug Jack Barron* was rejected by US editors as 'unpublishable' before Moorcock took a chance on it (Spinrad 1968: 13); the novel's serialisation in *New Worlds* – and the controversy this provoked – made the manuscript suddenly marketable, with Walker and Avon releasing hardcover and paperback editions, respectively, in 1969. Other young American authors, such as Disch and Sladek, submitted their work first to Moorcock because they felt he would give them freer rein than stateside editors. This fruitful synergy – with *New Worlds* blithely pollinating the field via its disseminated reprints – lasted only a few years, but it served to show that an SF magazine with a forward-looking agenda could still fill an important niche in the new publishing ecology.

Dangerous Visions or Ribald Limericks?

The New Wave took a slightly different tack in the US, in large part because the SF 'establishment' retained control of all the major magazine venues. This could lead, as in the case of Campbell's *Analog* (renamed from *Astounding* in 1960), to a stultifying conformity, with second-rate writers such as Randall Garrett, Christopher Anvil, and Dean McLaughlin churning out competent but ephemeral works of hard SF month after dreary month. Yet even in such a dry climate, the occasional bloom could appear, as when Campbell serialised Frank Herbert's ecological parable 'Dune World' (1963) – which, reprinted in book form as *Dune* (1965) **[6.2]**, became one of the decade's enduring classics.

The most vital of the old-school magazines was undoubtedly *Galaxy*, where ailing Horace Gold had finally relinquished the keys to his editorial assistant, seasoned SF professional Frederik Pohl. Wisely, Pohl gave one of the field's most eccentrically gifted talents, Cordwainer Smith, full licence to indulge his baroque fantasies, and the result was a series of prodigiously strange stories: 'The Ballad of Lost C'Mell' (1962), 'Think Blue, Count Two' (1963), 'The Dead Lady of Clown Town' (1964). He also permitted two young authors, Robert Silverberg and Harlan Ellison, who during the late 1950s had seemed content to produce amiable hackwork, to push the boundaries in their fiction; Ellison in particular crafted several ferocious counterculture allegories for *Galaxy* – and its sister publication, *If* – during the mid-1960s, such as '"Repent, Harlequin!" Said the Ticktockman' (1965), a tart harlequinade about social regimentation, and 'I Have No Mouth, and I Must Scream' (1967), a corrosive vision of a computer-generated hell. Yet for all Pohl's editorial

Figure 6.2 Cover by John Schoenherr depicting the giant sandworm from Frank Herbert's *The Prophet of Dune*, for *Analog* magazine, March 1965.

openness, he remained wedded to some of the old pulp constraints, blue-pencilling salacious language and anti-religious sentiment in ways that infuriated the always combustible Ellison.

A genre gadfly as well as a shrewd self-promoter, Ellison began to beat the drums for change in a series of barn-burning speeches at SF conventions, such as his Guest of Honour talk at the 1966 Westercon in San Diego, later published as 'A Time for Daring'. Boldly calling out the genre establishment to its face, Ellison opined that the best contemporary SF writers – Vonnegut, Burroughs, Anthony Burgess – had the good sense to avoid the field entirely 'for the very simple reason that they're too big and talented to be constrained by our often vicious, often ungrateful little back water eddy'. If genre authors wanted to keep pace, to publish 'something new and fresh and different and inventive', then they were going to have to resist and disrupt the status quo that had for so long muzzled them (Ellison 1967a: 33). Having butted heads with mulish editors for many years, Ellison realised that, if he truly wanted to shake things up, he would have to become an editor himself, and so he pitched, to Doubleday and Company, an all-original anthology, *Dangerous Visions*, that would be geared to smash every taboo inherited from the pulps. As he put it in the introduction to the volume, 'no one has ever told the speculative writer, "Pull out all the stops. No holds barred, get it said!" Until this book came along' (Ellison 1967b: xxiv).

The concept of an anthology publishing all-new fiction was not unique to Ellison: Pohl had edited a series for Ballantine in the 1950s, entitled *Star*, which drew considerable attention and acclaim. But by the mid-to-late-1960s, the conditions were ripe for a serious challenge to the priority of the magazines, and a number of major anthologies emerged that offered viable platforms free of prevailing shibboleths. Several of these – for example, Damon Knight's *Orbit* (1966–80) **[6.3]**, Silverberg's *New Dimensions* (1971–81), and Terry Carr's *Universe* (1971–87) – became durable series that provided stout competition to the remaining magazines, which were compelled to liberalise their

Figure 6.3 Cover for Damon Knight's *Orbit* anthology, vol. 2, 1967.

editorial policies to keep pace. But Ellison's *Dangerous Visions* had a massive impact, largely due to the editor's singular personality, which permeated the volume in the form of hectoring headnotes that talked up the brilliance of the thirty-three authors and the originality of their contributions.

Some of the stories were strident, wearing their rebelliousness rather too starkly on their sleeves, especially the handful of tales that evangelised for atheism; the most daring treatment of religious themes was undoubtedly Philip K. Dick's 'Faith of Our Fathers', with its drug-induced vision of an identity-devouring cannibal god. A few of the sex stories – especially Sturgeon's chatty brief for an incestuous utopia, 'If All Men Were Brothers, Would You Let One Marry Your Sister?' – were likewise purely provocative, although a couple were genuinely trailblazing: Farmer's 'Riders of the Purple Wage' offered a bawdy, pun-filled romp through a near future dominated by artsy libertines, while Samuel R. Delany's 'Aye, and Gomorrah . . .' brilliantly managed the difficult feat of inventing a wholly new form of sexual fetishism. Both of these stories, along with the anthology itself, received major awards from SF authors and fans, proving that there was an appetite in the field for such cutting-edge fare.

The book had its detractors, of course, and not only among the usual suspects. Indeed, the critical reception of *Dangerous Visions* pointed to an emerging split between the British and American New Waves, with the former seen as more committed to formal experiment while the latter favoured scandalous kinds of content. Merril, who had warmly embraced Moorcock's *New Worlds*, felt that Ellison's tome tended to 'substitute shock for insight' (Merril 1967: 33), while Aldiss went further, arguing that, although the stories might 'appear quite shocking. . .[,] it was rather like shocking your maiden aunt with ribald limericks' (Aldiss 1988: 298). This jibe was unfair, and the stark division it drew between transatlantic cousins tended to obscure their commonalities: Moorcock's *New Worlds* kept stumbling into controversy not because it ran startling photo collages but because its fiction was brazen and raunchy. That said, it is true that the American New Wave was less stylistically extreme, considered in the mass; there is nothing like *The Atrocity Exhibition* in the US canon, for example. But a revolution can proceed on two fronts, and attempts to introduce sexually frank and politically forthright content was as strategically important as efforts to disrupt linear narrative and settled point-of-view. And of course the beleaguered champions of the pulp tradition loathed both of these tactics, intensely.

Patterns of Reaction

As we have seen, resistance to the New Wave agenda can be traced back to 1950s critiques of the 'Milford Mafia' as a clique of pretentious literateurs whose tenets purportedly imperilled the core values of old-school SF. This resistance amounted to little more than catty backbiting in fanzines and at SF conventions, however; it was hardly an organised opposition. But as the advocates for change grew more numerous and voluble – issuing incendiary manifestoes attacking the status quo, hailing the likes of William S. Burroughs as an SF genius, filling the once-conservative *New Worlds* with borderline seditious material – the old guard reached for their cudgels in a more concerted fashion. Every fresh provocation from Moorcock or Merril or Ellison summoned an outraged response, and unsympathetic commentators with prominent platforms made their contempt for the new SF abundantly clear.

One of the most well-placed ripostes was published in the December 1966 issue of *Galaxy* magazine. Reviewing Disch's 1965 novel *The Genocides* [6.4], which Merril had praised to the skies in her own review column in *The Magazine of Fantasy and Science Fiction*, SF author Algis Budrys excoriated the book as both puerile and dangerous. In the first place, its vision of a future Earth colonised and subjugated by remorseless aliens was 'unflaggingly derivative' of Ballard's bleak disaster stories. More troublingly, its fatalistic reduction of the human race to a cringing clutch of 'dumb, resigned victims' was an affront to the resilient spirit of the Golden Age, 'the school of science fiction which takes hope in science and in Man' (Budrys 1985: 92). As David Hartwell has observed, Budrys's passing mention of the melancholy tone of H. G. Wells's scientific romances suggested that the 'dark and pessimistic mode of Ballard and the New Wave' might actually be 'closer to the classical sources of SF than the optimistic, problem-solving literature of John W. Campbell' (Hartwell 1996: 208). But historical consistency was not Budrys's

Figure 6.4 Cover for Thomas M. Disch's *The Genocides*.

goal; rather, he was seeking to squelch the spread of Ballard's influence, especially among younger writers and fans, by polemically roasting a budding author's first novel in the pages of one of the genre's premier publications. Disch was still smarting decades later: 'Algis Budrys talked of me as a "nihilist." That's the word people use when they want to say, "this is our enemy. He believes nothing." Meaning, he believes nothing that we believe in (and we believe a lot of crap)' (quoted in Horwich 2001).

Disch's comments show how skirmishes over the New Wave could soon devolve into a seeming war of creeds. Always a small and contentious community, SF had been riven by internecine struggles before, going back to 'The Great Exclusion Act of 1939', wherein several left-leaning fans were expelled from the first World SF Convention. Pohl recounted his version of these events in *The Way the Future Was: A Memoir* (1978). Still, it seemed to many long-time observers that the current battles were more spiky and intense, amounting almost to a civil war between defenders of the true pulp faith and a pack of invaders with alien values. No major fanzine or SF convention could avoid the swelling controversy, and many prominent commentators seemed to relish stirring the pot. A few examples must suffice. In a 1967 fanzine letter, *New Worlds'* associate editor Charles Platt ranted against old-guard readers as a pack of 'dumb' reactionaries, of 'poor mind' and 'feeble and pitiful imagination' – 'illiterate masses, yearning for simple entertainment, scared of anything that remotely tries to stretch the[ir] mental abilities' (Platt 1967: 45–6). In response to such attacks, del Rey used his Guest of Honour address at the 1967 Worldcon to lambast New Wave SF as 'completely lacking in even the slightest trace of originality, while it claims to be something new and revolutionary. It has borrowed almost every cheap trick from the mainstream as taught today': stream-of-consciousness style, neurotic characters, 'plotless stories', and a general obsession with 'failure and ugliness' (del Rey 1968: 82). These examples could be multiplied, ad infinitum if not ad nauseam.

Along with prominent fans Sam Moskowitz and J. J. Pierce, del Rey was responsible for opening one of the bloodiest fronts in the New Wave campaigns: the establishment, in 1968, of the 'Second Foundation', named for the secret society in Isaac Asimov's classic series whose mission was to preserve the fruits of civilisation during a galaxy-wide dark age. By analogy, the real-world Second Foundation would come to the defence of 'genuine' SF – scientifically sound, clearly written, with a staunch focus on heroic action – against New Wave intrusions of 'anti-rationalism, nihilism and despair' (Pierce 1968: 33). According to Moskowitz, the group planned to mount 'overt and covert attacks on the New Wave ..., with the objective of its destruction as a viable force' (Moskowitz 1968: 1) – declaring, in Pierce's words, a 'Holy War' against the SF infidels (Pierce 1968: 40). Their official fanzine, *Renaissance*, which debuted in 1969, offered intellectual ammunition in the form of pithy debunkings of key New Wave claims. While some New Wavers responded to these incitements by bemoaning the (in Spinrad's words) 'insane factional bickering, vendettas, and personal ill feelings' that seemed to be consuming the field (Spinrad 1968: 17), others girded for battle, including – unsurprisingly – the ever-pugnacious Ellison, who taunted the Second Foundation as a pack of 'old farts' whose views were 'arteriosclerotic'. 'You want a Holy War?' he jeered. 'Then get it on, baby, get it on!' (Ellison 1968: 48, 44).

SF's Generation Gap

As Ellison's rhetoric suggests, the textures and tones of the controversy had, by the late 1960s, taken on all the resonances of the larger social struggle between the so-called Establishment and the youth counter-culture. Indeed, it is fair to say that a significant – seemingly unbridge-able – generation gap had opened within the field: despite the presence of ageing fellow-travellers such as Merril and Ballard, New Wave authors were generally younger, the first SF cohort to mature outside the sanctum of the pulps, in a climate of greater sexual freedom and with an abiding mistrust of technocratic agendas. Some, such as Disch and Delany, were openly gay; others, like Ursula K. Le Guin and Joanna Russ, were committed feminists; yet others had fought in Vietnam and returned with a worldly, bruised militancy – Joe Haldeman's 1974 novel *The Forever War* being this group's keenest literary testament. New Wave authors were much less likely than their pulp forebears to believe that modern technoscience was a panacea for social ills; to the contrary, Disch edited a 1971 anthology, *The Ruins of Earth*, that traced science's unwitting collusion in ecological catastrophe, while Barry N. Malzberg penned a series of novels, culminating in *Beyond Apollo* (1972), that arraigned the American space programme as a public relations exercise in masculinist egomania. In an almost surreal historical irony, *Beyond Apollo* was chosen to receive a new literary award named after recently deceased Golden Age titan John W. Campbell, a decision that sent the pulp-era partisans into fresh spasms of outrage.

Some of the furore over the New Wave can thus be put down to mutual incomprehension, a simple inability on the part of both factions to under-stand their opponents' world-view. A more poignant predicament was faced by SF authors who tried to bypass the conflict entirely. Combatants on both sides sought to conscript Le Guin, for example, largely due to the brilliance of her 1969 novel *The Left Hand of Darkness*, with its compelling vision of a gender-free utopia: while the old-guard fans appreciated her rigorous world-building and careful evocation of an alien species, the New

Wave crew embraced her multi-layered narrative scheme and critique of sexual binarism. Yet Le Guin persistently rebuffed attempts to enrol her, instead lamenting the sectarianism that had infected the field, and rejecting all literary labels as essentially meaningless in a letter to the *Science Fiction Review* (Le Guin 1970: 49). Some commentators wondered why the SF community couldn't just celebrate its ideological diversity, finding value both in 'hard' extrapolation and 'soft' speculation, but their voices were lost in the general racket. In this overheated atmosphere, with both sides citing the spectre of 'Chicago' – that is, the ruthless suppression of youthful protestors at the 1968 Democratic convention – as proof of the authoritarian tendencies of their opponents, a sudden access of universal amity was highly unlikely.

Yet Le Guin had a point with her resistance to labelling. One of the problems involved in writing about 1960s SF is the sheer centripetal power of the New Wave debates: they seem omnipresent and all-consuming, drawing attention inexorably towards the swirling commotion. But focusing on the works and statements of the ultimately small handful of identifiable combatants can obscure the true variety that was beginning to emerge and that would characterise the genre going forward. Prior to the full flowering of the book market, as Damon Knight once remarked, it was possible for dedicated readers to consume virtually everything published in the field; some time towards the middle of the 1960s this became impossible – there was too much new material sprouting up, in too many locations. Moreover, the burgeoning of the book market prompted waves of translation of 'foreign' SF that unsettled the presumed centrality of the anglophone canon: these were the years that made Stanisław Lem, Herbert W. Franke, Pierre Boulle, Kobo Abe, and the Strugatsky brothers, among others, recognisable names to readers in the US and the UK. And yet, at the very moment when SF was diversifying as never before, the genre's most vocal citizens seemed intent on cramming the entire field into a bipolar straitjacket.

Important developments during this period can disappear from the scholarly map if the only coordinates available are pulp versus New Wave. For example, between the mid-1960s and mid-1970s, there was a remarkable resurgence of hard SF, yet the work of Larry Niven, Gregory Benford, and John Varley – to name three major practitioners – rarely resembled that of their Golden Age predecessors; instead, it was dark, psychologically probing, and stylistically complex. To take another example, it might seem as if feminist SF – which emerged most powerfully, during the early-to-mid-1970s, in the fiction of Joanna Russ and Alice B. Sheldon (writing as James Tiptree, Jr) – can be plausibly roped into the New Wave camp due to its angry social consciousness. Such a conflation is highly misleading, however, since many feminist authors (for example, Vonda McIntyre, Pamela Sargent, Suzy McKee Charnas) were far from experimental in their narrative modes; indeed, they could be as dogged and didactic as Isaac Asimov. And then, because the vast, catholic book market made room for them, there were the writers who were simply *sui generis*, spinning out their feverish visions with an autistic intensity: R. A. Lafferty, for instance, is sometimes labelled a New Waver because his fiction is weird and delirious, but a careful reading of his work makes clear that the only faction he belonged to was extraterrestrial in origin. Alas, unique talents like Lafferty – along with D. G. Compton, David R. Bunch, Edgar Pangborn – are little read today, largely because they had the misfortune of living in interesting times.

The Wave Recedes

Ellison's gargantuan follow-up to *Dangerous Visions* – *Again, Dangerous Visions*, featuring forty-six original stories, along with the editor's trademark rambling headnotes – was released in 1972. Although the book contained its share of brilliant fiction (such as Russ's 'When It Changed', a fierce brief for lesbian separatism, or Kate Wilhelm's 'The Funeral', a mordant portrait of inter-generational strife), there was a distinct sense of belatedness about the proceedings, as if a garrulous guest had barged into a party already winding down. The genre, beset by half a decade of fratricidal angst, was simply exhausted. 1970 was perhaps the high-water mark of the New Wave whirlpool: the combatants were still fulminating, but now with an occasional tongue-in-cheek flippancy, as if embarrassed by the fracas. Moorcock, in an autumn issue of the British fanzine *Speculation*, facetiously floated the notion that the years-long skirmish had been little more than a conspiracy to gin up readership. By 1971, the Second Foundation had closed shop, suspending its Holy War and declaring the New Wave safely dead (Pierce 1971: 1–2).

This was wishful thinking, of course. While *New Worlds* had finally folded, worn down by its endless battles with jittery distributors and fickle readers, the project was immediately reborn as an anthology series that continued, under various editorial hands, until 1976. Far from falling silent, New Wave heroes such as Ballard and Delany moved on to greater enormities, with the former's *Crash* (1973) **[6.5]** and the latter's *Dhalgren* (1975) breaking startling new ground in the treatment of decadent eroticism; by the mid-1970s, both authors – along with Le Guin and Moorcock – were being celebrated as major literary novelists by mainstream critics. It seemed as if the New Wave had, at least for this cohort, begun to achieve Merril's vision of a cosmopolitan speculative fiction that transcended the genre.

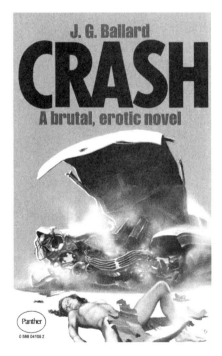

Figure 6.5 Artwork by Chris Foss for J. G. Ballard's *Crash*.

But this too was wishful thinking. Even before the advent of *Star Wars* (1977) flooded the field with waves of pulp nostalgia, not to mention rampant media-driven commodification, cultural and economic forces were conspiring to rebuild the ghetto walls as a trusty stronghold of marketable properties. By the mid-70s, a critical mass of crossover hits had convinced publishers that their two-decade investment in SF was poised for a pecuniary bonanza. Whereas, in the early 1960s, an SF author might receive a $2000 advance for a novel manuscript (with, in all likelihood, no subsequent royalties), several writers, starting in 1974, were landing six-figure sums based on little more than an outline – and a track record of proven success. In 1976, Frank Herbert's *Children of Dune*, third in the popular series, became the first SF novel to crack the *New York Times* hardcover bestseller list, and this opened the floodgates: by the early 1980s, trilogies or even open-ended series – Herbert's 'Dune' sequels, Asimov's later 'Foundation' and 'Robot' books, Anne McCaffrey's 'Pern' novels – became the norm as major names, seeking reliable income, established themselves on the charts as stable brands. While some New Wave authors – Haldeman, Delany, Le Guin – were lucky enough to catch this tide, if only intermittently, the major beneficiaries, as the list in the preceding sentence suggests, were pulp holdovers suddenly enjoying a singularly profitable second childhood.

This fiscal mainstreaming of the genre placed the New Wave in a strange predicament. On the one hand, an upmarket breakthrough could prove the concept of a cutting-edge SF 'unconventional in every sense' and 'relevant to the world of Now' (to quote Moorcock's early *New Worlds* editorials); on the other hand, avant-gardes by definition are minority tastes, and such a windfall could instead be seen as the movement 'selling out'. Looking back on the era, a cynical Disch viewed the issue in precisely these terms: Ballard's early brief for an experimental 'inner space' had become, one decade later, 'shorthand for sex, drugs, and rock and roll, that troika of '60s hedonism for the masses' (Disch 1998: 108). But this whole formulation ignores the sad fact that, in the publishing industry at least, a rising tide does not always lift all boats: indeed, the vast majority of New Wave authors were left behind with the backwash, and many of them resented it. Robert Silverberg, who had spent the late 1960s and early 1970s crafting gem after gem of brooding speculation (such as the 1972 *Dying Inside*, perhaps the finest treatment ever of the theme of telepathy), found that readers did not seem to appreciate his zealous efforts. '[They] don't want literary quality,' he complained, 'they want space adventure' (quoted in Thompson 1975: 7), and so he retired in protest – although his principled stance was somewhat undermined when he subsequently accepted a record advance from Harper & Row to write the dreamy pastel fantasy, *Lord Valentine's Castle* (1980).

Few others were so fortunate. Indeed, by the late 1970s, many prominent New Wave talents had abandoned the field entirely, some moving on to different genres – Disch essaying horror novels, Wilhelm penning courtroom thrillers, Delany and Russ taking up literary criticism – while others vanished into the weeds of the speciality presses, which reached at best a coterie market. Some, like Malzberg, simply fell silent, perhaps frazzled by the gauntlet of opprobrium the old guard reserved for particularly rebarbative individuals. Malzberg's valedictory, *The Engines of the Night* (1982), offered a gloomy assessment of the state of the field on the cusp of the 1980s, blaming his hasty departure on an 'effective counterrevolution which got some of us out of the temple right quick' (Malzberg 1982: xi). In the words of Damien Broderick, the mid-1970s ushered in a fitful 'interval of integration and bruised armistice' (Broderick 2003: 58), during which both factions counted their blessings – and licked their wounds.

Unquestionably, a significant amount of 'integration' occurred, at this time and after; indeed, though its revolution was short-lived and never wholly triumphant, the New Wave transformed the field in major ways. It did not drive doughty space opera into oblivion, but it carved out room for jazzy inner-spatial fabulations – dark expeditions into psychic extremity that have taken on more hard-edged textures in the wake of cyberpunk, with its wetware implants and virtual realities replacing the mass-media phantasms and 'spinal landscapes' of Spinrad and Ballard. After the decade's clamorous orgy of taboo-shattering, the genre has never reverted to its pre-1960s reticence about sexual matters; even pulp-inclined contemporaries, such as C. J. Cherryh and Lois McMaster Bujold, routinely feature gay and lesbian characters in their work, and hard SF writers such as Greg Bear have speculated freely on the implications of elective sex surgery and biotech porn. While outré experiments such as *The Atrocity Exhibition* have found few followers, SF writers now commonly attend to structural and stylistic matters in ways that are considerably more sophisticated, in the mass, than at any other time in the genre's history. It is probably fair to say that the New Wave 'reformed' rather than 'revolutionised' science fiction, but such is, as I have remarked elsewhere, the perennial fate of SF avant-gardes – to be defused and assimilated into a field they temporarily disrupt but, in the long run, help to refit and sustain.

References

Aldiss, Brian, with David Wingrove (1988), *Trillion Year Spree: The History of Science Fiction*. New York: Avon.

Ashley, Mike (2005), *Transformations: The Story of the Science-Fiction Magazines from 1950 to 1970*. Liverpool: Liverpool University Press.

Ballard, J. G. (1996), 'Which Way to Inner Space?' [1962], in *A User's Guide to the Millennium*. New York: Picador, pp. 196–8.

Brier, Evan (2010), *A Novel Marketplace: Mass Culture, the Book Trade, and Postwar American Fiction*. Philadelphia: University of Pennsylvania Press.

Broderick, Damien (2003), 'New Wave and Backwash: 1960–1980', in *The Cambridge Companion to Science Fiction*, ed. Edward James and Farah Mendlesohn. Cambridge: Cambridge University Press, pp. 48–63.

Budrys, Algis (1985), *Benchmarks: Galaxy Bookshelf*. Carbondale, IL: Southern Illinois University Press.

Cogswell, Theodore R., ed. (1992), *PITFCS: Proceedings of the Institute for Twenty-First Century Studies*. Chicago: Advent.

del Rey, Lester (1968), 'Art or Artiness?,' *Famous Science Fiction: Tales of Wonder* 8, pp. 78–86.

_____ (1980), *The World of Science Fiction, 1926–1976: The History of a Subculture*. New York: Garland.

Disch, Thomas M. (1998), *The Dreams Our Stuff Is Made Of: How Science Fiction Conquered the World*. New York: Touchstone.

Ellison, Harlan (1967a), 'A Time for Daring', *Algol* 12, pp. 27–34.

_____. (1967b), 'Introduction: Thirty-Two Soothsayers', in *Dangerous Visions*, ed. Harlan Ellison. New York: Doubleday, pp. xix–xxix.

_____.(1968), 'Letter to the Editor', *Science Fiction Review* 28, pp. 43–4.

_____.(1969), 'Letter to the Editor', *Science Fiction Review* 30, pp. 48–50.

_____ (1983), Preface to 'I Have No Mouth, and I Must Scream', in *I Have No Mouth, and I Must Scream*. New York: Ace, pp. 1–3.

Hartwell, David G. (1996), *Age of Wonders: Exploring the World of Science Fiction*. New York: Tor.

Horwich, David (2001), 'Interview: Thomas M. Disch', *Strange Horizons*, http://strangehorizons.com/non-fiction/articles/interview-thomas-m-disch/ [accessed 26 January 2017].

Latham, Rob (2006), '*New Worlds* and the New Wave in Fandom: Fan Culture and the Reshaping of Science Fiction in the Sixties', *Extrapolation* 47, pp. 296–315.

_____ (2009), 'Fiction, 1950–1963', in *The Routledge Companion to Science Fiction*, ed. Mark Bould, Andrew M. Butler, Adam Roberts, and Sherryl Vint. New York: Routledge, pp. 80–9.

_____ (2010), '"A Rare State of Ferment": SF Controversies from the New Wave to Cyberpunk', in *Beyond Cyberpunk: New Critical Perspectives*, ed. Graham J. Murphy and Sherryl Vint. New York: Routledge, pp. 29–45.

_____ (2013), 'Inside the New Wave Wars: John J. Pierce and the Second Foundation', *The Eaton Journal of Archival Research in Science Fiction* 1: 1, <http://eatonjournal.ucr.edu/articles1/lathamfinal.pdf> [accessed 27 January 2017].

Le Guin, Ursula K. (1970), 'Letter to the Editor', *Science Fiction Review* 35, pp. 48–9.

Luckhurst, Roger (2005), *Science Fiction*. Malden, MA: Polity.

Malzberg, Barry N. (1982), *The Engines of the Night: Science Fiction in the Eighties*. New York: Doubleday.

Merril, Judith (1967), 'Books', *The Magazine of Fantasy and Science Fiction* 33: 6, pp. 28–34.

Moorcock, Michael (1964), 'A New Literature for the Space Age', *New Worlds* 142, pp. 2–3.

_____ (1965), 'Symbols for the Sixties', *New Worlds* 148, pp. 2–3, 25.

_____ (1983), 'Introduction', in *New Worlds: An Anthology*, ed. Michael Moorcock. London: Flamingo, pp. 9–26.

Moskowitz, Sam (1968), 'The Second Foundation', *Different* 3: 3, p. 1.

Pierce, J. J. (1968), 'Science Fiction and the Romantic Tradition', *Different* 3: 3, pp. 2–40.

_____ (1971), 'The End of the Beginning', *Renaissance* 3: 4, pp. 1–2.

Platt, Charles (1967), 'Letter to the Editor', *Habakkuk* 2: 3, pp. 45–6.

Pohl, Frederik (1978), *The Way the Future Was: A Memoir*. New York: Ballantine Del Rey.

Spinrad, Norman (1968), 'Letter to the Editor', *The SFWA Forum* 7, pp. 16–18.

_____ (1969), 'The *Bug Jack Barron* Papers', *Algol* 15, pp. 9–14.

Thompson, Donald C. (1975), 'Spec Fic and the Perry Rhodan Ghetto', *Science Fiction Review* 15, pp. 6–10.

What to Read Next

Brian W. Aldiss, *Barefoot in the Head: A European Fantasia* (New York: Open Road Media, 2009).

J. G. Ballard, *The Atrocity Exhibition* (London: Flamingo, 2002).

Samuel R. Delany, *Dhalgren* (Middletown, CT: Wesleyan University Press, 2001).

Thomas M. Disch, *Camp Concentration* (New York: Vintage, 1999).

Ursula K. Le Guin, *The Left Hand of Darkness* (New York: Ace, 1987).

Michael Moorcock, ed., *New Worlds: An Anthology* (London: Flamingo, 1983).

Joanna Russ, *The Female Man* (Boston: Beacon, 2000).

Robert Silverberg, *Dying Inside* (New York: Orb, 2009).

Chapter 7

From the New Wave into the Twenty-First Century

Sherryl Vint

Between the end of the New Wave and the beginning of the twenty-first century, SF transformed into a more diverse genre community that was no longer synonymous with the fandom that emerged during its Golden Age, but nonetheless retained a connection to it. The New Wave disrupted habituated ideas about what SF could or should be, and even if fervour about its revolution was fading by the 1970s, the field left in its wake was different. The stylistic innovations it promoted shaped writers who followed and continued to experiment with prose forms: Joanna Russ, James Tiptree Jr (Alice Sheldon), William Gibson, and Gene Wolfe were each celebrated for their distinct styles, producing SF attentive to the literary as much as to the scientific. The intensified focus on social and political issues that characterised the New Wave similarly continued into the 1970s and beyond, informed by contemporary activism such as the environmental movement and feminist struggle, just as an earlier generation of writers responded to countercultural impulses in the anti-war and Civil Rights movements. Feminists and people of colour began to see in SF a tool for articulating alternative visions of the world freed from systemic discrimination, and this diverse group of writers and their audiences inevitably changed the field.

The 1980s were a time of technological change, especially related to personal computing and media entertainment. Although games were played on computers as early as the 1950s, the emergence of the gaming industry dates to the 1970s, with early games migrating from arcade machines to home PCs in the 1980s; the first video game console was released in 1972 and a second generation, using microprocessors, in 1976. The CD was invented in 1981, the Walkman in 1981, the World Wide Web in 1989, the first browser in 1991, and the DVD in 1995; smartphones, social media, and YouTube all lay in the future, although PayPal opened the door to this coming digital world in 1998. The first ARPANET (precursor to the Internet) email was sent in 1971, but it was not until the 1990s that email was widely adopted. The first registered dotcom company, Symbolics, took the first domain name in 1985, quickly followed by IBM, AT&T and Hewlett Packard; Apple joined in 1987, and its 1984 launch of the Macintosh (the 'Mac'), the first personal computer with a graphical user interface, famously drew on George Orwell's *Nineteen Eighty-Four* (1949) in a high-profile commercial, directed by Ridley Scott, which promised Apple would give us freedom rather than conformity. The computer was named *Time* magazine's Person of the Year in 1991, and the anticipated Y2K crisis (fears of massive computer failure if internal computer clocks failed to recognise 01.01.00) fuelled millennial anxiety about the potential crash of the IT infrastructure upon which we had already come to rely. Through the 1970s and into the 1990s, quotidian life was shaped more and more by the kinds of technologies once envisioned only in the pages of SF.

The 1980s were a time of the big – big hair, shoulder pads, conspicuous consumption and Wall Street excess, big speakers on boom boxes, blockbuster films. Science fiction of this period also tended towards the big: the ascendency of the novel over short fiction as the dominant form, and long novels at that; a tendency towards trilogies or longer series in established worlds, which included the last hurrah for Golden Age authors who published final volumes, such as Isaac Asimov's Foundation (1942–86) and Robot (1939–84) series, and Arthur C. Clarke's Odyssey (1968–97) and Rama (1973–93) series. Yet this kind of SF was waning, and a new community of writers and fans – many who mainly came to SF through film and television – increased the

presence of women and people of colour in the genre, shifts that ultimately paved the way for a new kind of SF in the twenty-first century. Writers respected by the mainstream, such as Doris Lessing and
Margaret Atwood, published overtly SF books during this period,
while other contemporary writers who got their start within SF, such
as William Gibson and Jonathan Lethem, were later embraced by the
literary establishment.

The 1990s was the era of the alternative, albeit one that was rapidly
becoming mainstream, and this ethos informed SF of that decade as
well. The genre became more multicultural and increasingly experi-
mented not only with alternative political stances but also with new
forms and topics, influenced by the Japanese manga and anime that
were now reaching America markets. An even more diverse Japanese
SF flourished, much of it responding to the trauma of the bombing
of Hiroshima and Nagasaki, but little of this was translated into English. The genre did become increasingly global, spread by digital technologies, and the globalisation of markets during the period strongly
informed, and increased the influence of, anglophone SF.

The ascendency of postmodern literary modes generated greater
space for SF motifs not only within anglophone literature but also in
Russia, where Victor Pelevin published self-reflexive satires of technology and modernity – such as *Homo Zapiens* (1999) – that blurred
the line between SF and mainstream literature, work embraced by
Russian and anglophone audiences alike. Acclaimed Japanese novelist Haruki Murakami began his career during this period, drawing
as much on Western authors (such as Franz Kafka) and Russian ones
(such as Fyodor Dostoyevsky) as he did upon a prior Japanese tradition. Like Pelevin, Murakami writes what we might now think of as
the literature of globalisation, each of them exploring how their own
culture responded to the disruptions of modernity and the post-World
War II global order. Murakami's work attempts to come to terms with
a disenfranchising modernity; his SF-inflected *Hard-Boiled Wonderland
and the End of the World* (1985) beautifully captures a contemporary
feeling of reality collapsing into its representation. The most prominent
contemporary Russian SF writers, Boris and Arkady Strugatsky, had
been embraced by an anglophone readership, paving the way towards

a genuine grasp of international SF. France was influenced by New Wave writers, but it was largely publishing translations – Thomas M. Disch, Norman Spinrad, Philip K. Dick – at this time, although Pierre Boulle's *La planète des singes* (1963; translated as *Planet of the Apes* in 1964) and Robert Merle's *Un animal doué de raison* (1967; translated as *Day of the Dolphin* in 1969) both achieved significant anglophone audiences through film adaptations. Other European countries such as Spain, Italy, and Germany published translations of Golden Age American SF, and some native imitations. A truly international SF, however, was yet to emerge. Although the terrorist attacks of 2001 massively shifted Western cultures towards renewed nationalism and conservative, militarised stances, the alternative visions nurtured in 1990s SF persist as well.

Legacies of the New Wave

The New Wave opened to door for SF to rediscover its roots in the utopian tradition. Environmental SF emerged almost simultaneously with the movement itself. Earth Day was officially pronounced in 1970 **[7.1]**, linked to countercultural movements on campuses that had ties to SF – Frank Herbert's *Dune* (1965) and Robert Heinlein's *Stranger in a Strange Land* (1961) found large audiences – and to the iconic image of the planet from space. Rachel Carson's fundamental *The Silent Spring* (1962) drew on SF techniques in its speculations about possible futures, and SF scholar Eric Otto argues that it might be understood as the origin of environmental SF. The first UN conference on human environments was held in 1972, the same year that Greenpeace activists adopted this name; the Endangered Species Act in the US followed in 1973; the UK Wildlife and Countryside Act came later in 1981. As early as 1973 the anthology *The Ruins of Earth*, edited by Thomas M. Disch, collected stories organised into sections entitled 'The Way It Is', 'Why It Is the Way It Is', 'How It Could Get Worse', and 'Unfortunate Solutions', which sought to catalyse protest against the rapid disappearance of the natural world and the alienation of humans in societies of overcrowded automation.

Ernest Callenbach's *Ecotopia* (1975) was written out of environmental activism and quickly found an enthusiastic audience. As much a

Figure 7.1 'Earth Help' banner for Earth Day, April 1970.

handbook as a work of speculation, it took pains to think through the transition from contemporary modes of production to its ecologically sustainable vision of how Americans might live. Anticipating arguments made only decades later by economic scholars, Callenbach's protagonist argues that:

> our system is considerably cheaper than yours, if we add in *all* the costs. Many of your costs are ignored or passed on through subterfuge to posterity or the general public. We on the other hand must acknowledge all costs. Otherwise we could not hope to achieve the stable-state life systems which are our fundamental ecological and political goal (Callenbach 1975: 23).

Recent critical discussions of notions such as 'natural' or 'green' capitalism use a similar logic, although they suggest proper accounting will enable capitalism to become the defender of nature, while Callenbach sees profit-driven development as its chief destroyer. The need to balance economic growth with environmental limits preoccupied contemporary culture, following the Club of Rome's *Limits to Growth* report in 1972. Frank Herbert's wildly successful Dune series (1965–85; relaunched by Herbert's son in 1999 and continuing to this day) is largely a tale of imperial struggle, but the first novel especially relied on the mythology of limited resources on a desert world to shape its societies. It is now widely remembered as a novel of environmentalism. In the UK, John Brunner's *The Sheep Look Up* (1972), depicting a dystopian future of environmental collapse, savagely satirised the predatory emerging order of globalisation at the root of this damage, concluding 'We can just about restore the balance of the ecology, the atmosphere, and so on – in other words, we can live within our means instead of on unrepayable overdraft as we've been doing for the past half century – if we exterminate the two hundred million most extravagant and wasteful of our species' (Brunner 2003: 363)

Without question, the writer who stands out on themes of environmentalism and social justice is Kim Stanley Robinson, especially his indispensable *Mars* trilogy, which established his place as one of the most important writers of his generation. The story of the colonisation and later independence of Mars told over many decades, Robinson's potent work shows how deeply political, social, and environmental questions are entwined, while retaining a commitment to 'hard SF' – that is, scientifically informed and plausible speculation – in his careful thinking about the technologies that could enable the terraforming of Mars and sustain a community there physically and economically. Although the hard SF tradition often sees itself as 'purely' interested in science (that is, separate from politics), Robinson's work here and elsewhere combines both meticulously researched and accurate scientific details and a sense of how science is shaped by the values of its surrounding culture. Robinson sees in science a hope for transforming the patterns of living that have caused the environmental crisis, and so his commitment to accuracy springs from his desire to see such ameliorative techniques put into practice.

Red Mars (1993) focuses on how an early scientific research station staffed by the 'First 100' settlers grows into a diverse community. This is not simply a matter of executing a predetermined plan: Robinson gives voices to a variety of ideologies and agendas, using differences among his characters to show the many possible futures for the planet, including arguments for respecting its existing, if sparse, ecology. Mirroring the diversity of opinion within the environmental movement, Robinson's Martians make both a new physical and a new social world. As one of his characters argues in the first book, it is ridiculous to be 'twenty-first-century scientists on Mars ... living within nineteenth-century social systems, based on seventeenth-century ideologies. ... we must terraform not only Mars, but ourselves' (Robinson 1993: 89). *Green Mars* (1994) **[7.2]** picks up the story after the Martian revolution and focuses on the first Martian-born generation. Even as this generation transforms Mars by terraforming, it seeks socially to transform an Earth suffering economic, social, and environmental collapse, offering to manage the 'bioinfrastructure' of nations in return for labour. The detailed information about environmental engineering on Mars thus clearly stands in for possible ways to alleviate damage on Earth. Finally, *Blue Mars* (1996) focuses on the new constitution negotiated among competing interests on a now-free Mars, a political order that includes a substantial voice for the

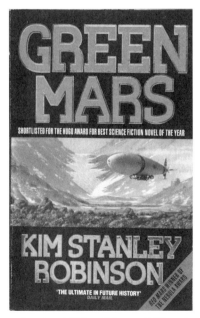

Figure 7.2 Cover for the 1992 edition of Kim Stanley Robinson's *Green Mars*.

natural world in things such as its environmental courts and a consti-
tutional commitment to landscape having a right of place. Robinson's
later *Antarctica* (1997) draws on many of the same technologies and
political structures, evidence that we can enact such transformative
change on Earth.

The second-wave feminist movement found in SF an equally powerful tool, and some works, such as Joan Slonczewski's *A Door into
Ocean* (1986), were explicitly ecofeminist in their orientation. Although
women writers and feminist themes have been part of the genre since
its origin, such visions flourished during this period. Ursula K. Le
Guin's *The Left Hand of Darkness* (1969) imagined a world that did not
view gender as a primary rubric for organising society: the inhabitants
of Gethen take on a gendered identity only during periods of mat-
ing and any individual can become either male or female, inhabiting
both over a lifetime. Joanna Russ's *The Female Man* (1970) explores
how gender shapes personality by looking at the differences among
four versions of what began as the 'same' woman; they become diverse
individuals based on how gender ideology does – or does not – deform
them. One version, Janet, lives in a world populated only by women,
and other novels followed which explored the consequences of living
in gender-segregated societies, both propitious and harmful, such as
Suzy McKee Charnas's *Holdfast* chronicles (1974–99) and Sheri S. Tepper's ecofeminist *The Gate to Women's Country* (1988), a tradition that
began with Charlotte Perkins Gilman's *Herland* (1915). Russ was also
an important critic of SF whose essays on gender and sexuality inaugurated a new critical consciousness about these topics. Pamela Sargent's
Women of Wonder anthologies **[7.3]** (1974, 1976) drew attention to the
wealth of work by women in the field, and her retrospective *Women of
Wonder: The Classic Years* (1995) restored earlier writers to visibility.

Dystopian visions of the future of gender discrimination also thrived,
and Marge Piercy's *Woman on the Edge of Time* (1976) explores the two
possibilities dialectically. Her protagonist, Connie, is pulled between her
1970s present, in which she is incarcerated in a mental institution via a
legal structure that discriminates against women, especially women of
colour, and a future in which the radical vision of contemporary countercultural movements has created a world beyond sexism, homophobia,

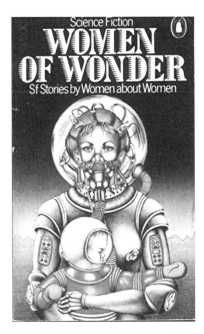

Figure 7.3 Cover for the 1978 Penguin edition of the *Women of Wonder* anthology, with introduction and notes by Pamela Sargent.

racism, consumerism, poverty, and environmental collapse. Connie – and readers – understand the contemporary moment to be one of pivotal importance, able to materialise either this idealised future or one of intensifying injustice, depending on the choices made. Piercy's later *Body of Glass* (1991), inspired by Donna Haraway's influential 'Cyborg Manifesto', continues to explore how gender ideologies are foundational to whether society is organised in ways that enhance or detract from equity, engaging with the IT technology contemporary to its publication.

An important but often overlooked novel from this period is Zoë Fairbairns's *Benefits* (1979), a projection of a dystopian future Britain that is disconcertingly like our present. The British economy is in collapse and the infrastructure of the welfare state is rapidly dismantled, leading to struggles over how to restore social order within austerity frameworks. The novel was written in response to the contemporary social and political unrest and in response to a particular proposal to introduce child benefit in Britain, a weekly stipend to be paid to primary caregivers, usually women. Resisted by unions, the proposal revealed a fractured left in which gender and labour politics did not align; this tension between class struggle and the politics of gender lies at the heart of the novel, which follows Lynn Byers, mother of a special-needs child, as she resists a government that tries to resolve the economic crisis by forcing women to return to the home. Beginning with the contemporary situation and projecting into a future in which the gains of the feminist movement are undone in response to rhetoric about economic crisis, Fairbairns's novel explores the same themes as Margaret Atwood's later and better-known *The Handmaid's Tale* (1989), without the emphasis on theocracy. Both texts seem eerily prescient in a twenty-first century that has materialised their predictions of eroding social welfare and renewed state desire, at least in the US, to control women's bodies and reproduction.

Equally strong was a tradition that addressed themes of sexuality, influenced by an increased openness towards depictions of sexuality in the genre following the radicalism of the New Wave (Golden Age SF tends to be rather prudish) as well as strong connections between feminist and LGBTQ activisms. Angela Carter explored the fluid boundaries of gender and sexual identities in her metafictional and surrealist *The Infernal Desire Machines of Doctor Hoffman* (1972) and *The Passion of New Eve* (1977) **[7.4]**. The latter transforms a sexist man, Evelyn, into the debilitating identity of femininity *as he fantasises* it. David Gerrold's *The Man Who Folded Himself* (1973) is a time-travel romp about self-creation like Robert Heinlein's 'All You Zombies' (1959), but made poignant by its tender depiction of homosexuality and sexual love. Nicola Griffith's *Ammonite* (1992) follows an anthropologist to a colony inhabited entirely by women that has been out of contact with the rest of humanity for more than 200 years. She is sent as part of a colonial project to exploit the planet's resources, but becomes involved in their resistance movement. Along with its celebration of lesbian community, the novel is notable for its vision of a technology that enables sexual reproduction between women. Similar ideas were explored earlier in stories by James Tiptree Jr, the pseudonym for Alice Sheldon, and the SF community acknowledged her role in expanding our imagination around gender and sexuality in the Tiptree Award, founded in 1991, which annually recognises the best work on this theme.

Figure 7.4 Cover for the 1977 first American edition of Angela Carter's *The Passion of New Eve*.

Samuel R. Delany, mostly identified as the most prominent writer of colour at the time, is equally noteworthy for his identity as a gay man. His masterful *Dhalgren* (1975), a stream-of-consciousness trip through Bellona, a fictional city somehow cut off from the rest of the world, defeats summation but is centrally about sexual joy beyond the limits of orientation and identity politics, experiences that enable moments of utopian possibility and personal change within this damaged world. *Triton* (1976), like *The Left Hand of Darkness*, explores a world in which individuals can experience either gender, but in Delany's novel gender is complicated and remade, rather than simply erased. His characters can decide to be male or female, and most switch between, but desire shapes Delany's world in a way that is overlooked by Le Guin, producing a more nuanced and entangled exploration of how much ideology shapes – and at times deforms – gender and sexuality.

Delany subtitles his work 'an ambiguous heterotopia', a term he takes from French theorist Michel Foucault, meaning 'other' place or place 'of difference' rather than the 'good' or 'perfect' place connoted by (e)utopia. The heterotopic spaces are ones of multiplicity and contradiction, a recognition of the complexity of trying to create a 'good' society given the multiplicity of human goals and passions. New thinking about utopias and dystopias is another legacy of the New Wave. Delany's subtitle alludes to Le Guin's *The Dispossessed* (1974), subtitled 'an ambiguous utopia', one of the most celebrated novels of the period, which explores the planets of Anarres and Urras, whose differences enable an examination of the relative merits of capitalism and collectivism, anarchism and hieratical governance. Protagonist Shevek, a physicist, moves between these two worlds, working on a revolutionary theory of temporality, and much of the book concerns what kind of science is made possible by their rival political and economic systems. Le Guin carefully avoids making either Anarres or Urras wholly 'good' or wholly 'evil' and instead reveals how each system enables and constrains in its own distinct way.

Other writers reinvented SF by playing with its form. Russell Hoban's *Riddley Walker* (1980) is a gutting depiction of a post-literature Kent 2,000 years into the future, struggling to remake itself after a nuclear war. The only technology is salvage of items from earlier eras, and church and state have fused into one oppressive order maintained through a bowdlerised version of the legend of Saint Eustace, a Roman general who converted to Christianity, largely misremembered and conflated with Punch and Judy shows. *Riddley Walker*'s stunning achievement is its depiction of the (d)evolution of language, making it challenging to read, which aptly conveys a vision equally as bleak as the one in the contemporary film *Threads* (Mick Jackson 1984). Kim Stanley Robinson's *Three Californias* trilogy extrapolated Marge Piercy's technique of making the reader's present the turning point for diverse possible futures, each novel depicting a different future for Orange County. *The Wild Shore* (1984), his first published novel, depicts the future after a nuclear war, one in which the US struggles to rebuild, policed by a victorious Soviet Union that refuses to allow technological development. *The Gold Coast* (1988) envisions the future as an intensification of the urban sprawl, gridlock, and economic injustice of the contemporary Reagan-era America and focuses on a protagonist who benefits economically from this social order but nonetheless finds it empty of meaning. *Pacific Edge* (1990) depicts a heterotopia that has been achieved by 2065 in a California that embraced ecological values and transformed its infrastructure towards a more sustainable life.

New World Orders

Even as some elements of SF continued in the countercultural tradition of the New Wave, however, other SF, especially into the 1980s, embraced the spirit of this decade of privatisation and deregulation, ushered in by Thatcher and Reagan. Territorial empires were dismantled through the 1960s, but Michael Hardt and Antonio Negri argue that by the 1990s they were replaced by a nexus of economic entanglements and rule via transnational corporations, a system they call 'Empire' in their 2000 book. This rising global capitalism fuelled by information technology is at the centre of the most influential SF of the 1980s, cyberpunk, a subgenre embodied most clearly in William Gibson's acclaimed *Neuromancer* (1982). Gibson himself hesitated to embrace the rhetoric that gave cyberpunk its name, most visible in Bruce Sterling's fervent introduction to the anthology *Mirrorshades* (first published in 1986). For Sterling it is a fusion of the new horizons opened up by cybernetic media with the cultural resistance of the punk movement. Taking its cue from shifts towards austerity in both the US and the UK, cyberpunk declared an end to techno-optimism and projected the harsh future to come, memorably summed up in *Neuromancer*'s description of the city as 'like a deranged experiment in Social Darwinism, designed by a bored researcher who kept one thumb permanently on the fast-forward button' (Gibson 1984: 7).

Cyberpunk reinvented SF in several ways, not only in the shift from earlier visions of technological transcendence via space travel towards the more intimate technologies of personal computers (ones that fused with their users), but also in its implacably pessimistic tone. Cyberpunk envisioned futures of corporate dominance and expendable human lives, with people either barely making ends meet or else subsuming themselves to the demands of capital to achieve success on its terms – such as Ricky in Gibson's story 'Burning Chrome' (1982), who sells sexual encounters with her body (her mind cordoned off elsewhere) in order to afford to upgrade her eyes to recording implants that will enable her to become a media star. Cyberpunk owes tremendous debts to feminist and New Wave SF: Ricky, for example, descends from the protagonist of James Tiptree Jr's caustic 'The Girl Who Was Plugged In' (1973). Cyberpunk rose quickly to unprecedented prominence both within and beyond the field, fuelled by the poststructuralist turn in literary theory, producing a generation of critics for whom cyberpunk emblematised the contemporary. Leading American Marxist critic Fredric Jameson famously called it 'the supreme literary expression, if not of postmodernism, then of late capitalism itself' (Jameson 1991: 419). Unlike earlier dystopias, cyberpunk simply diagnosed contemporary discontent rather than tried to use its anticipations to prompt social change.

Bruce Sterling's Mechanist/Shaper stories and related novel, *Schismatrix* (1985) took cyberpunk into the twenty-third century and beyond, examining two branches of posthumans, one that augments their bodies via technology and the other that uses biological engineering. Lewis Shiner, whose work was heavily influenced by music culture, explores anarchist themes in *Deserted Cities of the Heart* (1988) and *Slam* (1990). He was a central cyberpunk figure at the time, but his work is often overlooked today, perhaps because he was also among the first to pronounce cyberpunk's death. Pat Cadigan was the most prominent woman writing in this mode, in works such as *Mindplayers* (1987) and *Synners* (1991), and her greater attentiveness to embodiment was celebrated by the academic community who worried at revulsion towards 'meat' in some cyberpunk fictions. Yet perhaps the most interesting take on cyberpunk is Raphael Carter's *The Fortunate Fall* (1996), which follows journalist Maya Andreyeva, whose augmented body is her recording device, as she investigates a political conspiracy. The novel is prescient in understanding how the media shape the way we experience and understand history, and its focus on issues of how queer individuals survive within an oppressively heteronormative social order offers a vital reimagining of a subgenre critics were already identifying as implicitly misogynistic. George Alec Effinger's Marîd Audran series (1987–91) fuses hard-boiled detective fiction with sophisticated brain implants that allow one to instantly install skills and/or personalities, set in a futuristic Middle East where the West is in decline and the Muslim world ascendant.

Cyberpunk was especially influential on a broader media culture that was rapidly becoming many people's introduction to SF. The longevity of academic and popular interest in it was fuelled by the rapidity with which cyberpunk visions seemed to become material realities with the invention of digital games and personal computers, the emergence of online communities, and experiments creating immersive multi-participant online worlds and virtual reality experiences. Gibson and Sterling's collaborative *The Difference Engine* (1990), an alternative history in which Charles Babbage's analytical engine oriented Victorian society towards conceptualising the world as data, established the steampunk subgenre – reinventions of the past premised on steam-powered versions of IT technology having been invented in the nineteenth century. Steampunk rose to greater prominence after 2000.

Computer scientist and SF author Vernor Vinge published his essay 'The Coming Technological Singularity' (1993) just as cyberpunk was morphing into something else, and this concept of the singularity has been central to early twenty-first-century SF. Vinge argued that technology was improving at such a significant rate that we were approaching the end of the 'human era' and entering a new society created by superhuman intelligence, a theme amplified and widely disseminated in works by computer scientist Ray Kurzweil, such as *The Age of Spiritual Machines* (1999) and *The Singularity is Near* (2006). The new social order that is to emerge from these transcendent machines cannot be imagined by mere humans on this side of the dividing line, but this barrier did not stop SF writers from offering possible visions; Vinge's own *Marooned in Realtime* (1986) does so. Such SF, often called 'singularity fiction', is more prevalent after the turn of the millennium. During the 1990s advocates of directed 'evolution' through technology, a group known as the Extropians, were a small subculture whose recommended reading list was a heady mix of futurist speculation, popularised science, cognitive self-help, and SF by authors such as Sterling, Vinge, and Larry Niven. By the twenty-first century, such technologised fantasies of augmented human bodies and life extension have become research projects funded by venture capital, such as the 2045 Initiative and Humanity+, much of it from Silicon Valley entrepreneurs who made their fortunes in IT industries. 'Transhumanism' is now the preferred moniker for this subculture.

We can see in cyberpunk's anxious vision of the future anticipations of our twenty-first-century reality, and it is not a coincidence that the subgenre appeared just as Reagan and Thatcher were reorganising global markets and introducing austerity politics at home. Economics is as important to cyberpunk's emergence as IT. Jack Womack is often loosely associated with this subgenre because his fiction emerges from a similar vision of the future dominated by corporations for whom the financial bottom line is the only ethical imperative. His Dryco series (1987–2000) explores a brutal and violent future America in which the middle class has disappeared, corporate elites indulge in the most grotesque acts of conspicuous consumption, and the impoverished live on the edge of desperation. The first book, *Ambient* (1987), launches us into this future and its desperate economic choices, anchored by the point of view of bodyguard Jake, whose sister is an ambient: a person whose morphology is deformed, either by radiation or voluntarily, part of a subgroup that arose after a major meltdown. Womack's novels are set in an alternative future (in reality, the 1979 Three Mile Island meltdown was only partial; in the novels, the Civil War never happened) but the correlations between the real world and this future are more meaningful than such differences.

These novels are critical dystopias, defined by Tom Moylan as a form that 'takes on the present system and offers not only astute critiques of the order of things but also explorations of the oppositional spaces and possibilities from which the next round of political activism can derive imaginative sustenance' (Moylan 2000: xv). Womack's novels enable us to see negative elements of the contemporary more clearly, and he intensifies this effect by playing with chronology, especially in *Ambient*, *Heathern* (1990) and *Random Acts of Senseless Violence* (1993). Their internal chronology is the reverse of their order of publication: *Ambient* launches us into a frightening dystopian future, then *Heathern* moves back a generation, as does *Random Acts*, creating an alarming sense of continuity between this world and the our present as their temporalities almost overlap. The most powerful of the series, *Random Acts,* is written as the diary of an adolescent girl (an allusion to Anne Frank) as her family slides from middle-class security to poverty. A response to both the dismantling of the welfare state and a 1970s-era vision of New York City as a space of ubiquitous and senseless violence, the novel explores how the quotidian world contemporary with its publication could become the nightmare world of its future. The novel's style is memorable, beginning with a recognisable English vernacular and incorporating more and more of the futuristic slang and 'verbing' of language (as in this example) Womack uses for the series.

Not all contemporary SF was critical of such economic developments, however. A group of writers associated with the hard SF tradition, and especially with stories of space exploration and military conflict with aliens, wrote SF that aligned with the political shift towards the right. Many were members of the Citizens Advisory Council on National Space Policy, a right-wing think tank interested in militarised space exploration aimed at commercial profit, and which advised President Reagan directly. Chaired by SF author Jerry Pournelle, this group included astronauts, retired military officers, people associated with the aerospace industry, computer scientists, and several SF writers, including Greg Bear, Gregory Benford, Robert Heinlein, Dean Ing, and Larry Niven. Pournelle and Ing co-authored a popular book, *Mutually Assured Survival* (1984), which sought to counter the anti-nuclear lobby and its rallying cry 'mutually assured destruction', by arguing that only increased militarisation of space could protect us from nuclear war. The efforts of this group helped to launch the ill-conceived Strategic Defence Initiative that put weapons in space. This non-fictional volume paints a heady vision of a future of space weapons, a permanent Moon base paid for by lunar mining, and the inevitable triumph of 'that driving force of the American economy, the small entrepreneur' (Pournelle and Ing 1984: 136), all freed from pesky government oversight. They conclude that this 'rediscovery of progress' (Pournelle and Ing 1984: 185) and a refusal to accept limits to growth will ensure the ongoing hegemony of the US. Niven and Pournelle's *Oath of Fealty* (1981), a vindication of a prosperous future city that walls itself off from a suffering, remnant population no longer necessary to the economy, provides the domestic policy analogy to this new-right vision.

We thus see in some 1980s SF the seeds of our present and a rising right for whom market logic trumps all, and who believe the power of 'innovation' will inevitably find a way to solve crises such as climate change, so that we do not need to contemplate political solutions. There is no question that the 9/11 attacks in 2001 jolted Western cultures, and especially the US, into a paranoid security state of zero-sum game politics and cynical profiteering, but the SF of the two decades before demonstrates that these tendencies were already thriving. We see this kind of thinking, for example, in Francis Fukuyama's ambitious proclamation of *The End of History and the Last Man* (1992), which celebrated the triumph of capitalism – entirely equated with democracy – over Communism.

Yet another response to these shifts came in the reinvention of space opera, a term coined in 1941 to describe – pejoratively – space adventure SF that partook too much of romance and military action and not enough of scientific extrapolation. By the 1990s, the subgenre was regarded more favourably, in part influenced by media SF such as *Star Wars* (1977): in America such works tended towards the right, such as David Weber's Honor Harrington series (1993–2012). This form, however, was subverted by other writers, such as Lois McMaster Bujold in her Miles Vorkosigan series (1986–2012), which features a protagonist with limited mobility and storylines related to gender and reproductive rights. Orson Scott Card's Ender series, which continues to this day, explores the future of warfare imagined as digital gaming. *Ender's Game* (1985), about the education of this new generation of child soldiers, was warmly received by the SF community and by the US military, who saw in it a model of leadership and the values of martial culture.

Other writers sought to reorient space opera away from its military and imperialist underpinnings, and this mode came to be called New Space Opera. The best examples were published by authors based in Britain: Iain M. Banks, Gwyneth Jones, Ken MacLeod, Ian McDonald, and Alastair Reynolds, among others. They were central to a trend dubbed by Andrew Butler and other critics the 'British Boom' in the

1990s, a judgement that the best contemporary SF was written in the UK. Often seen as a left-wing answer to the imperialism of traditional space opera, these works fused the adventure narrative with reflections on military and political power, renewing the form.

Banks' Culture series (1987–2012) imagined an inclusive, post-scarcity intergalactic society run by AIs, in which all necessary labour is done by non-sentient machines, leaving intelligent humans, machines, and aliens to pursue lives of hedonistic pleasure and satisfying avocation. Banks troubles his seeming paradise by focusing on its relationships with external polities, thus using space opera to reflect on the politics of globalisation, probing the axiom of non-intervention versus an ethical imperative to transform oppressive societies. Gwyneth Jones is perhaps best known for her *Aleutian* trilogy (1991–7), a first-contact story that emphasises the risks of miscommunication across cultural difference. It scrutinises how systemic sexism shapes human identity, by depicting an encounter between humans and aliens who cannot parse human gender diffences. MacLeod's publications are notable for their visions of anarchist political formations and commitment to a left libertarianism, and provide an important counterpoint to the conflation of political and market freedoms in American space opera. This New Space Opera continues to be important into the twenty-first century, with McDonald rising to prominence as a writer whose fiction directly explores histories of colonial occupation and resource extraction through stories set in the future of previously colonised nations such as India and Brazil. His Chaga series (1990–2000), for example, explores a future Kenya transformed by alien invasion and questions the justice of United Nations interventions.

Anticipating the Twenty-First Century

Much of what shaped late-twentieth-century SF remains important to the genre today. Reinventions of space opera continue but are no longer central; similarly, approaches to the genre that were a minor part of the field in the 1990s have grown, especially works that complicate boundaries among speculative genres and between them and 'mainstream' literature. In retrospect, it is clear that science fiction was in transformation during the 1990s, changed by an influx of new writers and fans, many of whom did not have a strong connection to Golden Age writers such as Isaac Asimov, Arthur C. Clarke, and Robert Heinlein. This period saw a few manifestos and short-lived subgenres, such as Geoff Ryman's 'Mundane SF', a revitalisation of hard SF that focused on near-future settings, urgent real-world problems, and rigorously extrapolated visions of how science could be oriented towards solving them. Another such subgenre was the 'New Weird', a fusion of SF, horror, and surrealism inspired by the work of H. P. Lovecraft (the term first coined in 2003 by the writer M. John Harrison), which similarly emphasised the need to model its fictional worlds on complex, real-world problems (for a useful anthology of stories and discussions on the term, see the Ann and Jeff VanderMeer 2008 anthology). Both movements were oriented towards seeing science, speculation, and the social world as co-constitutive and thus rejected earlier version of speculative genres, which they saw as unrealistic wish-fulfilment fantasy or escapist consolation.

The New Weird had greater longevity as a term, but Mundane SF tendencies are at least as – if not more – apparent in recent SF. The computer innovations that inspired cyberpunk fiction of the 1980s gave way to a focus on biology in the 1990s with the Human Genome Mapping Project. Nancy Kress's Sleepless series (1993–6), beginning with *Beggars in Spain*, quickly understood the implications of an anticipated future of genetically optimised babies, which would allow the privileged to engineer even greater advantage for their offspring. Premised on the idea that simply removing the need for sleep would enable greater accomplishment, Kress explores a future world in which the Sleepless easily outperform their baseline human counterparts, who then resent and attack these augmented humans. Such themes had been explored in SF since Aldous Huxley's *Brave New World* (1932), but took on a new urgency as techniques in IVF, cloning, and other genetic therapies developed. Amitav Ghosh's *The Calcutta Chromosome* (1995) similarly helps us to see how science and the social are entwined. Its plot moves between the near future and the nineteenth century to show

how malaria research relied on the invisible labour of colonised people, who are present in official records only as research subjects or anonymous technicians.

Works focusing on the possibilities of nanotechnology began to appear into the 1990s. Greg Bear's *Blood Music* (1985) was one of the earliest, fusing nanotechnology and biotechnology in a tale about microbial computers, noocytes, that escape containment and remake, first, the body of their inventor who smuggles them out of the lab, then the entire world of matter which becomes a fused collective that can take on various forms. The novel is notable for its transition from horror, in which the takeover of human bodies and the collapse of individual identity into collectivity inspires fear, into a posthumanist tale that finds new promise in life thus reinvented. Neal Stephenson, who was associated with cyberpunk for his *Snow Crash* (1992), envisioned nanotech manufacture in *The Diamond Age* (1995). Set in a future of balkanised micro-states premised on a diverse economics, the novel tells the story of how an interactive educational primer creates class mobility for a young girl, Nell, into whose hands it accidentally falls. John Varley's *Steel Beach* (1993), set on the Moon in a future in which humans are displaced from Earth by aliens, posits a society that relies on nanotech to ensure the health and safety of citizens. Nanobots live within humans and continually monitor and adjust for optimal health, but they are controlled by a centralised computer that proves to be conducting unauthorised experiments. Greg Bear's *Queen of Angels* (1990) similarly posits a future in which continual minute adjustments made by nanobots are integral to the social order. Citizens are expected to be thus 'therapied' and the novel's focus on the 'untherapied' asks questions about how to balance freedom with stability. The untherapied often suffer from trauma, but the therapied may simply be productive cogs in society's economic machine.

Perhaps the most rigorous extrapolator from science is Greg Egan, whose works focus on neuropsychology and theories of cognition, often extrapolating from quantum physics. *Quarantine* (1992) is premised on the idea that human consciousness collapses wave functions of quantum systems, reducing potentiality to the quantum state that

Figure 7.5 Cover for the 1996 edition of Greg Egan's *Axiomatic*.

materialises. In Egan's novel, modification of the brain allows conscious control over this process. His short story collection *Axiomatic* (1995) **[7.5]** meditates on the fantasy of uploading one's consciousness into a computer to live forever. 'Learning to Be Me' changes narrative voice midway to confront readers with the recognition that there will always be a gap between digitised and organic versions of the self, while the title story envisions temporary brain implants, like those in George Alec Effinger's work, to explore the fragility of personal convictions if the mind is understood to be merely data. *Permutation City* (1995) questions what happens to notions such as self and morality if the human mind can be digitally simulated, asking if there is any difference between 'real' and simulated people. It explores a world of Copies – intelligent programs that began as non-sentient medical models – in which economic inequality persists even in one's virtual life. *Diaspora* (1997) explores a distant future in which transhumanism becomes the default.

Authors not centrally associated with SF began to take up questions about how contemporary science was remaking the human, perhaps literally, although this trend did not fully flourish until the twenty-first century. Yet there are hints of this coming convergence. Doris Lessing turns explicitly to SF in her *Canopus in Argos* novels (1979–83), which explore the evolution of human societies, often from the point of view of alien observers. Many of Don DeLillo's works, such as *Ratner's Star* (1976), about a maths prodigy deciphering a message from space, or *White Noise* (1985), organised around the 'airborne toxic event', are propelled by scientific events even if their focus is not on plausible extrapolation. Similarly, Richard Powers took inspiration from new discoveries in science, the chemical structure of DNA in *The Gold Bug Variations* (1991), AI research in *Galatea 2.2* (1995), and links between the chemical industry and cancer in *Gain* (1998). The tone of such postmodern works is often absurdist or surreal, such as Mark Leyner's *My Cousin, My Gastroenterologist* (1990), a loose collection of narratives about advanced medical therapies, such as stimulated growth of red-blood cells in patients undergoing radiation treatment, which deliberately mixes contemporary science with futuristic speculations to comment on how rapidly social and physical norms are being rewritten by medical practice.

The emergence of such works points to the increasingly central role of science in daily life, prompting writers to respond, whatever their genre identification. Even as the gap between SF and literary culture narrowed, the genre was also changing internally, focusing more explicitly on narrating alternative visions of the social world. This new emphasis emerged from multiple impulses. One was the recognition that remaking the human via technology could fundamentally change a culture that had been premised on humanism. Another was the counterculture values infused into the genre by the New Wave, which led to new organisations and awards that recognised the value of the genre to social justice movements: the Tiptree Award, founded in 1991 to recognise work that expands thinking about gender and sexuality; and the Carl Brandon Society, founded in 1995, focused on fiction that addressed issues of race and ethnicity, which began to give its own awards in the twenty-first century.

The increasing visibility and greater numbers of writers of colour is perhaps the most important legacy of this period, measured in terms of how much it has shaped the genre today. Science fiction of earlier eras tended to be a project of white writers and fans, albeit with exceptions, and it was not until the twenty-first century that a larger tradition of speculative writing in African American, indigenous, and other communities was conceptualised as part of SF, through ground-breaking anthologies such as Sheree R. Thomas's *Dark Matter* anthologies (2000, 2004) and Grace L. Dillon's *Walking the Clouds* (2012). Although postwar SF responded to shifting relations of colonial power – independence movements in former colonies, and related demands for racial justice in Civil Rights, American Indian, and Chicano movements – such responses usually reflect what David Higgins calls imperial masochism, that is, imagining that the historical subject of privilege is in the position of those who were victimised by this history. Such works explore historical trauma via affect, but position white characters as revolutionaries against tyranny, rather than acknowledging historical complicity in colonialism, a sleight of hand perhaps most easily visible in *Star Wars* (1977).

Nonetheless, these narratives opened the door to thinking about how the colonial mindset shaped the genre, which ultimately resulted in greater space for writers of colour to enter the field and tell different kinds of stories. Samuel R. Delany, whose work was associated with the New Wave, was joined by Octavia E. Butler, one of the most significant writers of this era, as well as Steven Barnes and Nalo Hopkinson. Butler's Patternist series (1976–84) explores the bifurcation of humans into three biologically distinct branches and explores the history of slavery by including two long-lived characters who witness changing racial regimes. *Kindred* (1979) is an eloquent reflection on the still-open wounds of slavery, told through a protagonist who travels from the bicentennial year of 1976 to the antebellum period to experience first-hand what her ancestors endured so that she might live at all. The *Xenogenesis* trilogy (1984–9) hybridises humans with aliens who rescue a few survivors from a planetary nuclear war, exploring our (lack of) capacity to embrace difference in a story about the necessary biological transition of humanity into something new. Butler is best remembered now for her Parables series (1993–8), set in a near-future California in economic and ecological crisis, in which the poor have become permanently displaced migrants. This future now seems distressingly close to the realities of the twenty-first century. It narrates the creation of a new community/religion, called Earthseed, that provides guidelines for a less violent way of living in a heterogeneous community.

Work by African American writers was more prominent than that by other writers of colour in this period, but other traditions were present. Ernest Hogan fused cyberpunk with Latin American history and mythology in *Cortez on Jupiter* (1990) and *High Aztech* (1992). Both are notable for their neologisms, which use Spanish and Nahuatl, creating futuristic discourse that is different from familiar techno-speak and thus reinforces how the future will be different as we extrapolate from multiple cultures. The protagonist of *Cortez on Jupiter*, Pablo, is a graffiti artist and trickster, who explores the transformative power of art. He is the only one who can communicate with aliens, perhaps pointing to the alienation of minority experience in contemporary US culture. Leslie Marmon Silko's *Ceremony* (1977) and *Almanac of the Dead* (1990) fuse indigenous speculative traditions with narratives about the impact of technology on indigenous communities. Sherman Alexie's collection *The Lone Ranger and Tonto Fistfight in Heaven* (1993) uses surrealist and other speculative techniques to humorously, yet pointedly, interrogate how popular culture shapes perceptions of indigenous identity, beyond these communities but also within them. Not explicitly science fictional, the book illustrates many of the techniques that will be embraced in a more expansive definition of SF in the twenty-first century.

As the twentieth century ended, SF was rapidly becoming a vernacular for conceptualising a world that had come to resemble many of the SF visions published as it commenced. More importantly, it was posed to become a mode used by diverse communities, generating a more robust and inclusive socio-technical world view to shape speculations about the future into the twenty-first century.

References

Bear, Greg (2001), *Blood Music*. [1985] London: Gollancz.

Brunner, John (2003), *The Sheep Look Up* [1972]. Dallas: BenBella.

Butler, Andrew M. (2003), 'Thirteen Ways of Looking at the British Boom', *Science Fiction Studies* 30: 3, pp. 374–93.

Butler, Octavia E. (2000), *Lilith's Brood*, containing the novels in the Xenogenesis trilogy, *Dawn, Adulthood Rites* and *Imago*. London: Warner Books.

Callenbach, Ernest (1975), *Ecotopia*. New York: Bantam Books.

Carter, Angela (1977), *The Passion of New Eve*. London: Virago.

Fairbairns, Zoe (1979), *Benefits*. Harmondsworth: Penguin.

Foster, Thomas (2005), *The Souls of Cyberfolk: Posthumanism as Vernacular Theory*. Minneapolis: University of Minnesota Press.

Foucault, Michel (1971), *The Order of Things*. New York: Vintage.

——— (1986), 'Of Other Spaces'. *Diacritics* 16, pp. 22–7.

Gibson, William (1984), *Neuromancer*, New York: Ace.

——— (1995), *Burning Chrome*. [1982] London: HarperCollins.

Haraway, Donna (1991), 'A Cyborg Manifesto: Science, Technology, and Socialist-Feminism in the Late Twentieth Century', in *Simians, Cyborgs and Women: The Reinvention of Nature*. London: Routledge.

Hardt, Michael, and Antonio Negri (2000), *Empire*. Harvard: Harvard University Press.

Hawken, Paul, Amory Lovins and L. Hunter Lovins (1999), *Natural Capitalism: Creating the Next Industrial Revolution*. Boston: Little, Brown and Company.

Higgins, David (2016), 'Survivance in Indigenous Science Fictions', *Extrapolation* 57: 1–2, pp. 51–72.

Hoban, Russell (1980), *Riddley Walker*. London: Jonathan Cape.

Jameson, Fredric (1991), *Postmodernism, or the Cultural Logic of Late Capitalism*. London: Verso.

McCaffery, Lawrence (1991), *Storming the Reality Studio: A Casebook of Cyberpunk and Postmodern Science Fiction*. Durham: Duke University Press.

Moylan, Tom (2000), *Scraps of the Untainted Sky: Science Fiction, Utopia, Dystopia*. Boulder: Westview Press.

Murphy, Graham J., and Sherryl Vint, eds (2012), *Beyond Cyberpunk: New Critical Perspectives*. London: Routledge.

Nixon, Nicola (1992), 'Cyberpunk: Preparing the Ground for Revolution or Keeping the Boys Satisfied?', *Science Fiction Studies* 19: 2, pp. 219–35.

Otto, Eric (2012), *Green Speculations: Science Fiction and Transformative Environmentalism*. Columbus: Ohio State University Press.

Pournelle, Jerry, and Dean Ing (1984), *Mutually Assured Survival*. New York: Baen.

Rieder, John (2008), *Colonialism and the Emergence of Science Fiction*. Middletown: Wesleyan University Press.

Robinson, Kim Stanley (1993), *Red Mars*. New York: Bantam.

——— (1994), *Green Mars*. New York: Bantam.

——— (1996) *Blue Mars*. New York: Bantam.

Sterling, Bruce, ed. (1988), *Mirrorshades: The Cyberpunk Anthology*. New York: Ace Books.

VanderMeer, Ann and Jeff (2008), *The New Weird*. San Francisco: Tachyon.

Vinge, Vernor (1993), 'The Coming Technological Singularity'. Lecture freely available on the internet, for example at: https://ntrs.nasa.gov/archive/nasa/casi.ntrs.nasa.gov/19940022855.pdf (accessed 23 January 2017).

What To Read Next

Raphael Carter, *The Fortunate Fall* (New York: St Martin's, 1996).

Samuel R. Delany, *Dhalgren* (London: Gollancz, 2010).

Nicola Griffith, *Ammonite* (London: Gollancz, 2012).

Kim Stanley Robinson, *Red Mars* (New York: Bantam, 1998).

Marge Piercy, *Woman on the Edge of Time* (New York: Del Rey, 2016).

Jack Womack, *Random Acts of Senseless Violence* (London: Gollancz, 2013).

Chapter 8

New Paradigms, After 2001

Gerry Canavan

We live in an era of obsolete futures and junked dreams. It has now been over fifteen years since 2001 with nary a monolith in sight, much less manned missions to Jupiter or increasingly malevolent computer superintelligences refusing to open the pod bay doors. The Moon was *not* torn out of Earth orbit in 1999, nor did genetic superman Khan Noonien Singh become absolute ruler of more than a quarter of the globe during the bloody Eugenic Wars of the early 1990s (before, of course, fleeing into space on the sleeper ship *Botany Bay* following his overthrow in 1996). We've missed at least three separate Judgement Days, dodging *The Terminator's* Skynet and the scheduled rise of the machines each time. Manhattan Island is not a maximum security prison; Dr Sam Beckett did not invent the Quantum Leap Accelerator and vanish; Doc Brown and Marty arrived in 2015 to find a world totally bereft of flying DeLoreans, hoverboards, or sleep-inducing alpha rhythm generators (and the Cubs didn't even win the World Series until 2016). *Blade Runner 2049* (2017) came over a year after replicant Roy Batty completely failed to roll off the assembly line at the Tyrell Corporation as prophesied.

A century of science fiction predicted space missions, first contacts, robot uprisings, and nuclear wars that were all dated before *now*. To live in the twenty-first century is thus in a very real sense to live *after* the future – after the future we invented together, the one that never happened.

And yet despite this slightly melancholic sense of thwarted futurity it cannot be denied that we live in science-fictional times, from the incredible supercomputers we all carry in our pockets (able to access the totality of world knowledge in an instant from anywhere on the planet, by either touch or voice command), to the algorithmic military–corporate surveillance apparatus that tracks our movements (using those very devices), to the increasingly dire state of the planetary ecosystem in multiple crisis (which is also registered in and intensified by the accelerating upgrade cycle of those same smart phones and tablets, among many other contemporary sites of resource-extraction and trash-generation). In many ways the world has been utterly transformed since it rang in the new millennium on 1 January 2001, almost to the point of unrecognisability; Francis Fukuyama's proclamation of 'the end of history' in 1992 following the end of the Cold War has been largely replaced by a vertiginous mood of constant, uncontrollable change, the dread of a world that seems to be spinning out of control, and SF since 2001 in some sense is still struggling to catch up.

How can one even *write* science fiction when, in 2016 alone, Britain unpredictably voted to exit the European Union, a planet was discovered around Alpha Centauri in the habitable zone, the Arctic ice sheet went through further catastrophic reduction, bee colonies further collapsed, and Donald Trump was elected President of the US? How can our science fictions hope to keep up with a world that increasingly seems beyond prediction, beyond parody, beyond reason, and beyond redemption? 'Reality is broken,' Charles Stross declared in 2016, describing the way that Britain's decision to leave the European Union had forced him to rewrite a novel he'd *thought* was a biting dystopian satire of the future, only to wake up one morning to discover the present had already outpaced his wildest, darkest dreams (Stross 2016). On the other hand in such strange times as these the pull of science fiction may be all the stronger; the genre becomes, as Kim Stanley Robinson put it in an interview with the *Guardian* in 2009, not fanciful speculation but 'the realism of our time' (Flood 2009), a collective first draft of the worlds we hoped to make and the worlds we feared, instead, that we were actually making.

This chapter differs somewhat from the other chapters in this volume in its attempt to articulate a history that is very much still being written; unlike earlier periods in science fiction the 'literary history' of the 2000s era is still very much up for grabs. What follows is an attempt to trace major trends in the genre and project those texts and authors that may *become* canonical, from the perspective of future fans and scholars of SF. Such a project is necessarily speculative, on two fronts: it must extrapolate the consensus that might someday crystallise out of our current, often contentious debates about the genre, as well as imagine the interests and reading habits of a future that will some day look back on our time with (one hopes) more bemusement and appreciation than bitterness, resentment, and rage.

Climate Change: Science Fiction at the End of Civilisation

In September 2016 scientists at the University of California, San Diego reported that carbon in the atmosphere had reached a concentration unheard of in human history: 400 parts per million (Monroe 2016). This threshold was widely heralded as a point of no return for the climate, not only in the sense that a return to the 'normal' climate context in which our agricultural and architectural practices evolved looks increasingly impossible, but also in the sense that we may now be on the cusp of triggering feedback loops (such as the release of stored methane in what was once permafrost, or change in the ice-albedo loop that tends to make cooler periods cooler and warmer periods warmer) that will intensify the shifts further, perhaps radically. And the rise in average global temperatures is only one of the many interrelated ecological crises that we face – ocean acidification, water pollution and scarcity, mass extinctions, and so on – that are popularly grouped together under the heading 'climate change'. While the causes, severity, and solutions of these crises remain controversial – and the recent right-wing political victories in Britain, Europe, and the US suggest that no action to tackle them will be taken any time soon – we appear to be entering a period that the writer and critic Ziauddin Sardar has designated, with startling incision, as 'postnormal' (Sardar 2010).

The dread of climate change and its attendant effects on nature and society permeates SF of the twenty-first century. Even the optimism of Kim Stanley Robinson – one of very few contemporary writers in the genre whose political and philosophical orientation might be described as 'utopian' – has grown increasingly tempered by climate change since the Red Mars trilogy of the 1990s (which itself already featured a cataclysmic climate event in the form of the collapse of the West Antarctic Ice Sheet). His Science in the Capital trilogy (2004–7, slightly abridged and published as a single volume, *Green Earth,* in 2015) imagined rapid climate change following the 'shutting off' of the Atlantic Gulf Stream, forcing direct intervention via geoengineering in an effort to restore something like normal climate. In *Galileo's Dream* (2009), a future human civilisation living around Jupiter's moons is moved to attempt to meddle in its own past in the name of preventing the cataclysmic wars and ecological devastation that characterised its rise to the stars. In *2312* (2010) the techno-optimistic futurity of the Mars trilogy is reimagined in similar but less utopian terms; a lucky few, benefiting from immense wealth, ply the larger solar system while billions languish on a climate-ravaged 'Earth, the Planet of Sadness' (Robinson 2010: 303). Robinson's next book, *Shaman* (2013), set in the Neolithic, imagined human beings confronting the end of the Ice Age, while *New York 2140* (2017) is set in a flooded Manhattan, post-ice-sheet-collapse. Robinson's overall best work of the period, *Aurora* (2015), is perhaps his darkest vision yet, once again refashioning the imagined 'Accelerando' of the Mars books but this time twisting it into a brutal deconstruction of the generation-ship fantasy that argues, as Robinson has argued before, that despite what generations of space-operatic SF has trained us to believe, the solar system will always be our species's only home.

In the hands of writers who were already less inclined to optimism, the growing reality of climate change makes a much more brutal shutting-off of the possibilities of the future. This sort of necro-futurological imagining is perhaps best registered in Cormac McCarthy's slipstream novel *The Road* (2006) – one of many 'literary' novels in the period not treated as SF by critics despite its narrative situation and themes – featuring the hopeless wanderings of a father and his son after an unspecified disaster has destroyed the planetary ecology (at least in the US) and inaugurated instead a world of starvation, cannibalism, and maximum death. The renowned Canadian author Margaret Atwood turned to a similarly brutal vision of the future in her acclaimed Oryx and Crake (or MaddAddam) trilogy (2003–13), which she provocatively insisted was not SF at all due to the plausibility of the horrors it described. *Oryx and Crake* (2003), the first in the series, takes what slim optimism it still allows from its vision of a 'Humanity 2.0', designed by its creator (the titular mad scientist Crake) to be a cognitively limited successor species for *Homo sapiens* that will never again outstrip the carrying capacity of the planet. Crake then engineers a plague to wipe out humanity to let the Crakers take over, and by the end of the novel the reader is nearly convinced he made the right decision. In a flash fiction composed for the *Guardian* on the occasion of the Copenhagen climate talks, 'Time Capsule Found on the Dead Planet', Atwood was even more uncompromising, imagining the last message of a human species to the aliens who might someday find our ruins: 'You who have come here from some distant world, to this dry lakeshore and this cairn, and to this cylinder of brass, in which on the last day of all our recorded days I place our final words: Pray for us, who once, too, thought we could fly' (Atwood 2009). Atwood's unforgiving epitaph for humanity is reprinted as the closing piece in *Loosed Upon the World* (2015), an anthology of recent climate-change-centred short fiction edited by John Joseph Adams that also includes Robinson. *Loosed Upon the World* joins *Welcome to the Greenhouse* (2011), *The Apocalypse Reader* (2007) and *Wastelands: Stories of the Apocalypse* (2008) in its gathering of a new canon of apocalyptic short fiction registering collective dread for the future. These form an emergent genre that journalist Dan Bloom has dubbed 'cli-fi'.

In generic terms, such necro-futurological fictions trace a path away from the New Frontier of outer space to the No Frontier of a blank future, perhaps a Planet Earth devoid of human life entirely. The superhistorical era that is now commonly called 'the Anthropocene', first proposed by Paul Crutzen in 2002 as a scientific proposition about human effects on geological history (Crutzen 2002: 23), thus always generates a structure of feeling about the deep future that is being created out of our present. Accordingly, much SF of the Anthropocene is a Neo-Romantic fascination with how a place – this place, *our* place – becomes a ruin. Richard McGuire's graphic novel *Here* (2014) is a perfect example of the melancholic attitude this way of thinking produces, as well as the difficulty of slipping out of that knot: the nearly wordless book uses its three-dimensional spatiality to create the corner of a room of a house, which we then witness across a billion-year span of time ranging from the deep past to the near future to the deep future. What we discover is that there isn't much of a future for human civilisation; the house (located in New Jersey) is wrecked by rising sea levels around 100 years from now, in 2111; a resurgent human civilisation reclaims the site around 2213, but is gone again (this time seemingly destroyed by nuclear war) by 2314. The world of 10,175 is a dark and barren one, populated by a forlorn mammal (a South American bear now living in New Jersey) that looks directly at the reader with a sort of indescribable sadness, as if to demand an apology. When we get as far as the 22,000s we are relieved to find a bizarre, almost unrecognisable ecology on the site, which is filled with weird, dinosaur-like giant mammals and brightly coloured jungle plants – an ecology totally not 'right' for New Jersey, and not a place *we* could live, but at least there's *something* still alive. At least we didn't kill everything.

A similar preoccupation with the status of animal life, and the need for human beings to redirect their energies to protecting the creatures endangered by our activities, can be felt not only in Atwood's MaddAddam series and Robinson's *2312* and *New York 2140*, but also in other works such as Lauren Beukes's inventive animal-familiar novel *Zoo City* (2010), James Patterson's all-humans-vs.-all-animals thriller *Zoo* (2012), and Karen Joy Fowler's quasi-science-fictional, gut-wrenching *We Are All Completely Beside Ourselves* (2013). In Ted Chiang's spellbinding 'The Great Silence' (2015), narrated by a parrot, a rumination on the Fermi Paradox – our ongoing inability to detect any signs of alien life, suggesting that civilisations all die out before they create the sort of Galactic Empire that SF tells us is the human destiny – becomes a sad rumination instead on the Great Silence of the many companion species on Earth we have driven to extinction: 'Hundreds of years ago, my kind was so plentiful that the Rio Abajo forest resounded with our voices. Now we're almost gone. Soon this rainforest may be as silent as the rest of the universe' (Chiang 2015).

Likewise, in Chiang's utterly haunting novella 'Exhalation' (2008), a non-human civilisation with very human cognition must confront the fact that it is simply and irrevocably doomed to total disappearance. Chiang's characters in that story are artificially intelligent robots, whose kinaesthetic and mental operations depend on a complex system of pneumatic switches, valves, and tubes. The robots live inside some sort of sealed chromium canister, which is filled with pressurised argon gas; thus they can speak literally, not figuratively, about reaching 'the edge of the world' (Chiang 2010, 744). As far as the robots can tell they are the only life forms that exist. They discover that time appears to be slowing down; rituals that used to take precisely one hour to perform now take longer, all over their world. What they discover is that the problem is not time, but themselves: their apprehension of time is changing as the atmospheric differential inside their heads (which gives them movement and consciousness) equalises with the pressure outside. They further realise that there is no possible fix for this condition; because they are permanently trapped inside the canister, there is no way for them to repressurise it, no way for them to reverse entropy and turn back time. 'Which is why I have written this account,' Chiang's narrator tells us; he hopes that the records he leaves behind will inspire the visitors to the canister to understand what happened, and, through the power of the written word, make his people live again, if only in the imagination. 'Though I am long dead as you read this, explorer, I offer to you a valediction. Contemplate the marvel that is existence, and rejoice that you are able to do so. I feel I have the right to tell you this because, as I am inscribing these words, I am doing the same' (Chiang 2010: 756).

There has been a spate of similarly cataclysmic novels about utterly ruined futures of one kind or another. These range from Ben H. Winters's *The Last Policeman* trilogy (2012–14), which details the last days of humanity in anticipation of the asteroid strike that will wipe out all life, to Emily St. John Mandel's acclaimed *Station Eleven* (2014) about life in a collapsed America among the handful of survivors of a plague, and N. K. Jemisin's Hugo-award-winning *The Fifth Season* (2015), which describes the cataclysmic downfall of a civilisation on another world as a result of a cyclical climatological event. Neal Stephenson's cosmic *Seveneves* (2016) is perhaps especially noteworthy in this category for its unforgettable opening line, which wonderfully captures the dark mood of the zeitgeist: 'The Moon blew up without warning and for no apparent reason' (Stephenson 2016: 3) – though it is in its own way also surprisingly optimistic, given the unrelenting scope of the catastrophe the Moon's destruction unleashes on the human race. As with Chiang's 'Exhalation', such books frequently avoid the techno-miracle that can save humanity in the nick of time, and kill off most or all of the planet, daring us to find philosophical or aesthetic consolation in the face of the inevitability of our own species extinction.

Other ecologically minded writers have cut more of a middle path, of course, pulling back from the blank necro-future of human extinction towards the nearer term. Paolo Bacigalupi, for instance, one of the best new writers to emerge during the 2000s, has written two excellent novels about adaptation to the new climate normal, *The Wind-Up Girl* (2010) and *The Water Knife* (2015), as well as an equally excellent short story collection *Pump Six* (2008), all of which envision human societies struggling to adapt to the new scarcity, miseries, and investment opportunities brought about by the collapse of the climate and energy paradigms that made twentieth-century technoculture possible. Robert Charles Wilson's *Julian Comstock: A Story of 22nd-Century America* (2009) **[8.1]** combines, as Bacigalupi does, the dread of climate change with the dread of the loss of the carbon-based fuels that have made technological modernity possible. The people of 2172 remember the twentieth century dyspeptically as the 'Efflorescence of Oil' (Wilson 2009: 30). The word 'efflorescence' describes the evaporation of water that leaves behind a thin layer of salty detritus, the remains of our own twentieth- and twenty-first-century lives: the hardship and dislocation of global economic collapse, the inscrutable plastic junk that litters their countryside, their myths that man once walked on the Moon, a generally ruined world. William Gibson's remarkable time-travel thriller *The Peripheral* (2014) has an especially dark take on this kind of speculation; the survivors on the other side of the multi-pronged apocalypse call it

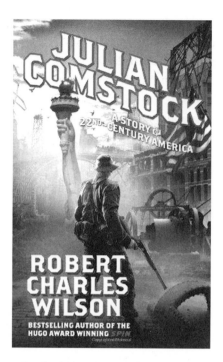

Figure 8.1 Cover for the 2009 edition of Robert Charles Wilson's *Julian Comstock: A Story of 22nd-Century America*.

the Jackpot (because *they* hit it, even if the rest of us did not). These are stories about innovation, resilience, and adaptability that nonetheless put a ceiling on what is achievable post–climate-change, and that even at their most optimistic tend to depressively place our moment as a high-water mark for human civilisation that will end soon, that perhaps has already begun to end in ways we are only just coming to realise.

Other stories sidestep the paradigm of realistic prediction altogether in favour of metaphorical or allegorical confrontation with the weirdness of the postnormal future. China Miéville, in conversation with Mark Bould, noted in 2016 that the late 1990s and early 2000s phenomenon of the 'New Weird' – transgenre stories which are neither clearly fantasy nor clearly science fictional, which partially harken back to the 'weird tales' of writers such as H. P. Lovecraft – now looks less like a surrealist, symbolic response to the anti-globalisation activism that started in the 1999 Seattle protests and much more like a very literal anticipation of a coming world of disruption and transformation caused by climate change (Bould 2016: 17). Paradigmatic New Weird writers include M. John Harrison, Steph Swainston, and Kelly Link. Miéville himself probably remains the most distinguished practitioner working in this mode, even though he himself has lost some interest in the New Weird as an aesthetic category. Perhaps the post-2001 SF writer most certain to be considered canonical in coming decades, Miéville has produced wide-ranging work that stands atop the period, from horror-fantasy (the New Crobuzon books, 2000–4) to hybridic noir (*The City and the City*, 2009) to space opera (*Embassytown*, 2011) to madcap apocalyptic romp (*Kraken*, 2010).

Another exemplary New Weird writer, Jeff VanderMeer, long known among genre fans as a writer and editor (often with his wife Ann), seems to have crossed over into the highest tier of global recognition with his acclaimed Southern Reach trilogy, *Annihilation*, *Authority*, and *Acceptance*, all released in 2014 and adapted for film by Alex Garland in 2017. The Southern Reach trilogy depicts an unexplained ontological transformation in Florida that has caused the region to be 'lost' to the ordinary workings of global capitalism; the first book begins with the inauguration of the twelfth expedition into the Southern Reach to try to learn its sequence, missions that inevitably result in the deaths of all involved either within the Reach itself or in their acquisition of a highly aggressive cancer upon leaving the zone. The production of the image of a cursed place, a haunted ecology that has transformed in ways we cannot understand or ameliorate and which is now making us all sick, is a pitch-perfect example of how the New Weird is not so much 'weird' as it is an intensification and literalisation of the changes that are already happening around us daily.

The Singularity (and Empire)

The above list of texts, wholly inadequate to the scale of contemporary science-fictional cultural production, sketches out the emergence of a canon of SF dealing directly or indirectly with climate change, naming only a tiny sliver of the many texts that exemplify the darkly apocalyptic futurological mood of the period. Climate disaster and its attendant crisis produce a sort of interpretive black hole in 2000s-era science fiction. The transformations that will be caused by climate change are so over-awing, in the near term, as to threaten to swamp any other futurological possibility. In the 2000s environmental critique has become a crucial component of work in the humanities generally, becoming a part of the social justice mission alongside race, gender, class, and sexuality – but this is especially true of SF studies, where the idea of the future that is so central to SF now seems overdetermined by environmental crisis. Ecological crisis hangs over the genre now in the way that, at an earlier moment, the spectre of nuclear war did – the centre of gravity for many lines of speculation.

Peter Frase's essential *Four Futures: Life after Capitalism* (2016) offers a useful framework to discipline this impulse so as to allow climate change to exist in conversation with other futurological concerns. To the opposition between abundance (which we once had, but which now seems lost) and scarcity (which now seems inevitable and permanent) he adds a new dimension, the binary between equality and hierarchy. This produces a classic semiotic square, with four options: abundance–equality (the *Star Trek* future that climate change has ruined); scarcity–hierarchy (exterminism, the zombie future); scarcity–equality (the constrained but ecotopian future, something perhaps like Le Guin's anarcho-socialist masterpiece *The Dispossessed* from 1974); and abundance–hierarchy (rentism, or the utopia of elite tech billionaires who hoover up all the intellectual property that the mass of the population then rents back). Indeed, the one major futurological competitor to the disaster of climate change takes place entirely on that spectrum between abundance–equality and abundance–hierarchy. It is most commonly called the Singularity.

The Singularity, broadly stated, holds that we are on the cusp of a period of exponential social and technological transformation that will be fuelled by the advent of self-augmenting artificial intelligence. The Singularity originated in the 1980s cyberpunk of writers such as Vernor Vinge and is perhaps more popularly known in vulgar negative form in rise-of-the-robots-style movie fantasies such as *Terminator* and *The Matrix*. The concept has tremendous currency among tech capitalists such as Ray Kurzweil, Peter Thiel, and Elon Musk, many of whom have publicly stated that they believe the Singularity is imminent. Some of them have gone further, suggesting that they believe it is possible or even probable that the Singularity has in fact already happened, and we are all actually living inside a computer simulation in some unknowable deep-futurological context, after artificial intelligence has reduced the cost of computing power effectively to zero.

The central question of the Singularity becomes precisely that of equality vs. hierarchy, in two senses: first, the by-now quite familiar question of whether the emergent artificial intelligences of the Singularity will have much interest in upholding human values or serving human ends; and second, the often repressed question of whether the billionaires are going to share any of the bounty of the Singularity with the rest of us, and at what price. At its extreme the rentism of the abundance–hierarchy future squeezes back into a version of exterminism, if, as in the early twentieth century, the explosion of technological capability means that the rich eugenically, genocidally decide that perhaps they no longer need the rest of us at all.

Charles Stross's *Accelerando* (2005) **[8.2]** is almost certainly the best literary treatment of the Singularity, structured as it is by a running joke in which a hapless narrator fruitlessly attempts to prognosticate the exact moment the coming Singularity will soon happen, even as mind-body uploading becomes commonplace, functional immortality becomes a given, and the world becomes populated by digital clones and cosmic simulations. The great punchline at the end – a true gut punch – is that in Stross's view the Singularity is not the moment the machines become self-aware, but the moment the corporations do – and the fascinating latter half of *Accelerando* sees the spiralling out of the corporate Singularity as the machines begin trading incomprehensible financial products with each other at fantastically inhuman speeds, crashing the human economy and causing humanity to actually abandon the Earth as the machines convert more and more of the mass of the planet into themselves. Here at least Stross did get ahead of the curve; the corporations didn't manage to crash the global economy through derivatives trading until three years after the book was published, in 2008.

Figure 8.2 Cover for the 2005 edition of Charles Stross's *Accelerando*, published by Orbit.

Financial speculation has crossed over with speculative fiction in other works as well, including Robinson's *New York 2140*, Richard K. Morgan's *Market Forces* and *Altered Carbon,* and Francis Spufford's hybridic novel *Red Plenty* (which marries contemporary high-speed financial computing to the planned economy of the Soviet Union). William Gibson's 2000s trilogy *Pattern Recognition* (2003), *Spook Country* (2007), and *Zero History* (2010) all revolve in different ways around the intersection of cutting edge technology, global finance, internet culture, and the military-industrial-entertainment complex, loosely focalised around the machinations of billionare Hubertus Bigend and his cool-hunting marketing agency Blue Ant. Gibson's technosublime vision is one of the strongest articulations of the dark side of the internet age, in which network technology has proved as much an asset as a challenge to the surveillance state. The trilogy's treatment of the war on terror and its intersections with the technological advancements of the period – especially in *Spook Country* – and its tracing of the links between seemingly autonomous realms of commerce, technology, and statecraft marks it as a key cultural document of the Bush-era US. The books also crystallise Gibson's new intellectual project of seeking to predict the present in a time when, as one of his characters in *Pattern Recognition* puts it, 'Fully imagined cultural futures were the luxury of another day, one in which "now" was of some greater duration. For us, of course, things can change so abruptly, so violently, so profoundly, that futures like our grandparents' have insufficient "now" to stand on. We have no future because our present is too volatile' (Gibson 2003: 57). A pithier Gibsonian articulation of the collapse between future and present has circulated widely on the internet and become proverbial, an apt description of this moment in global culture: 'The future is here – it just isn't very evenly distributed.'

The use of autonomous drones in warfare, once purely science fiction, likewise has become a familiar component of real-life warfare, even if our science fictions have generally tended to stay focused on human-piloted, manned ships, and human crews in military SF. These drones still require human decision-making, but they are rapidly moving towards autonomy (whether that autonomy would be described as genuinely artificially intelligent or 'merely' algorithmic). The most significant extended treatment of drone warfare in literary SF is probably still Iain M. Banks's Culture series, which began in the 1990s and sadly ended with the novelist's death in 2013. The Culture also distinguishes itself as the most dedicated contemporary attempt to imagine a Star Trekian post-scarcity society: abundance–equality, in Frase's terms. Of course, this is somewhat paradoxical. Why does the Culture fight so many wars, and police its boundaries and limits so aggressively, if it is supposed to be a paradise? To the SF critic of the 2000s this is less of a paradox than it might initially seem. The utopia-focused critical paradigm of an earlier generation of scholars strongly gave way in the 2000s to an 'imperial turn' focusing on the ways in which SF has grown out of and reinforced, rather than challenged, the racist and militarist violence of the nation state. Istvan Csicsery-Ronay's article 'Science Fiction and Empire' applied the neo-Marxism of Michael Hardt and Antonio Negri to SF's longstanding dream of 'a single global technological regime' (Csicsery-Ronay 2003: 231) – a dream seemingly achieved in the US's open declaration, during the Bush administration, of a new global juridical regime ultimately subject to its military authority. John Rieder's *Colonialism and the Emergence of Science Fiction* traced this mutual imbrication between science fiction and colonialist-imperialist fantasy at the dawn of the emergence of the genre, and rapidly became a similarly essential reference among scholars.

Despite the importance of this moment, however, the wars in Iraq and Afghanistan have proved far less important as context for 2000s-era literary science fiction than science fiction film, television, and video games of the same period. The attacks of 9/11 – perhaps for similar reasons – have similarly figured much less importantly as a key event in prose SF (although see Douglas Lain's 2015 anthology, *In the Shadow of the Towers: Speculative Fiction in a Post-9/11 World*), while in films and television of the same period it has proved ubiquitous and unavoidable. 'In Spirit', a Hugo-nominated time-travel novella by Pat Forde published in *Analog* in 2002, tackled 9/11 directly. The PATRIOT Act, and fears of government creep, have proved much more crucial as a theme in literary SF; the Bush administration brought about tremendous interest in visions of dystopian governance, of which Suzanne Collins's *The Hunger Games* is probably the most famous, but Cory Doctorow's *Little Brother* (2009), Vinge's *Rainbows End* (2006), Ken MacLeod's *The Execution Channel* (2007), Max Barry's *Jennifer Government* (2003), M. T. Anderson's *Feed* (2002), Dave Eggers's social-media thriller *The Circle* (2013), and Jennifer Egan's *A Visit from the Goon Squad* (2010) are also standout entries in an endlessly popular subgenre.

The Bush administration also inspired a spate of alternate history novels from mainstream literary writers, such as Michael Chabon's *The Yiddish Policemen's Union* (2007), Paul Auster's *Man in the Dark* (2008), or

Philip Roth's *The Plot Against America* (2004), among others, especially the provocative work of Israeli novelist Lavie Tidhar in *Osama* (2011) and *A Man Lies Dreaming* (2014). The most novel and noteworthy of these alternate histories may be those that realign the presumed point of identification away from the US, like Matt Ruff's *The Mirage* (2013), which imagines Christian terrorists attacking a skyscraper in Baghdad, ushering in a military response from the United Arab States, or Abdourahman A. Waberi's *In the United States of Africa* (2008), which imagines a prosperous Africa and poverty-stricken Europe and US without ever asserting any concrete point of divergence between their history and ours.

This detour from the ostensibly utopian alternative to climate disaster into the shockingly adjacent world of mass surveillance and killer robots shows once again how fragile Singularitarian fantasy is. Even beyond the question of the potentially dystopian structures the Singularity might produce – to the extent that a given Singularity fantasy allows human beings to survive as discrete individuals at all (in whatever form) – it raises important questions about whether humans have an essential nature that it would be wrong (either practically or ethically) to edit or alter.

Cory Doctorow's *Down and Out in the Magic Kingdom* (2003) remains perhaps the most balanced and complete treatment of the Singularity in fiction, tackling everything from post-scarcity to novel finance to ubiquitous surveillance to functional immortality. *Down and Out* sees the emergence of a reputation economy, called Whuffie, after technological innovation has rendered the traditional economy obsolete. Its protagonists maintain Disney World for fun and Whuffie, debating whether and how to update the rides – a debate that turns deadly serious as the main character's computer implants become damaged and he is no longer able to continually 'backup' his memories and personality in the event of death. As with Stross's Singularity, in *Down and Out* the moment of the 'transhuman' constantly withdraws, and eludes any specific definition, prediction, or demarcation – but our rapid real-life technological explosion and previously unheard of capacities for prosthetic and genetic modification of the body make transhuman fantasy seem less like a flight of fancy and more like the premeditation of a future that is rapidly approaching.

The Classics and the Canon

Although the primary brief of this chapter is 'new paradigms', alongside climate change and the Singularity there has been ongoing interest in many of the 'old paradigms' of science fiction as well, among them (of course) the most classic milieu of SF, space opera. Ann Leckie's Ancillary series – *Ancillary Justice* (2013), *Ancillary Sword* (2014), and *Ancillary Mercy* (2015) – may be the most innovative and most celebrated new space opera milieu to come along in some time, centred on an artificially intelligent ship from the Radchaai space empire (which does not use gender pronouns, allowing for interesting social commentary on gender norms to permeate the narrative alongside the critique of empire and war). The popular Expanse novels (2011–) of James S.A. Corey (a pseudonym of Daniel Abraham and Ty Franck), recently adapted to television on the Syfy Channel, do space opera in the more limited space of the solar system, bringing a realistic aesthetic to traditional space fantasy through focus on the class struggle in and among the extra-planetary colonies. Other extremely popular space operas of the period include franchises from the 1990s that have extended into the post-2001 period, such as Lois McMaster Bujold's Vorkosigan saga and Banks's Culture series, as well as new properties like John Scalzi's Old Man's War series (2005–), Ken MacLeod's Engines of Light series (2000–), Alastair Reynolds's Revelation Space series (2000–), M. John Harrison's *Light* (2002), and Peter Watts's *Blindsight* (2006). Many of Charles Stross's novels have recognisably space-operatic settings, such as his stand-alone novel *Glasshouse* (2006) (which takes place in a twenty-seventh-century culture reminiscent of the end of *Accelerando*, which experimentally seeks to recreate the conditions of twentieth-century life) or his Saturn's Children series (2008–). I have already mentioned Robinson's *2312* and *Aurora,* Stephenson's *Seveneves,* and Miéville's *Embassytown* in the context of their environmental themes, but they are worthy of mention here too. Many such contemporary space opera narratives, including nearly all of the ones I have suggested here save *Embassytown,* include strong Singularitarian elements as well.

Another incredibly significant space opera of the period is Cixin Liu's Three-Body Problem series **[8.3]**, published in China beginning in 2006 and translated into English in 2014–16. Aside from its own

Figure 8.3 Cover for the Chinese edition of Cixin Liu's *Three-Body Problem (or Dark Forest)*.

ample merits, the trilogy marks a breakthrough moment for Chinese SF in the West (the Three-Body Problem series was even endorsed by Barack Obama as he left the American Presidency in January 2017). The first book in the series, *The Three-Body Problem* (2006/2014), depicts a SETI-style Chinese scientific collective that makes contact with an alien race living in the Alpha Centauri system. The first contact is with a Trisolaran pacifist who warns the scientists not to attempt to make contact again, as her civilisation is warlike and dangerous. However, one of the Chinese scientists, deeply embittered by her political persecution and by her horror of humankind's destruction of the environment, pursues contact anyway, leading to an alien invasion narrative that continues in *The Dark Forest* (2008/2015) and *Death's End* (2010/2016). *Death's End* in particular expands the story to a universal, quasi-theological scale, in a narrative that is reminiscent of the cosmic scope of Olaf Stapledon in *Star Maker* – becoming a deeply philosophical rumination on the nature of existence in the shadow of universal extinction. The translator of the first and third books in the series, Ken Liu, also published an anthology of Chinese short fiction titled *Invisible Planets* in 2016 that brought more attention to Chinese authors beyond just Cixin Liu.

Naturally other writers have continued to work in other classic science-fictional paradigms, perhaps most centrally time travel and other modes of imagining historical difference. Connie Willis won the Hugo award in 2011 for her two-part time-travel novel *Blackout/All Clear*, the same year Stephen King published *11/22/63* about the Kennedy assassination; these were only two standouts of the many time-travel novels published during the period (see especially Audrey Niffenegger's *The Time Traveler's Wife* of 2003 and Lauren Beukes's *The Shining Girls* of 2013). Iain Banks's non-Culture novel *Transition* (2009) deals with multiple timelines, as did Neal Stephenson's lengthy but brilliant *Anathem* (2008). Kate Atkinson's *Life after Life* (2013) – which, like many of the other time-travel novels listed here, was not marketed as genre SF but as mainstream literature – detailed the many reincarnations of a woman who slowly becomes aware she is living her life over and over again, ultimately leading her to attempt to assassinate Adolf Hitler. A similarly quasi-science-fictional reincarnation plot structures Jo Walton's *My Real Children* (2014) and Claire North's *The First Fifteen Lives of Harry August* (2014). Ted Chiang has risen in prominence to become one of the best-known, best-loved, and most widely respected writers of short SF in the period – especially after the release of *Arrival* in 2016, based on his 1998 short story 'Story of Your Life', which also lent its name to his first collection. His recent stories have similarly opened the door on alternative worlds: of time travel in 'What's Expected of Us' (2005) or 'The Merchant and the Alchemist's Gate' (2007); of novel cognitive improvements in 'Liking What You See: A Documentary' (2002) or 'The Truth of Fact, The Truth of Feeling' (2013); and even of worlds where the Singularity has happened in 'The Lifecycle of Software Objects' (2010) or where religion is an empirical, measurable fact of the universe in 'Hell Is the Absence of God' (2001).

This ongoing interest in – one might even say hunger for – historical difference suggests that, despite the imperial turn, the utopian approach to science fiction is not dead after all. Indeed, much imperial-turn

criticism contains within itself utopian anti-racist and anti-war ambitions, and the utopian school of SF criticism may well have had its
greatest articulation in the 2000s period in the publication of Fredric
Jameson's magnum opus, *Archaeologies of the Future: The Desire Called
Utopia and Other Science Fictions* (2005).

Alongside these earnest attempts at constructing and innovating
classic SF structures, the period has also seen several noteworthy metafictional dissections of the traditional assumptions of the genre, as in John
Scalzi's *Redshirts* (2012), set in a pastiche of *Star Trek* in which some of
the famously endangered red-shirted support staff discover they are the
disposable extras in a television series, or Charles Yu's *How to Live Safely in
a Science Fictional Universe* (2010), in which a character also named Charles
Yu (a time machine mechanic) navigates a grandfather paradox amidst a
backdrop of classic SF narratives. Adam Roberts's *The Thing Itself* (2015)
uses John Carpenter's *The Thing* as the springboard for a consideration of
Kantian philosophy as a counter to Lovecraftian dread. Roberts's *Yellow
Blue Tibia* (2009), set among SF writers in Soviet Russia, is an unexpect-
edly moving rumination on the transcendent possibilities of the genre.
Ernest Cline's *Ready Player One* (2011) **[8.4]** is a cyberpunk novel set in
a near-future culture that has become a nostalgic soup of 1980s pop culture references – a troublingly accurate prediction of mid-2010s reboot
culture. Miéville's *Kraken* takes that sort of nostalgia and transforms it to
the level of an ontology, depicting a universe in which all the beloved
science-fictional, fantasy, and horror stories are happening simultaneously,
in the context of the multiple apocalypses.

These revisionist science fictions are the creative component of a
period of canon-formation and canon-revision within the genre, which
has seen not only the usual sorts of reprints, re-releases, and prestige
editions (like the Library of America's reprints of Philip K. Dick and
Ursula K. Le Guin), but also new attempts to formalise science-fictional
canons in the SF Masterworks imprint, as well as major retrospective
anthologies such as *The Wesleyan Book of Science Fiction* (2010) and *The
Big Book of Science Fiction* (2016). A similar movement is under way
critically; the 2000s have seen the release of major critical handbooks
from Routledge, Oxford and Cambridge University Presses, and Black-
well, devoted to the formalisation of academic approaches to SF. Also

Figure 8.4 Cover for the 2011 edition of Ernest Cline's *Ready Player One*.

significant were the 'Modern Masters of Science Fiction' at University of Illinois Press, devoted to single-author monographs of major writers in the genre, and the expansion of lists devoted to SF at Wesleyan University Press, Liverpool University Press, University Press of Mississippi, and elsewhere. Monographs and edited collections devoted to SF have proved a reliable bet, in part due to their crossover potential in the non-academic fan base, resulting in a proliferation of available criticism and a fruitful explosion of methods, approaches, and focuses.

One of the most important inflection points in genre history has to do precisely with this question of canonicity. While women and writers of colour have always been a part of SF, the 2000s period has marked a new diversity in the genre that has utterly exploded the always-false stereotype of straight white male writers writing for a straight white male fanbase. This is especially true of writers of colour, who in previous decades might have been represented in a canonical sense primarily by two African American authors: Samuel R. Delany, who returned to science fiction after a long absence with *Through the Valley of the Nest of Spiders* (2012); and Octavia E. Butler, whose last novel, the science-fictionalised vampire novel *Fledgling,* appeared shortly before her death in 2005, though a posthumous collection of two previously unpublished works appeared as the eBook *Unexpected Stories* in 2014. In the 2000s the ranks of black writers of SF have been swelled by newcomers such as Nalo Hopkinson, Nnedi Okorafor, Sofia Samatar, N. K. Jemisin, Nisi Shawl, and McArthur-grant-awardee Colson Whitehead, among many others, writing from both African American and African Afrofuturist perspectives. While some of these fit squarely into traditional science fiction paradigms – like Whitehead's *Zone One* (2011), a zombie novel, or Whitehead's *The Underground Railroad* (2016) and Shawl's *Everfair* (2016), both alternate history novels – others offer a more syncretic mix of Western technoscience with Africanist or Caribbean religion, as in Hopkinson's *Midnight Robber* (2000) or Okorafor's *Who Fears Death* (2010), *Lagoon* (2014), and 'Binti' (2015).

Critical and creative interest in Afrofuturism has also sparked growing interest in Latin futurism, techno-Orientalism, postcolonial science fiction, and indigenous futurism as paradigms for SF, the last of which was the subject of a special issue of the journal *Extrapolation* in 2016. Science fiction from non-white and non-European perspectives has also been the subject of a boom period in short fiction anthologisation, including the *Dark Matter* books edited by Sheree R. Thomas and the *Apex Book of World SF* series edited by Lavie Tidhar, as well as *So Long Been Dreaming, Long Hidden, Mothership,* and *Octavia's Brood,* a collection of social justice science fiction inspired by Octavia Butler. *Terra Incognita: New Short Speculative Stories from Africa,* edited by Nerine Dorman, appeared in 2015, while the anthology *Iraq +100: Stories from a Century after the Invasion,* edited by Hassan Blasim, signalled a new exploration of SF tropes by writers from the Middle East and its diaspora. 'Gulf Futurism', a term coined by writer and artist Sophia al-Maria, whose work is saturated in SF, has had significant global traction in the 2010s.

Unfortunately, the new recognition of talent in the field has not proved uncontroversial. As in many other arenas of culture ranging from the so-called 'Gamergate' movement in video games to the revanchist political coalitions that elected Trump and voted for Brexit in 2016, a backlash movement comprised largely of straight white men has arisen to challenge the new diversity of SF. These 'Sad Puppies' – who take their name from a post mocking an ad from the Society for the Prevention of Cruelty to Animals – claim to be taking SF back for its original fans, against a new cohort who (they feel) has been manipulating awards and prestige in the genre for political purposes. Beginning in 2013 and sharply intensifying in 2015, this group has focused its attention primarily on the Hugo Awards, named for Hugo Gernsback, which choose the best SF works of the year using an unusual two-stage voting process: the nominating stage is open to all, while the final selection stage is voted on only by registered Worldcon members (mostly attendees of that year's Worldcon convention), using a ranked ballot. By coordinating their nomination slates, the Sad Puppies were able to create shortlists comprised mostly or entirely of right-wing, white writers, sometimes with profiles quite marginal to the larger body of science fiction.

The Sad Puppies (along with an even more right-wing group, the Rabid Puppies, coordinated by American white supremacist Vox Day) were 'defeated' in 2015 and 2016 primarily through another quirk in the Hugo's voting system: the 'No Award' line, which allows voters to 'rank' works below the Award line. In 2015 and 2016 many awards went either to the nominees who were not Sad Puppy-endorsed or, in cases where the Sad Puppies had managed to nominate their entire slate, to 'No Award'. Meanwhile Worldcon is attempting to change its voting system to prevent further manipulation (changes to the Worldcon rules must be endorsed by two consecutive Worldcon fan assemblies, hence the delay). Still, even if their susceptibility to coordination has been fixed, the sudden eruption of 'No Award' after 'No Award' in the list of

Hugo winners will always record the strange politics of this moment in SF history.

Conclusions

Any 'literary history' tackling the early twenty-first century will be challenged by the breakdown of traditional publishing categories – including, in extremis, the physical form of 'the book' as a material object one owns, as opposed to a digital download one 'rents' from Amazon or Apple and reads on a device, subject to emendation or revocation at any time – as well as by shifts in consumption habits towards digital platforms that have made prose fiction, if not quite obsolete, certainly less hegemonic as a media form than it once was. These tendencies seem especially disruptive for the study of SF as a genre. Many books that in another era would have been clearly SF are now marketed, branded, and critiqued as if they were not SF but mainstream literary fiction – as, for instance, David Foster Wallace's paradigm-shifting *Infinite Jest* (1996), which was rarely described as science fiction despite taking place in a dystopian near future filled with world-transformative technological innovations, or David Mitchell's *Cloud Atlas* (2004), Kazuo Ishiguro's *Never Let Me Go* (2005), Gary Shteyngart's *Super Sad True Love Story* (2010), or Don DeLillo's *Zero K* (2016). What Bruce Sterling once called 'slipstream' fiction is now hard to distinguish from the bodies of either genre fiction or literary fiction, perhaps befitting an era in which the whole world has become SF, as J. G. Ballard once said. Science fiction has become respectable enough to merit annual collections in the 'Best American' imprint, and even a special issue of *The New Yorker* entirely devoted to SF in 2012 (perhaps most notable for another slipstream work, Junot Díaz's postcolonial zombie story 'Monstro').

Likewise, in the wake of J. K. Rowling's transformation of the culture industry it has become difficult to draw lines between 'literary' works and the form of the 'young adult' novel, which are increasingly marketed to and read by adults as well and which frequently take up science-fictional themes, most notably in the blockbuster *Hunger Games* franchise by Suzanne Collins, but also in similar series such as *Divergent, The Scorch Trials,* and more. The successful self-published works by Andy Weir ('The

Egg' in 2009 and *The Martian* in 2011) and Cory Doctorow are only the tip of a vast iceberg of self-published original and derivative (often fan-fictional) prose texts that are using the near-zero cost of digital publishing to sidestep traditional publishers altogether. This is a tendency that has not only transformed the production of fictional science fiction but also vastly proliferated and democratised its critical apparatus as well.

A parallel bleeding at the margins is happening on the level of media form: trends in science fiction as a genre are increasingly hard to discuss without reference to the sorts of visual SF media that have become global phenomena, in many cases viewed and discussed in numbers that utterly swamp prose fiction. This is true not only of the sort of franchise block-buster SF that has dominated box offices since *Star Wars* (1977) – includ-ing the return of Star Wars as an ongoing concern in *The Force Awakens* (2015) and the first of the Star Wars anthology spinoffs *Rogue One* (2016), but also the Marvel Cinematic Universe (2008–), *Avatar* (2009–), and so on – but also of the increasingly sophisticated and intellectual SF film and television that has emerged with the sharp decrease in the cost of digital film effects and the proliferation of platforms like HBO, Amazon Prime, and Netflix. Works in that field include *Primer* (2004), *District 9* (2009), the early seasons of *Battlestar Galactica* (2004–9), *The Expanse* (2015–), *Westworld* (2016) and *Arrival* (2016) **[8.5]**. The last of these was based on a prose work by Ted Chiang, which neatly makes the point that SF cannot be broken up by media form without losing some perspective on what the genre is now doing and how it is doing it. Storytelling forms such as the video game (perhaps most notably the *Mass Effect* series) and the comic (such as Robert Kirkman's *The Walking Dead* (2003–) or Brian K. Vaughan and Fiona Staples's acclaimed *Saga* (2012–) and even the podcast (for example, *LifeAfter* and *The Outer Reach*, both in 2016) have become significant ways in which to tell contemporary science-fictional stories. In addition to the bleeding between genres discussed above, firm bound-aries between SF and the mainstream, or between prose SF and other media forms, seem more and more difficult to sustain.

Still, the intense, ongoing fight over the Hugos shows that there is still something *special* about prose, the place where SF began, and the place where it still finds its most ambitious and elaborate long-form articula-tions. Something about prose SF still calls to us, even as readership num-bers and demographics transform, and even as the short story marketplace

Figure 8.5 Still from *Arrival*, 2016.

has largely bottomed out altogether. As assumptions about genre specificity, the materiality of the book, and the independence of the written word from other forms of communication continue to flux, prose SF stubbornly soldiers on, and with it the tradition of science fiction storytelling that began with Shelley, Poe, Verne, and Wells, 200 years ago.

References

Atwood, Margaret (2009), 'Time Capsule Found on the Dead Planet', *The Guardian* (25 September), https://www.theguardian.com/books/2009/sep/26/margaret-atwood-mini-science-fiction. Last accessed 9 February 2017.

Bould, Mark (2016), 'Not Just Some Viggo Mortensen of Desolated Left Politics: An Interview with China Miéville', *Paradoxa* 28: Global Weirding, pp. 15–40.

Chiang, Ted (2010), 'Exhalation' [2008], in *The Wesleyan Anthology of Science Fiction*, ed. Arthur Evans, Istvan Csicsery-Ronay, Joan Gordon, Veronica Hollinger, Rob Latham, and Carol McGuirk. Middletown, CT: Wesleyan University Press, pp. 742–56.

————— (2015), 'The Great Silence', e-flux (8 May): http://supercommunity.e-flux.com/texts/the-great-silence/ Last accessed 9 February 2017.

Crutzen, Paul (2002), 'Geology of Mankind', *Nature* 415 (31 January), p. 23.

Csicsery-Ronay, Istvan (2003), 'Science Fiction and Empire', *Science Fiction Studies* 30: 2, pp. 231–45.

Flood, Alison (2009), 'Kim Stanley Robinson: science fiction's realist', *The Guardian* (11 November), https://www.theguardian.com/books/2009/nov/10/kim-stanley-robinson-science-fiction-realist Last accessed 9 February 2017

Frase, Peter (2016), *Four Futures: Life after Capitalism*. London: Verso.

Gibson, William (2003), *Pattern Recognition*. New York: Berkley Books.

Monroe, Rob (2016), 'Note on Reaching the Annual Low Point', Scribbs Institute of Oceanography (23 September). https://scripps.ucsd.edu/programs/keelingcurve/2016/09/23/note-on-reaching-the-annual-low-point/ Last accessed 9 February 2017

Robinson, Kim Stanley (2012), *2312*. New York: Tor.

Sardar, Ziauddin (2010), 'Welcome to Postnormal Times', *Futures* 42: 5, pp. 435–508.

Stephenson, Neal (2016), *Seveneves*. New York: Harper Collins.

Stross, Charles (2016), 'Reality is Broken', antipope.org (14 August). http://www.antipope.org/charlie/blog-static/2016/08/reality-is-broken-1.html Last accessed 9 February 2017

Wilson, Robert Charles (2009), *Julian Comstock: A Story of 22nd-Century America*. New York: Tor Books.

What to Read Next

Margaret Atwood, *Oryx and Crake* (New York: Anchor, 2004).

Ted Chiang, *Stories of Your Life and Others* (New York: Vintage, 2016).

N. K. Jemisin, *The Fifth Season* (New York: Orbit, 2015).

Ann Leckie, *Ancillary Justice* (New York: Orbit, 2013).

Cixin Liu, *The Three-Body Problem*. Translated by Ken Liu (New York: Tor, 2014).

China Miéville, *The City & The City* (New York: Del Rey, 2010).

Kim Stanley Robinson, *Aurora* (New York: Orbit, 2015).

Notes on Contributors

Mark Bould is Reader in Film and Literature at UWE Bristol. He co-edits the *Science Fiction Film and Television* journal and the *Studies in Global Science Fiction* monograph series. His most recent books are *Solaris* (2014), *SF Now* (2014) and *Africa SF* (2013).

Gerry Canavan is an assistant professor of twentieth- and twenty-first-century literature at Marquette University, specialising in science fiction. He is the co-editor of *Green Planets: Ecology and Science Fiction* and *The Cambridge Companion to American Science Fiction*. His first monograph, *Octavia E. Butler*, appeared in 2016.

Caroline Edwards is Senior Lecturer in Modern and Contemporary Literature at Birkbeck, University of London. She is author of *Fictions of the Not Yet: Utopian Times in the 21st Century British Novel* (forthcoming) and has published articles in *Telos*, *Modern Fiction Studies*, *Textual Practice*, *Contemporary Literature*, *Subjectivity*, and the *New Statesman*.

Arthur B. Evans is a professor emeritus of French at DePauw University and managing editor of the journal *Science Fiction Studies*. He has published numerous books and articles on Jules Verne and early French science fiction, including the award-winning *Jules Verne Rediscovered* (1988). He is also co-editor of *The Wesleyan Anthology of Science*

Fiction (2010) and general editor of the Early Classics of Science Fiction for Wesleyan University Press.

Malisa Kurtz received her PhD in Interdisciplinary Humanities from Brock University. Her research focuses on the intersection of science fiction, globalisation, and postcolonialism. She has published articles in *Paradoxa, Science Fiction Studies*, and *Journal of the Fantastic in the Arts*.

Rob Latham is the author of *Consuming Youth: Vampires, Cyborgs, and the Culture of Consumption* (2002), the editor of *The Oxford Handbook of Science Fiction* (2014) and *Science Fiction Criticism: An Anthology of Essential Writings* (2017), and co-editor of *The Wesleyan Anthology of Science Fiction* (2010). In 2013, he received the Thomas D. Clareson Award for Distinguished Service to the Field from the Science Fiction Research Association.

Roger Luckhurst writes on Gothic and science fiction literature and film. He is the author of the cultural history *Science Fiction* (2005) and wrote the British Film Institute Classics on *The Shining* (2013) and *Alien* (2014). He is a professor at Birkbeck, University of London.

Adam Roberts is an award-winning science fiction author of many books including *New Model Army, By Light Alone, Jack Glass* and *The Thing Itself*. He is also a professor of nineteenth-century literature at Royal Holloway, University of London.

Sherryl Vint is Professor of Media and Cultural Studies at the University of California, Riverside, where she directs the Speculative Fiction and Cultures of Science programme. An editor of the journals *Science Fiction Studies* and *Science Fiction Film and Television*, she has published widely on speculative fiction, including, most recently, *Science Fiction and Cultural Theory: A Reader* and *The Walking Med: Zombies and the Medical Image*, co-edited with Lorenzo Servitje.

Picture Credits

Index

Italic page numbers refer to illustrations.

2001: A Space Odyssey (film; 1968) 55, 208

Abbott, Edwin, *Flatland* 48
Abe, Kobo 173
Ace Books (paperback publisher) 134–35, *134, 135*, 160
Ackerman, Forrest J. 12
Adams, John Joseph, *Loosed Upon the World* 212
advances and royalties, authors' 176, 177
Afghanistan 222
African-American writers 9, 78–81, 109–10, 153, 191, 204–5, 229
Afrofuturism 229
Aldiss, Brian W. 9, 13, 105, 146, 154, 163, 164, 168
Alexie, Sherman, *The Lone Ranger and Tonto Fistfight in Heaven* 205
aliens and extraterrestrials 16, 19, 120–22, 124–27, 142–43, 146; *see also* Mars and Martians
Alkon, Paul K. 23, 29, 37–38
Allen, Grant 50–51, 55–56

All-Story Magazine/Weekly 64, 104, 121; *see also Argosy* (magazine)
al-Maria, Sofia 230
Alvim-Correa, Henrique *53*
Amazing Stories (magazine) 15, 33, 102, 103–6, *104*
Amis, Sir Kingsley, *New Maps of Hell* 9, 13
Analog (magazine) 165, *166*, 222
Anderson, M.T., *Feed* 222
Anderson, Poul 136, 159
Angenot, Marc 36
animal extinctions 213
anime and manga 183
anthology publishing 151, 160, 164, 166–69, 174, 188, *189*, 212, 228, 229–230
anthropocene 212–13
Anvil, Christopher 165
Apex Book of World SF (anthologies) 229
apocalypse: *see* end-of-the-world scenarios; post-apocalypse scenarios
Apocalypse Reader, The (anthology) 212

Argosy (magazine) 45, 104, 115; *see also All-Story Magazine/Weekly*

arms races 47, 68, 144

Arnold-Foster, Hugh, *In a Conning Tower* 25

Arrival (film; 2016) 232, *233*

artificial intelligence (AI) 137, 195, 199, 203, 214, 218

Ashbee, C.R., *The Building of Thelema* 74

Asimov, Isaac 114, 127, 130, 174, 176, 200; *The Caves of Steel* 137, 140; *Foundation* series 171, 182; *The Naked Sun* 137; *Robot* series 158, 182; 'Social Science Fiction' 137; Three Laws of Robotics 137

Astounding (magazine) 105, *123*, 127, 133, 135, 138, 158, 159, 161

astronomy 15–16, 17, 19, 22, 32, 53, 87

Atkinson, Kate, *Life After Life* 226

Atlantis (lost world) 16, 119, 121

atomic and nuclear warfare 68, 116, 131, 141–42, 143–47, 148, 183, 197; *see also* post-apocalypse scenarios

Atwood, Margaret 9, 183; *The Handmaid's Tale* 190; *MaddAddam* series 212, 213; 'Time Capsule Found on Dead Planet' 212

Auster, Paul, *Man in the Dark* 222

Australia, as unexplored land 18–19

Avatar (film series; 2009–) 6, 232

awards, literary 172, 190, 203, 215, 226, 230–31, 232

Babbage, Charles 195

Bacigalupi, Paolo 215

Back to the Future (film; 1985) 208

Bacon, Sir Francis 28; *New Atlantis* 16

Bailey, J.O. 12

Ballantine Books (paperback publisher) 134, 135, 158, 167

Ballard, J.G. 9, 154, 162, 169–170, 172, 176, 231; *The Atrocity Exhibition* 162, 168, 178; *The Burning World* 146; *Crash* 175, *175*; *The Drowned World* 146, 162; 'The Terminal Beach' 162; 'The Voices of Time' 162

balloon flight 33, 34, 36

Balzac, Honoré de: *The Centenarian* 32; *The Quest of the Absolute* 32

Banerjee, Anindita 65, 86–87, 90

Banks, Iain M. 198, 199, 221, 224, 226

Bantam Books (paperback publisher) 134

Barnes, Steven 204

Barrows, Gertrude ('Francis Stevens') 114, 121

Barry, Max, *Jennifer Government* 222

Battlestar Galactica (television series) 232

Baudelaire, Charles 34

Baxter, Stephen 127

Bear, Greg 69, 178, 197; *Blood Music* 201; *Queen of Angels* 201

Bebel, August, *The Society of the Future* 87

Behn, Aphra, *The Emperor of the Moon* 17

Bell, Alexander Graham 47

Bell, Neil ('Miles'), *The Seventh Bowl* 106

Bellamy, Edward 103; *Looking Backward 2000–1887* 23, 24, 55, 73, 87

Benford, Gregory 173, 197

Berdyaev, Nicolas 93

Beresford, J.D. 102; *The Hampdenshire Wonder* 54

Berlin Conference (1885) 61

Berthet, Elie, *The Pre-Historic World* 22
Bester, Alfred, 'The Demolished
    Man' 133
Beukes, Lauren: *The Shining Girls*
    226; *Zoo City* 213
Big Book of Science Fiction, The
    (anthology) 227
Blackwood, Algernon, *John Silence*
    stories 58
Blackwood's Magazine 66, *66*
Blade Runner 2049 (film; 2017) 208
Blade Runner (film; 1982) 7, 208
Blake, William 28
Blandin, André, *Timeslip Troopers* 108–9
Blasim, Hasan 230
Blatchford, Robert, *The Sorcery Shop*
    74
Blavatsky, Helena 60–61
Bleiler, Everett F. 33
Blish, James 114, 160; *Surface Tension*
    136
Bloom, Dan 212
Bodin, Félix, *The Novel of the Future* 24
Boer War, Second (1899–1902) 67
Bogdanov, Alexander, *Red Star* 88–89,
    97
Borges, Jorge Luis, 'The Garden of
    Forking Paths' 6, 8–9, 10
Boucher, Anthony 8, 130, 133, 159
Bould, Mark 7, 80, 102–28, 216–17,
    235; *Routledge Concise History of
    Science Fiction* 12, 14, 105, 137
Boulle, Pierre 173; *Planet of the Apes*
    184
Boussenard, Louis, *Monsieur Synthesis*
    39
Brackett, Leigh 143, 151
Bradbury, Ray 130, 147, 154, 159, 160;
    Fahrenheit 451 138; 'The Fireman'
    133, 138–39, *139*; *The Martian
    Chronicles* 134, 152–53, 158; 'And
    the Moon be Still as Bright' 153;
    'The Pedestrian' 138–39

Bradley, Marion Zimmer 151
Bradley Lane, Mary E., *Mizora: A
    Prophecy* 20–21
Bradshaw, William R., *The Goddess of
    Atvatabar* 21
'Brandon, Carl Joshua' (pseud.) 152
Braun, Lil, *Female Labor* 87
Breuer, Miles J. 112
Brexit (British exit from European
    Union) 209, 230
Brier, Evan 159
British Association for the
    Advancement of Science 46–47
Britten, Emma Hardinge 60
Broderick, Damien 157, 177
Brunner, John: *The Altar on Asconel*
    135; *The Sheep Look Up* 186
Bryusov, Valery, *The Republic of the
    Southern Cross* 87–88
Buck Rogers (television series) 131
Budrys, Algis 169–170
Bujold, Lois McMaster 177;
    Vorkosigan Saga 198, 224
Bukharin, Nikolai 91
Bukovinka, Ján Hofman, *The
    Conspirators of Peace* 96
Bulgakov, Mikhail 105; *The Fatal Eggs*
    91
Bulwer-Lytton, Edward, 1st Baron
    Lytton, *The Coming Race* 20, 64
Bunch, David R. 174
Burdekin, Katharine ('Murray
    Constantine'), *Swastika Night*
    95–96, 118–19
Burgess, Anthony 166
Burke and Hare murders (1828)
    57
Burroughs, Edgar Rice 104–5;
    Barsoom series 64–65, 120–21,
    120; *Caspak* series 119; *Pellucidar*
    series 22, 119
Burroughs, William S. 162, 166, 169
Bush, George W. 221, 222

Butler, Andrew 198
Butler, Octavia E. 204–5, 229

Cadigan, Pat 194
Callanbach, Ernest, *Ecotopia* 184–85
Campanella, Tommaso, *The City of the Sun* 16, 73, 75
Campbell, John W. 105, 106, 126–27, 130, 135, 153, 158, 159, 165, 169, 172; *Arcot, Morey and Wade* stories 126–27; *Islands of Space* 136; 'Who Goes There?' 127
Canavan, Gerry 7, 208–33, 235
Capek, Karel 105; *R.U.R.* 84, 111; *War with the Newts* 109
Card, Orson Scott, *Ender* series 198
Carl Brandon Society 203
Carnell, John 161, 162
Carpenter, John, *The Thing* 127, 227
Carr, Terry 152; *Universe* series 167–68
Carson, Rachel, *Silent Spring* 184
Carter, Angela 190, *191*
Carter, Raphael, *The Fortunate Fall* 194
Casanova, Giacomo, *The Icosameron* 20
cats, intelligent 106
Cavendish, Margaret, Duchess of Newcastle, *The Blazing World* 19
Chabon, Michael, *The Yiddish Policemen's Union* 222
Charcot, Jean-Martin 58
Charnas, Suzy McKee 174; *Holdfast* chronicles 188
chemical warfare 25, 110, 116
Cherryh, C.J. 177
Chesney, Sir George Tomkyns, *The Battle of Dorking* 25, 66, *66*
Chesterton, G.K., *The Napoleon of Notting Hill* 74
Chiang, Ted 213–14, 226, 232
Chicago, 1968 Democratic Convention 173

Chinese science fiction 65, 106, 224–26
Christianity 17, 24–25, 60, 61, 86, 103, 119
Christopher, John, *The Death of Grass* 144–46
Church Quarterly Review (journal) 63
Citizens' Advisory Council on National Space Policy (think tank) 197
Civil Rights movements 152–53, 181, 204
Clarke, Arthur C. 54–55, 105, 127, 130, 137, 147, 200; *Childhood's End* 55, 146; *A Fall of Moondust* 136; *Odyssey* series 182; *Rama* series 182; 'The Sentinel' 55
Clayton, William 105
Clement, Hal 136
climate change 210–17
Cline, Ernest, *Ready Player One* 227, *228*
Club of Rome (think tank) 185–86
Cogswell, Theodore 159
Cold War 83, 138, 142, 144
Collier, John, *Tom's A-Cold* 107
Collier's Weekly (magazine) 159
Collins, Suzanne, *The Hunger Games* 6, 222, 231
colonialism 46, 61–65, 67, 81, 108–10, 114, 119, 121, 152–53, 199, 201, 204–5, 222
Colored American Magazine, The 78
comets 33, 79
comic books 117, 127, 131, 232
Committee for the Political Advancement of Science Fiction 114
Compton, D.G. 174
computer and video games 13, 182, 195, 198, 222, 230, 232
Conrad, Joseph: *Heart of Darkness* 62; *The Inheritors* 49

Constantine, Murray: *see* Burdekin, Katherine

consumerism 138–141, 196–97

conventions, science fiction 166, 170, 171, 230–31

Copernicus 15, 17

Corbusier, Le, *Toward an Architecture* 86

Corelli, Marie 45, 59–61, 62

Corey, James S.A., *The Expanse* series 224, 232

counterculture 164, 165, 172, 181, 184, 188, 192, 204

Cousin de Grainville, Jean-Baptiste, *The Last Man* 23–24

Cromie, Robert, *A Plunge into Space* 39

Crutzen, Paul 212

Csiscery-Ronay, Istvan, 'Science Fiction and Empire' 222

Cummings, Ray 104–5; *The Girl in the Golden Atom* 121

Curse of Frankenstein, The (film; 1957) 29

Curval, Philippe 132

cyberpunk 177, 193–97, 200, 205, 218, 227

Cyrano de Bergerac, Savinien de, *Other Worlds* 14, 17–18, *18*

Daily Mail (newspaper) 44, 67

Daily Mirror (newspaper) 44

Dalton, Hugh, Baron 118

Dangerous Visions (anthologies) 166–68, 174

Dark Matter (anthologies) 204, 229

Darwin, Erasmus 29

Darwinism 32, 51, 54, 73, 102; social Darwinism 51, 65–66, 102, 115, 193

Dashner, James, *The Scorch Trials* 231

Day of the Dolphin, The (film; 1973) 184

de Camp, L. Sprague 127; *Lest Darkness Fall* 109

De Mille, James, *A Strange Manuscript Found in a Copper Cylinder* 39

Dean, Mal *163*

definitions of science fiction 12–14, 65

Defoe, Daniel, *Robinson Crusoe* 14, 16, 29

Defontenay, Charlemagne-Ischir, *Star: Psi Cassiopea* 22

del Rey, Lester 127, 160, 171

Delany, Samuel R. 9, 12, 154, 164, 172, 176, 177, 191–92, 204; 'Aye, and Gomorrah' 168; *Dhalgren* 175, 191; *The Einstein Intersection* 153; *Nova* 153; *Through the Valley of the Nest of Spiders* 229; *Triton* 191–92

DeLillo, Don 203, 231

Dent, Lester 117

Depression (1930s) 103, 111, 115–16

detective fiction 32, 33, 44–45, 46, 69, 91–92, 194–95

Díaz, Junot, 'Monstro' 231

Dick, Philip K. 8, 130, 134, 138, 154, 159, 184, 227; 'Faith of Our Fathers' 168; 'Foster, You're Dead' 141; 'Nanny' 141; 'Sales Pitch' 141; 'Some Kinds of Life' 141; *Ubik* 141; 'We Can Remember It for You Wholesale' 141

Dickens, Charles 26

digital publishing 231–32

Dillon, Grace, *Walking the Clouds* anthology 204

dinosaurs 22, 64, *64*, 213

Disch, Thomas M. 33, 154, 172, 176, 177, 184; *Camp Concentration* 163–64; *The Genocides* 169–170, *170*; *The Ruins of Earth* anthology 172, 184

District 9 (film; 2009) 232

Doctor Who (television series) 6

Doctorow, Cory 222, 223, 232

Dorémieux, Alain 132

Dorman, Nerine 229–230

Dos Santos, Joaquim Felício, *Pages from the History of Brazil Written in the Year 2000* 65

Dostoyevsky, Fyodor 183

Doubleday and Company (publishers) *149*, 158, 166

Doyle, Sir Arthur Conan 102; *The Land of Mist* 103; *The Lost World* 22, 64, *64*, 103; *Sherlock Holmes* stories 32, 44–45; 'When the World Screamed' 103

drone warfare 221

Du Bois, W.E.B.: 'The Comet' 79–80; *Dark Princess* 109

dystopias 24–25, 27, 47–48, 55, 72, 75, 81–88, 92–98, 112, 116, 133, 139–140, 184–86, 188–190, 194, 196, 222, 231

Earth Day (annual event) 184, *185*

e-books 231–32

ecology and environmentalism 39, 140, 184–88, 192, 210–17

Edison, Thomas 47, 54

Edwards, Caroline 7, 72–98, 235

Effinger, George Alec, *Marîd Audran* series 194–95, 202–3

Egan, Greg 201–3; *Axiomatic* 202

Egan, Jennifer, *A Visit from the Goon Squad* 222

Eggers, Dave, *The Circle* 222

Egypt, ancient 19, 24, 61, 79, 125

Ehrenburg, Ilya, *The Extraordinary Adventures of Julio Jurenito* 91

Ellery Queen's Mystery Magazine 8

Ellis, Edward S., *The Steam Man of the Prairies* 39

Ellison, Harlan 138, 147, 151, 166–68, 169, 171–72; *Dangerous Visions* anthologies 166–68, 174; 'I Have No Mouth, and I Must Scream' 165; '"Repent, Harlequin!" Said the Ticktockman"' 139–140, 165

end-of-the-world scenarios 24, 52, 75–76, 107, 143–46, 210–17

England, George Allan 104–5

England Swings SF (anthology) 151, 164

environmentalism: *see* ecology and environmentalism

eroticism and sexuality 159, 168–69, 172, 173, 175, 177–78, 188, 190–91; *see also* homosexuality; lesbianism

eugenics 54, 75, 78, 95, 111, 219; *see also* race and racial theory

Evans, Arthur B. 7, 11–40, 235–36

Everett, Hugh 9

evolutionary theory 32, 51, 54, 73, 102

Expanse, The (television series) 232

extinctions (of animals) 213

Extrapolation (journal) 229

extraterrestrials: *see* aliens and extraterrestrials

F&SF see Fantasy and Science Fiction, The Magazine of

Fabra, Nilo María, 'On the Planet Mars' 39

factory systems and mass production 84–86, 89, 94, 95, 115–16, 139–140

Fairbairns, Zoë, *Benefits* 189–190

Fantasy and Science Fiction, The Magazine of (*F&SF*) 8, 131, 132, *132*, 133, 138, 147, 159, 169

Farley, Ralph Milne, *The Radio Man* 121

Farmer, Philip José 159, 168

Farrère, Claude, *Useless Hands* 115–16
fascism 81, 92–93, 95–97, 103, 110,
    111–12, 115–19
Fawcett, Edgar 12
Fearn, John Russell 127
Federico, Annette 60
feminism and women's science fiction
    21, 51, 59–61, 65, 77–78, 95–96,
    107, 112–14, 147–152, 163,
    172–74, 188–191, 194
Fermi paradox 213
Ferreira, Rachel Haywood 65
Fiction (French magazine) 132
financial crash (2008) 219–220
First World War 27, 48, 67, 68–69,
    102, 103, 106
Fisher, Terence, *The Curse of
    Frankenstein* 29
Flammarion, Camille: *Omega: The
    Last Days of the World* 24, 52;
    Real and Imaginary Worlds 22
Flash Gordon (television series) 131
Foigny, Gabriel de, *The Southern
    Land, Known* 18
Fontenelle, Bernard le Bovier de,
    *Conversations on the Plurality of
    Worlds* 16
Ford, Ford Madox (Ford Madox
    Hueffer), *The Inheritors* 49
Ford, Henry 93; Fordism 84–85, 95,
    144
Forde, Pat, 'In Spirit' 222
Forerunner, The (magazine) 77
Forster, E.M., 'The Machine Stops'
    55, 81–83, 84
'Fósforos-Cerillos' (pseud.), 'Mexico
    in the Year 1970' 65
Foss, Chris *175*
Foucault, Michel 191–92
Fourier, Charles 89
fourth dimension, theories of 48–50
Fowler, Karen Joy, *We Are All
    Completely Beside Ourselves*
    213

Franco-Prussian War (1870–1) 66
Frank, Anne 197
Frank, Pat, *Alas, Babylon* 147
Franke, Herbert W. 173
Frankenstein (film; 1910) 29
Frankenstein (film; 1931) 29
Frase, Peter, *Four Futures: Life after
    Capitalism* 218, 221
Fukuyama, Francis, *The End of History
    and the Last Man* 198, 209
future-war stories 25, 66–69, 80, 107,
    110, 141, 143–47, 148
Futurian Science Literary Society 114

Galaxie (magazine) 132
Galaxy (magazine) 131, 132, 133,
    138–140, *139*, 159, 165, 169
Galileo Galilei 15
gaming: *see* video and computer
    games
Garland, Alex 217
Garnier, Charles Georges Thomas,
    *Imaginary Voyages, Dreams, Visions,
    and Cabalistic Novels* 14–15
Garrett, Randall 165
Gaspar, Enrique, *The Time Ship* 39, *40*
gender roles 114
genetic modification 200–201
Gernsback, Hugo 12, 13, 15, 33, 102,
    103–6, 112, 230
Gerrold, David, *The Man Who Folded
    Himself* 190
Ghosh, Amitav, *The Calcutta
    Chromosome* 200–201
ghost stories 50–51, 56, 58–61
Gibson, William 181, 183; 'Burning
    Chrome' 193–94; *The Difference
    Engine* 195; *Neuromancer* 193;
    Pattern Recognition 220–21; *The
    Peripheral* 215–16; *Spook Country*
    221; *Zero History* 221
Giesy, J.U., *Palos of the Dog Star Pack*
    121
Gilgamesh, Epic of 13

Gilman, Charlotte Perkins: *Herland* 77–78, 77, 188; 'The Yellow Wall-Paper' 58–59

Gissing, George, *New Grub Street* 45

Gloag, John, *To-Morrow's Yesterday* 106, 108

globalization 65, 183, 186, 193, 199, 216, 220, 222

Godwin, Francis, *The Man in the Moone* 13, 16

Godwin, Tom, 'The Cold Equations' 136–37, 148

Goebbels, Josef 112

Goering, Hermann 118

Goethe, Johann Wolfgang von, *Faust* 28

Gold, Horace 130, 133, 159, 165

Goncourt Brothers 11

Gordon, Charles George 67

Gosse, Sir Edmund 60

Gothic fiction 9, 28–29, 32, 46, 56–59, 61, 63, 64, 69

Gottlieb, Erica 98

Gove, Philip, *The Imaginary Voyage in Prose Fiction* 14

Graffigny, Henry de, *Extraordinary Adventures of a Russian Scientist Across the Solar System* 39

Graham, P. Anderson, *The Collapse of Homo Sapiens* 108

Graham, Peter 152

graphic novels 13, 183, 213

Greece, ancient 13

Greg, Percy, *Across the Zodiac* 22–23

Griffith, George 102; *The Angel of the Revolution* 39; *The Raid of Le Vengeur* 25

Griffith, Nicola, *Ammonite* 190

'Gulf Futurism' 230

Gunn, James 135, 135–36

Haggard, Sir Henry Rider 22, 45, 46, 62–63; *King Solomon's Mines* 56, 62–63, *62*, 103, 119; *She* 63, 119; *When the World Shook* 103

Haldeman, Joe 176; *The Forever War* 172

Hale, Edward Everett, *The Brick Moon* 39

Halley, Edmund 19

Halley's comet 79

Hamilton, Cicely, *Theodore Savage* 106–7

Hamilton, Edmond, *Interstellar Patrol* stories 125–26

Haraway, Donna, 'A Cyborg Manifesto' 189

hard science fiction 33, 39, 135–37, 173–74, 186, 197–98, 200

Hardt, Michael, *Empire* 193, 222

Harmsworth, Alfred, Viscount Northcliffe 44

Harris, Clare Winger 148

Harrison, M. John 217; *Light* 224

Hartwell, David 169

Hastings, Milo, *The City of Endless Night* 110–11

Hawthorne, Nathaniel, 'Rappaccini's Daughter' 32

Hearst, William Randolph 44

Heinlein, Robert A. 9, 12, 127, 130, 137, 138, 159, 197, 200; 'All You Zombies' 190; 'The Puppet Masters' 133; *Starship Troopers* 152; *Stranger in a Strange Land* 132, 160, 184

Herbert, Frank, *Dune* series 132, 165, *166*, 176, 184, 186

Hermes (god) 61

heterotopias 191–93

Hetzel, Pierre-Jules 15, 34–36, *35*, 38; *Frankenstein* 28–31

Higgins, David 204

Hinton, Charles Howard 11–12, 48–50, 55–56

Hiroshima, bombing of (1945) 183

Hitler, Adolf 92, 95, 96, 111, 118, 226

Hoban, Russell, *Riddley Walker* 192

Hodgson, William Hope 69, 102; *Carnacki, The Ghost Finder* 58; *The Night Land* 69
Hoffman, Abbie 164
Hoffmann, E.T.A., 'The Sandman' 32
Hogan, Ernest 205
Holberg, Ludvig, *The Journey of Niels Klim to the World Underground* 14, 19–20
Holland, Leslie *93*
hollow-Earth narratives 19–22, 64, 119
Holmberg, Eduardo Ladislao, *The Marvellous Voyage of Mr Nic-Nac* 39, 65
Holtby, Winifred, *Take Back Your Freedom* 95
homosexuality 114, 119, 159, 172, 177, 190–91, 194
Hopkins, Pauline 9; *Of One Blood* 78–79, 80
Hopkinson, Nalo 204, 229
Horace 15
horror fiction 30, 32, 46, 56–57, 59, 69, 177
Horwich, David 170
Huang Jiang Diao Suo, *Tales from the Moon Colony* 65
Hubbard, L. Ron 127
Hugo Awards 215, 226, 230–31, 232
Hulme-Beaman, S.G. *57*
Human Genome Mapping Project 200
Hunger Games, The (book/film series) 6, 222, 231
Huxley, Aldous 105; *Brave New World* 55, 75, 93–95, *93*, 98, 103, 200

If (magazine) 165
Illustrated London News (magazine) *73*
imaginary voyages 15–23, 34–39, 61–66, 121–22

imperialism: *see* colonialism
In the Shadow of the Towers (anthology) 222
indigenous science fiction 204, 205, 229
Industrial Revolution 15, 23, 28
information and communication technologies, developments in 47, 61, 82, 182, 194–96, 199, 209, 218, 221
Ing, Dean 197
Internet 82, 182, 221
interplanetary travel 7, 15–16, 22, 37, 60, 61, 65, 87, 88–89, 120–21, 124–27, 140, 142–43, 148–150, 211; *see also* Mars and Martians; Moon, voyages to; space operas
Invisible Planets (anthology) 226
Ionesco, Eugène 160
Iraq War (2003–2011) 222
Ishiguro, Kazuo, *Never Let Me Go* 128, 231
Ivoi, Paul d' 39

Jackson, Mick, *Threads* 192
Jaeger, Muriel, *The Man with Six Senses* 117
James, Edward 13, 131
James, Henry 56
James, P.D., *The Children of Men* 128
James Tiptree Jr Award 190, 203
Jameson, Frederic 194, 227
Jameson, Storm: *In the Second Year* 95, 118; *Then We Shall Hear Singing* 118; *The World's End* 107
Japanese science fiction 65, 183
Jemisin, N.K. 229; *The Fifth Season* 215
Jetsons, The (television series) 26
John of Patmos 86
John W. Campbell Memorial Award 172

Jones, Gwyneth 127, 198, 199
Jones, Langdon *163*
Joyce, James 163
Jünger, Ernst 68

Kafka, Franz 105, 163, 183
Karloff, Boris 29
Kasack, Hermann, *The City Beyond the River* 96
Keating, Peter 46
Kelvin, William Thomson, Baron 102
Kennedy, John F., assassination 226
Kepler, Johannes, *Somnium* 13, 15–16
Ketterer, David, *New Worlds for Old* 13
Kidd, Virginia 114
Kincaid, Paul 13
King, Stephen, *11/22/63* 226
Kipling, Rudyard 45, 55, 91
Kirkman, Robert, *The Walking Dead* 232
Knight, Damon 12, 114, 138, 160, 173; *Orbit* anthologies 167–68, *167*
Koestler, Arthur, *Darkness at Noon* 97
Kornbluth, C.M. 114; *The Space Merchants* 134, 140, 141
Kraft, Robert, *From the Realms of the Imagination* 39
Krakatoa eruption (1883) 75
Kress, Nancy, *Beggars in Spain* series 200
Kubrick, Stanley, *2001: A Space Odyssey* 55, 208
Kurtz, Malisa 7, 130–154, 236
Kurzweil, Ray 195, 219
Kuttner, Henry 127

Lafferty, R.A. 174
Lain, Douglas, *In the Shadow of the Towers* 222
Lamb, William: *see* Jameson, Storm

Lamont, Victoria 150
Lang, Andrew 59
Lang, Fritz, *Metropolis* 112
Lao She, *Cat Country* 106
Lasser, David 105, 112
Latham, Rob 7, 157–178, 236
Latin American science fiction 39, 65, 205
Le Fanu, Sheridan, 'In A Glass Darkly' 58
Le Faure, Georges, *Extraordinary Adventures of a Russian Scientist Across the Solar System* 39
Le Guin, Ursula 151, 172–73, 176, 227; *The Dispossessed* 192, 218; *The Left Hand of Darkness* 172, 188, 191
Le Queux, William 67, 102
Leavis, F.R. 55
Leckie, Ann 224
Leinster, Murray 104–5; *Colonial Survey* 136
Lem, Stanislaw 138, 142, 154, 173
Lenin, Vladimir 88, 118
lesbianism 114, 174, 177, 190, 194
Lessing, Doris 183; *Canopus in Argos* series 203
Lethem, Jonathan 183
Lewis, C.S. 105; *Cosmic Trilogy* 61
Lewis, Sinclair, *It Can't Happen Here* 110
Leyner, Mark, *My Cousin, My Gastroenterologist* 203
Library of America (publisher) 227
Life After (podcast) 232
Limits to Growth (report; 1972) 185–86
Lindsay, David, *A Voyage to Arcturus* 61
Link, Kelly 217
Liu, Ken 226
Liu Cixin, *Three Body* trilogy 224–26, *225*

London, Jack: *Before Adam* 22; *The Iron Heel* 83–84; *The People of the Abyss* 83; 'The Red One' 121

Long, Huey 110

Loosed Upon the World (anthology) 212

Lorraine, Lilith 112–13, 148

lost worlds 22, 64, 119, 121–22

Loudon, Jane Webb, *The Mummy!* 24

Lovecraft, H.P. 8, 69, 104–5, 121, 122–24, 200, 216, 227; 'Cthulhu mythos' stories 122–24; *At the Mountains of Madness* 122–24, *123*, 127

Lowell, Percival, *Mars* 23

Lowndes, Robert A.W. 114

Lucian of Samosata, *True History* 14

Luckhurst, Roger 6, 7, 8–10, 13, 44–69, 105, 157, 236

Lyell, Sir Charles 102

MacDonald, Ramsay 118

Machen, Arthur 59

Mackenzie, Norman and Jeanne 68

MacLeod, Ken 198, 199, 222, 224

mad scientist (character type) 28–32, 38, 54, 212

Madden, Samuel, *Memoirs of the Twentieth Century* 23

Mader, Friedrich Wilhelm, *Distant Worlds* 39

Magasin d'Éducation et de Récréation (periodical) 34

magazine and newspaper publishing 44–45, 46, 127, 130–34, 138–140, 158–161, 161–65; *see also* pulp magazines

Magazine of Fantasy and Science Fiction: *see Fantasy and Science Fiction, The Magazine of* (F&SF)

Malzberg, Barry N. 177; *Beyond Apollo* 172; *The Engines of the Night* 177

Mandel, Emily St John, *Station Eleven* 214–15

Mandeville, Sir John 61

manga and anime 183

'many worlds' theory 9

Marco Polo 61

Mars and Martians 22–23, 53–54, *53*, 64–65, 68, 88–90, 120–21, 125, 152–53, 186–88

Marvel Comics/Cinematic Universe 6, 232

Marvell, Andrew, *Minimum Man* 116

Marxism 114, 222

Mass Effect (video game) 232

mass market literature 44–46, 55, 60, 158–161

Matrix, The (film series) 218

McCaffrey, Anne 151, 176

McCarthy, Cormac, *The Road* 211–12

McCarthyism 138–39

McClure's Magazine 47, 60

McComas, Jesse Francis 133

McDonald, Ian 198, 199

McGuire, Richard, *Here* 213

McIntyre, Vonda N. 174

McLaughlin, Dean 165

McLuhan, Marshall 164

Mercier, Louis-Sébastien, *Memoirs of the Year Two Thousand Five Hundred* 23

Merle, Robert, *The Day of the Dolphin* 184

Merril, Judith 12, 114, 130, 138, 144, 160, 164, 168, 169, 172, 175; 'Daughters of Earth' 148, 150; 'Dead Center' 148–150; *Shadow on the Hearth* 144, 148, *149*, 150; 'That Only a Mother' 144; 'Year's Best' anthologies 151, 160

Merritt, Abraham 104–5, 121–22, 124

mesmerism 25, 33, 34, 58, 59

Metropolis (film; 1927) 112
middlebrow literature 46, 127
Miéville, China 69, 216–17, 224, 227
'Miles' (Neil Bell), *The Seventh Bowl*
      106
Milford Writers' Workshop 160, 169
Mill, John Stuart 81
Miller, P. Schuyler 136
Miller, Walter M. 8; *A Canticle for*
      Leibowitz 143, 146, 147, 160
Millin, Sarah Gertrude 65
Milner, Henry M., *Frankenstein; or*
      The Man and The Monster 29,
      30, 31
mind control 58, 112, 113, 116, 118
Mirrorshades (anthology) 193
Mitchell, David, *Cloud Atlas* 231
Mitchell, J. Leslie 116
Mitchison, G.R., *The First Workers'*
      Government 115
Mitchison, Naomi 148, 151
Mitford, Bertram 64
'Modern Masters of Science Fiction'
      (publishing series) 228
Modernism 105, 161
Moon: destruction of 215; voyages
      to 13, 15–16, 17–18, 22, 33, 37,
      148–150, 197, 201
Moorcock, Michael 161–65, 168,
      169, 174, 175, 176
Moore, C.L. 124, 127, 148
More, Sir Thomas, *Utopia* 13, 16, 72,
      73, 92–93
Morgan, Monique R. 76
Morgan, Richard K. 220
Morris, William, *News from Nowhere*
      55, 72, 73, 74
Morrisson, Mark S. 60
Moskowitz, Sam 13, 171
Mosley, Sir Oswald 118
Mouhy, Charles de Fieux de, *Lamekis*
      14, 19

Moylan, Tom, *Scraps of the Untainted*
      Sky 83, 84, 196
mundane science fiction 161, 200
Munro, H.H. ('Saki') 67
Munsey, Frank 45
Murakami, Haruki 183
Musée des Familles (periodical) 34
Musk, Elon 219
Myers, Frederic W.H. 58

Nagasaki, bombing of (1945) 183
names for science fiction literary
      genre 11–12, 14, 46
nanotechnology 201
narrative form 12, 25, 29, 161–62,
      169, 173, 174, 192, 202
Native Americans 153, 204, 205
Nature and People (magazine) 65
Nazism 92, 95–96, 111, 112, 115, 118
Negri, Antonio, *Empire* 193, 222
neurological science 58, 201–2
New Dimensions (anthologies) 167–68
New Negro movement 78–81
New Space Opera 198–99
New Wave science fiction 136,
      151–52, 157–178, 184, 191,
      192
New Weird genre 69, 200, 216–17
New Woman movement 77–78
New Worlds (magazine) 132, 161–65,
      163, 168, 169, 171, 175, 176
New York Times bestseller list 176
New Yorker, The (magazine) 231
Newell, Dianne 150
Newnes, Sir George 44–45, 51
newspaper and magazine publishing
      44–45, 46, 127, 130–34, 138–140,
      158–161, 161–65; *see also* pulp
      magazines
Newton, Sir Isaac 15, 19
Nicolson, Marjorie Hope, *Voyages to*
      the Moon 17

Niffenegger, Audrey, *The Time Traveler's Wife* 226
Niven, Larry 173, 195, 197–98
Nordau, Max, *Degeneration* 47–48, 51, 102
North, Claire, *The First Fifteen Lives of Harry August* 226
Norton, Andre 151
nuclear warfare: *see* atomic and nuclear warfare
Nyby, Christian, *The Thing from Another World* 127

O'Brien, Fitz-James, 'The Diamond Lens' 32
Obruchev, Vladimir, *Plutonia* 39
occult fiction 14, 46, 50, 59–61
Okorafor, Nnedi 229
O'Neill, Joseph, *Land Under England* 116
Orbit (anthologies) 167–68, *167*
Orwell, George, *Nineteen Eighty-Four* 74, 96–98, 140, 182
Otto, Eric 184
Ouspensky, P.D. 50
Outer Reach, The (podcast) 232

Paget, Walter *62*
Paltock, Robert, *The Life and Adventures of Peter Wilkins* 14, 20
Pangborn, Edgar 174
paperback publishing 127, 131–35, 158–161
PATRIOT Act (2001) 222
Patterson, James, *Zoo* 213
Peake, Richard Brinsley, *Presumption; or The Fate of Frankenstein* 29
Pelevin, Viktor 183
physics 9, 32, 49, 102, 136; quantum physics 9, 201; thermodynamics 151
Pierce, John J. 13, 171, 174–75

Piercy, Marge 77, 192; *Body of Glass* 189; *Woman on the Edge of Time* 188–89
Pittsburgh Courier (newspaper) 80, 110
plagues and epidemics 24, 68, 87, 212, 214–15
Planet of the Apes (film; 1968) 184
Plato, *Republic* 73, 75
Platt, Charles 171
podcasts 232
Poe, Edgar Allan 24, 32–34, 103, 105, 122
Pohl, Frederik 8, 114, 165–66, 167, 170; *The Space Merchants* 134, 140, 141
pollution, environmental 39, 81, 184–88, 210
Positivism 28, 34
post-apocalypse scenarios 143–47, 151, 192–93, 201–2
postmodernism 8, 183, 191–92, 194
Pournelle, Jerry 197–98
Powers, Richard 203
prehistoric fiction 22, 116, 122–24, 211
Primer (film; 2004) 232
Protazanov, Yakov, *Aelita: Queen of Mars* (film; 1924) 89, *90*
psychiatry 76
psychical research and parapsychology 58–59, 60, 114, 119
pulp magazines 7, 13–14, 45, 102, 103–6, 127, 130, 131, 135, 147, 158, 159, 160

Quantum Leap (television series) 208
quantum physics 9, 201–2
quest motifs 36–37

race and racial theory 48, 51–52, 76, 78–81, 108–10, 111–12, 112–14, 152–53, 204–5; *see also* eugenics

Radio News (magazine) 104
Reagan, Ronald 192, 193, 196, 197
Renaissance (fanzine) 171
Renard, Maurice 12
Reporter, The (magazine) 138
Restif de la Bretonne, Nicolas Edme,
    *The Discovery of the Austral
    Continent by a Flying Man* 18–19
Revelation, Book of (biblical text) 86
Reynolds, Alastair 198, 224
Reynolds, Mack, *Black Man's Burden*
    153
Rhodes, Cecil 65
Rieder, John: *Colonialism and the
    Emergence of Science Fiction* 62;
    'On Defining SF, or Not' 10
Roberts, Adam 6–7, 105, 227, 236
Robida, Albert 25–27; *The Electric
    Life* 26–27, *26*; *The Engineer Von
    Satanas* 27; *The Twentieth Century*
    25–26; *The Very Extraordinary
    Adventures of Saturnin Farandoul*
    25; *War in the Twentieth Century* 25
Robinson, Kim Stanley 209, 211,
    212; *2312* 213, 224; *Antarctica*
    188; *Aurora* 211, 224; *Galileo's
    Dream* 211; *Mars* trilogy 186–88,
    187, 211; *New York 2140* 211,
    213, 220; *Science in the Capital*
    trilogy 211; *Shaman* 211; *Three
    Californias* trilogy 192–93
robots and robotics 84–85, 111, 137,
    199, 214, 218, 221
Rodchenko, Alexander *92*
Röhm, Ernst 118
Rokheya Shekhawat Hossain,
    Begum, *Sultana's Dream* 65
romans scientifiques 34–39
Romanticism 23–25, 28, 34, 38;
    Neo-Romanticism 213
Röntgen, Wilhelm 47, 60
Roosevelt, Franklin D. 118

Roshwald, Mordecai, *Level 7* 147
Rosny, J-H *aîné*: *The Death of the
    Earth* 24; *The Xipehuz* 22
Rostand, Edmond, *Cyrano de Bergerac*
    17
Roth, Philip, *The Plot Against America*
    223
Roth, Veronica, *Divergent* trilogy 231
Roumier-Robert, Marie-Anne de,
    *The Voyages of Lord Seaton to the
    Seven Planets* 14, 22
Rountree, Harry *64*
Rousseau, Jean-Jacques 28
Rowling, J.K. 231
Ruff, Matt, *The Mirage* 223
Ruins of Earth, The (anthology) 172,
    184
Rupert, M.F., 'Via the Hewitt Ray'
    113
Russ, Joanna 77, 151, 172, 174, 177,
    181, 188
Russell, Eric Frank 105
Russell, W.B. *52*
Russen, David, *Iter Lunare* 16
Russian science fiction 65–66, 84–92,
    138, 142–43, 183
Ryman, Geoff 200

Sad Puppies (campaigning group)
    230
Saga (comic book) 232
Saint-Simon, Claude Henri de
    Rouvroy, Comte de 28
Saki (H.H. Munro) 67
Samatar, Sofia 229
Sardar, Ziauddin 211
Sargent, Pamela 174; *Women of
    Wonder* anthologies 188, *189*
Saturday Evening Post, The (magazine)
    138, 159
Scalzi, John 224, 227
Schachner, Nat 111–12

Schiaparelli, Giovanni 23, 53
Schleicher, Kurt von 118
Schoenherr, John *166*
Scholes, Robert 12
Schuyler, George S. 9, 80–81, 109–10
Science and Invention (magazine) 104
Science Fantasy (magazine) 132, 161
Science Fiction Review (periodical) 173
Science/Air Wonder Stories (magazines):
    see Wonder Stories Magazine
scientific discoveries and
    developments 15–16, 28–29,
    46–48, 58–59, 60, 61, 87–88,
    102, 200–204
Scott, Sir Ridley 182
Scott, Sir Walter 11
Seaborn, Captain Adam (pseud.),
    Symzonia 20
Seattle, anti-globalization protests
    (1999) 217
Second Foundation (writers' group)
    171–72, 174–75
Second World War 92, 103, 127, 183
self-publishing 231–32
Senarens, Luis P. 39
serialization 158
Serviss, Garrett, *Edison's Conquest of
    Mars* 54
sexuality and eroticism 159, 168–69,
    172, 173, 175, 177–78, 188,
    190–91; *see also* homosexuality;
    also lesbianism
SF Masterworks (publishing imprint)
    227
Shaginian, Marietta, *Mess Mend*
    91–92, *92*
Shanks, Edward, *The People of the
    Ruins* 106
Shaw, Debra Benita 96
Shawl, Nisi 229; *Everfai* 229
Sheldon, Alice ('James Tiptree Jr')
    174, 181, 190, 194

Shelley, Mary: *Frankenstein* 13, 56, 58;
    The Last Man 24
Sherard, Robert H. 36
Shiel, M.P. 102; *The Purple Cloud*
    75–76, *76*
Shiner, Lewis 194
Shteyngart, Gary, *Super Sad True Love
    Story* 231
Shuster, Joe 117
Shute, Nevil, *On the Beach* 147
Siegel, Jerry 117
Silko, Leslie Marmon 205
Silverberg, Robert 138, 165,
    176–77; *Dying Inside* 177; *New
    Dimensions* anthologies series
    167–68
Simak, Clifford 127
Sinclair, Upton 115
Singer, Isaac Bashevis 160
Singularity (technological) 195,
    218–223, 224, 226
Slade, Henry 50
Sladek, John 163, 165
slavery 81, 93, 111
slipstream fiction 12, 148, 151,
    211–12, 231
Slonczewski, Joan, *A Door into Ocean*
    188
Smith, Clark Ashton 124–25
Smith, Cordwainer 165
Smith, E.E. 'Doc' 105, 126
Snell, Edmund, *Kontrol* 116
'social science fiction' 133, 137–143,
    147–154, 160
socialist fiction 74, 81–84, 88–92,
    97–98, 112–15, 218
Society for Psychical Research 58
Souvestre, Emile, *The World as It Shall
    Be* 24–25
Soviet science fiction: *see* Russian
    science fiction
Space: 1999 (television series) 208

space operas 105, 125–27, 198–99, 224–26

Speculation (fanzine) 174

Spencer, Herbert 50, 102

Spinrad, Norman 164–65, 171, 177, 184; *Bug Jack Barron* 164–65

spiritualism 49–51, 60, 103

Spufford, Francis, *Red Plenty* 220

St John, J. Allen *120*

Stableford, Brian 26, 54

Stalin, Joseph 118; Stalinism 97, 103, 115

Stapledon, Olaf 54, 105, 127; *Last and First Men* 54, 103; *Odd John* 117; *Star Maker* 103, 225–26

Staples, Fiona 232

Star Trek (television/film series) 208, 218, 227

Star Wars (film series) 6, 65, 176, 198, 204, 232

Statten, Vargo (John Russell Fearn) 127

Stead, W. T. 50

steampunk 195

Steinbeck, John 160

Steiner, Rudolf 50

Stephenson, Neal 201, 215, 226

Sterling, Bruce 148, 193, 194, 195, 231

Stevens, Francis (Gertrude Barrows) 114, 121

Stevenson, Robert Louis 45, 56–58, 59; 'The Body Snatchers' 57; 'Markheim' 56; *The Strange Case of Dr Jekyll and Mr Hyde* 32, 57–58, *57*; *Treasure Island* 56

Stites, Richard 87

Stockton, Frank R., *The Great War Syndicate* 39

Stoker, Bram, *Dracula* 58

Stone, L. F. 113–14, *113*

Strand Magazine 44–45, 51, *64*

Strategic Defense Initiative (weapons programme) 197

Stross, Charles 209, 224; *Accelerando* 219, *220*, 223, 224

Strugatsky, Arkady and Boris 138, 142–43, 173, 183–84

Sturgeon, Theodore 127, 159; 'If All Men Were Brothers, Would You Let One Marry Your Sister?' 168; *More Than Human* 133; 'Thunder and Roses' 144; *Venus Plus X* 159

subterranean worlds 7, 19–22, 64, 81, 116, 119, 121, 124–25

superman narratives 116–17

surveillance technology 86, 96–97, 209, 221, 223

Suvin, Darko 9, 12, 29, 86, 124

Swainston, Steph 217

Swift, Jonathan, *Gulliver's Travels* 14, 16, 31

Syfy Channel (television channel) 224

Symmes, John Cleves 20

Taylorism 85–86, 144

technocracies 55, 84–86, 93–95, 111–12, 115

television 6, 26, 131, 154, 222, 224, 232

Tepper, Sheri S., *The Gate to Women's Country* 188

Terminator, The (film; 1984) 208, 218

terrorism 184, 198, 222

Thatcher, Margaret, Baroness 193, 196

theosophy 60–61

thermodynamics 151

Thiel, Peter 219

Thing, The (film; 1982) 127, 227

Thing from Another World, The (film; 1951) 127

Thomas, Sheree R., *Dark Matter* anthologies 204, 229
Thompson, Donald C. 177
Thompson, Mark Christian 81
Thoreau, Henry David, 'Civil Disobedience' 140
Threads (film; 1984) 192
Three Mile Island accident (1979) 196
Tidhar, Lavie 223, 229
Times Literary Supplement (newspaper) 46
time-travel 7, 23–25, 39, 50–52, *52*, 55, 62–63, 72, 109, 111–12, 116, 190, 215–16, 222, 226
Tiphaigne de la Roche, Charles-François, *Amilec* 22
Tiptree, James Jr (Alice Sheldon) 174, 181, 190, 194
Tiptree Award 190, 203
Tit-Bits (magazine) 44, 51
Todd, Ruthven, *Over the Mountain* 95
Tolstoy, Alexei: *Aelita* 89–91, 97; *Engineer Garin's Death Ray* 90–91
Total Recall (film; 1990) 141
transhumanism 196, 202–3, 205, 223
Tremaine, F. Orlin 105
Trump, Donald 209, 230
Tsiolkovsky, Konstantin 39
Tucker, Wilson, *The Long Loud Silence* 144
Twain, Mark, *A Connecticut Yankee at King Arthur's Court* 109
Twilight Zone, The (television series) 131
Tyndall, John 46–47

underground worlds: *see* subterranean worlds
Universe (anthologies) 167–68
university presses (publishing houses) 227–28

utopias 16, 17, 19, 20, 21, 23, 51, 55, 65, 72–98, 191–93, 211, 227

Vairasse d'Alais, Dénis, *The History of the Sevarambians* 18
Van Vogt, A.E. 127, 130; *The Voyage of the Space Beagle* 158
Vance, Jack 159
VanderMeer, Ann 200, 217
VanderMeer, Jeff 200, 217
Varlet, Théo, *Timeslip Troopers* 108–9
Varley, John 173; *Steel Beach* 201
Vaško, Alexander, *The Payback* 96
Vaughan, Brian K. 232
Verne, Jules 9, 11, 13, 34–39, *35*, 87, 91, 103, 105; 'Edgard Poë and his Works' 34; 'Master Zacharius' 38; *Paris in the Twentieth Century* 38
Voyages extraordinaires novel series 15, 25, 34–39, *35*; The *Adventures of Captain Hatteras* 25, 37; *Around the Moon* 37; *Around the World in 80 Days* 25, 37; *The Castle of the Carpathians* 39; *The Children of Captain Grant* 31, 37; *From the Earth to the Moon* 36, 37, 38, 65; *Family Without a Name* 38–39; *Five Weeks in a Balloon* 36; *Foundling Mick* 39; *Hector Servadac* 25, 37; *The Ice Sphinx* 37; *The Invasion of the Sea* 37; *The Janganda* 37; *Journey to the Centre of the Earth* 20, *21*, 28, 36; *The Last Will of an Eccentric* 39; *Master of the World* 37, 38; *Meridiana* 37; *Michel Strogoff* 25; *The Mighty Orinoco* 37; *Mistress Branican* 37; *The Mysterious Island* 25, 28, 36, 37; *The Purchase of the North Pole* 38; *Robur the Conqueror* 36, 37,

38; *The Self-Propelled Island* 38; *The Steam House* 37; *Twenty Thousand Leagues Under the Sea* 25, *35*, 36, 37; *A Two-Year Vacation* 37; *The Village in the Treetops* 39

Versailles, Treaty of (1919) 106

Versins, Pierre 17

video and computer games 13, 182, 195, 198, 222, 230, 232

Vietnam War 163–64, 172

Vinge, Vernor 195, 218, 222

Vint, Sherryl 7, 181–205, 236; *Routledge Concise History of Science Fiction* 12, 14, 105, 137

volcanoes 20, 51, 75

Voltaire, *Micromégas* 14, 19

Vonnegut, Kurt 134, 138, 144, 147, 159–160, 166

Vox Day (activist) 230

voyages, imaginary: *see* imaginary voyages

Waberi, Abdourahman A., *In the United States of Africa* 223

Walking Dead, The (comic book) 232

Walking the Clouds (anthology) 204

Wallace, David Foster, *Infinite Jest* 231

Walpole, Horace, *The Castle of Otranto* 56

Walther, Daniel 132

Walton, Jo, *My Real Children* 226

Wastelands: Stories of the Apocalypse (anthology) 212

Watts, Peter, *Blindsight* 224

Weber, David, *Honor Harrington* series 198

Weinbaum, Stanley G. 125

Weir, Andy 231–32

weird fiction 121–25, 200, 216–17

Weird Tales (magazine) 104, 125

Welcome to the Greenhouse (anthology) 212

Wells, H.G. 9, 11, 13, 36, 40, 45, 46, 50–56, 72–75, *73*, 87, 102, 103, 133, 169; *Anticipations* 55; 'Filmer' 54; *The First Men in the Moon* 22–23; *God the Invisible King* 103; *The Holy Terror* 117–18; *The Invisible Man* 54; *The Island of Dr Moreau* 32, 54; 'The Land Ironclads' 25; *Love and Mr Lewisham* 55; *Men Like Gods* 74–75, 78, 81, 88, 97; *A Modern Utopia* 55, 73–74, 81, 97; 'The Plattner Story' 50; 'The Remarkable Case of Davidson's Eyes' 50; *The Sleeper Awakes* 72; *A Story of the Days to Come* 55; *The Time Machine* 45, 50–52, *52*, 55, 72, 82; *The Undying Fire* 103; 'Utopias' 72; *The War in the Air* 87; *The War of the Worlds* 51, 53–54, *53*, 68, 81, 146; *The Wheels of Chance* 55; *The Wonderful Visit* 55

Wesleyan Book of Science Fiction (anthology) 227

westerns (genre) 39, 69, 124, 133

Westfahl, Gary 13–14

Westworld (television series) 232

Whale, James, *Frankenstein* 29

Whewell, William 46

White, Ted, *Android Avenger 134*

Whitehead, Colson 229

Wilde, Oscar, *The Picture of Dorian Gray* 48

Wilhelm, Kate 177; 'The Funeral' 174; 'No Light in the Window' 148

Wilkins, John, *The Discovery of a World in the Moon* 16

Williamson, Jack 127
Willis, Connie, *Blackout/All Clear* 226
Wilson, Robert Charles, *Julian Comstock* 215, *216*
Winters, Ben H., *The Last Policeman* trilogy 214
Witkiewicz, Stanislaw Ignacy, *Insatiability* 116
Wolfe, Gary K., *Evaporating Genres* 10
Wolfe, Gene 181
Wollheim, Donald A. 114, 134
Womack, Jack 196–97
Women of Wonder (anthologies) 188, *189*
women's science fiction: *see* feminism and women's science fiction
Wonder Stories (magazine) 105, 112, 113, *113*, 127
Wootton, Barbara, Baroness Wootton of Abinger, *London's Burning* 115
Worldcon (World Science Fiction Convention) 171, 230–31
Wright, Sydney Fowler, *Deluge* 107–8

Wylie, Philip 117, *117*
Wyndham, John 127, 138, 147; *The Day of the Triffids* 127, 143–46, *145*

X-rays 47, 59, 60

YA (young adult) novels 231
Yaszek, Lisa 148
'Year's Best' anthologies 151, 160
Yefremov, Ivan, *Andromeda Nebula* 142–43, *143*
Yu, Charles, *How to Live Safely in a Science Fictional Universe* 227

Zagat, Arthur Leo 111
Zamyatin, Yevgeny 84–86, 105; *We* 84–86, *85*, 87, 97, 98
Zola, Émile 56
Zoline, Pamela, 'The Heat Death of the Universe' 150–51, 163
Zöllner, Johann 50
zombies 218, 229, 231
Zulu uprising (1879) 63, 67